R I Lord

Decorative And Fancy Textile Fabrics

R I Lord

Decorative And Fancy Textile Fabrics

ISBN/EAN: 9783741125317

Manufactured in Europe, USA, Canada, Australia, Japa

Cover: Foto ©Thomas Meinert / pixelio.de

Manufactured and distributed by brebook publishing software (www.brebook.com)

R I Lord

Decorative And Fancy Textile Fabrics

DECORATIVE AND FANCY

TEXTILE FABRICS

WITH DESIGNS AND ILLUSTRATIONS

LONDON
SCOTT, GREENWOOD & SON
8 BROADWAY, LUDGATE HILL, E.C.

CANADA: THE COPP CLARK CO., LTD., TORONTO
UNITED STATES: D. VAN NOSTRAND CO., NEW YORK
1898

D. VAN NOSTRAND COMPANY
8 WARREN ST., NEW YORK

CONTENTS.

CHAPTER | PAGE

I. A Few Hints on Designing Ornamental Textile Fabrics 1

II. A Few Hints on Designing Ornamental Textile Fabrics (*continued*) 11

III. A Few Hints on Designing Ornamental Textile Fabrics (*continued*) 20

IV. A Few Hints on Designing Ornamental Textile Fabrics (*continued*) 30

V. Hints for Ruled-paper Draughtsmen 40

VI. The Jacquard Machine 50

VII. Brussels and Wilton Carpets 63

VIII. Tapestry Carpets 77

IX. Ingrain Carpets 89

X. Axminster Carpets 99

XI. Damask and Tapestry Fabrics 111

XII. Scarf Silks and Ribbons 127

XIII. Silk Handkerchiefs 143

XIV. Dress Fabrics 149

XV. Mantle Cloths 166

XVI. Figured Plush 178

XVII. Bed Quilts 187

XVIII. Calico Printing 198

CHAPTER I.

A FEW HINTS ON DESIGNING ORNAMENTAL TEXTILE FABRICS.

It is a matter of surprise that there are hundreds of designers whose work lies entirely in the construction of patterns for certain classes of woollen, worsted, cotton, linen, silk and other materials, who, when asked to depart from their regular routine and launch forth into ornamental designing, of however simple a character, are entirely at a loss how to proceed. This has been forcibly brought before our notice time after time by manufacturers, who, desiring to introduce innovations into their trade, have applied to us for ornamental designs, that their own designers might work out on point paper ready for weaving. The designers at such establishments had not, previously, been required to extend beyond a few shafts in the composition of patterns, because the cloths made were mostly of a stereotyped class, *viz.*: corkscrews, diagonals, checks and similar effects, and, as every one knows, the scope is limited and the requirements of the fabrics such that ornamental designs are not desirable, but in many cases positively objectionable. Therefore designers of these materials have prosecuted their studies so far and no further, and, having perfected themselves in one particular line, have had no thought for the future.

FREEHAND DRAWING NECESSARY.

Changes often occur which have the effect of inducing producers of fabrics to enter into styles of manufacture new to them, in order to keep trade together. Thus, an employer, who for a generation has been engaged entirely in the production of gentlemen's cloths, may suddenly decide to cater for the ladies or for other branches, where ornamental patterns are required. The designer finds himself nonplussed, because, being wanting in the knowledge required for constructing an ornamental pattern, he may also be entirely deficient in the first requirement, namely drawing. This seems somewhat incredible, but we have personally met with designers who were unable to draw a simple scroll or flower. In such a case, what results? The manufacturer must either procure

FIG. 1.

outside aid or look out for another man whose abilities lie in the direction specified. It is therefore necessary that every designer, no matter in what particular line he may be, should be proficient in the first of all requirements, *viz.* drawing. When this has been attained, practice in the technical details of ornamental pattern construction is required, and much may be done in one's spare time.

Professors at technical schools will bear out the statement that the student who comes out at the head of his fellows at the end of each session is the one who has given attention to ornamental designing, providing, of course, that his other knowledge is up to the requisite standard.

SUGGESTIONS FOR DESIGNS.

There are many experienced designers who possess abundant stores of material—illustrated art works, scraps of fabrics, wall papers, Christmas cards, and such like helps of artistic merit which have been gathered together at various times. These are intended to assist the imagination, the fertility of which is often a matter of surprise to the outsider. There

FIG. 2.

is no doubt such things are a great help to some designers. There are others who look to nature for much of their "material" in forming patterns, whose spare time is spent in the fields, the woods, or in gardens—studying trees, flowers, foliage, birds, insect life, light and shade, etc., etc., and who seldom or never depend on artificial aids in their work. Then again, others utilise art and nature—sometimes one, sometimes another, and sometimes a combination of the two aids.

There are others who refer to nothing visible, but will commence with a blank sheet of paper before them and, with great rapidity, will sketch object after object until a complete design is the result. This ability and power of imagination, however, are not attained readily, but are the result of much study, practice and natural aptitude. The "easy way" for a beginner is to look about and notice what objects surround him from which he may take a suggestion upon which to build up his design. It is remarkable how easily such suggestions occur to one. Anything of an ornamental nature,

FIG. 3.

however simple, is of sufficient importance to be noticeable. As an instance, we take one's home. There are curtains, carpets, table covers, wall papers, the picture frames upon the walls, the plants or flowers in the garden, the carving upon the furniture. These are all suggestive, and from a scrap of any of them the student may find a "motif," and, when once his pattern is in progress, he will probably be surprised to see how little resemblance it possesses to that which gave him his idea. There are no end of everyday objects which will strike the observant mind as of use. The windows of shops are a fruitful source of suggestion to some designers, whilst a mind ever on the alert will find, even in the streets, that ideas strike him as he walks along. A lady's dress or mantle, the ornamental carving upon a building, and the thousand and one things which one meets with are all sources of inspiration.

CORRECT STYLES OF ORNAMENT.

A designer will usually possess one or two good illustrated books of designs, which will serve to educate him in the

FIG. 4.

various periods or styles of ornament, as also in the correct effects of colour incidental to the respective periods or styles. In these works, the primitive, the Persian, the Indian, the Egyptian and the various other styles are profusely illustrated, and although in most branches of what we may term "commercial" designing not much attention is paid to "correct style" or "period," it is necessary for a student to be well up in such matters, as they tend to educate and enlarge the mind, and ideas occur more freely, and finally he does not know how soon a call may be made upon him for any distinct style. There are many works published, the one known as *L'Ornament Polychrome* being amongst the most useful. This work contains an immense number of beautifully coloured designs, which will be found an education to students.

A SUGGESTION CARRIED OUT.

I have spoken upon the ease with which a designer may receive suggestions, and it may be interesting and instructive to give an illustration of the manner in which a simple suggestion may be carried to a complete design. Fig. 1 shows a simple spray of lilac, which we may have noticed upon a Christmas card, or as an illustration in a book, or in its natural form in the garden. To construct a design from this is an easy matter to the experienced hand, but to a young student it is not so easy. In Fig. 2 a design is constructed from the lilac. Of course, it is not necessary to hold fast to the one particular flower. It is only the "motif"—other flowers may be introduced as desired to relieve what might otherwise be a monotonous pattern. The example is given simply to illustrate how a design may be drawn from any given object. Having dealt with the suggestive aspect of designing, I will pass on to the practical construction of patterns, giving a few particulars and illustrations of the readiest methods of sketching designs.

AN ELEMENTARY DESIGN.

In the designing of a pattern, the first point to be taken into account is the size it must assume when woven. The design must be drawn to that particular size. Before proceeding further, I may say that those which repeat across or straight over form the simplest style of designing, and therefore samples of such are given. Take in the first place an elementary pattern, and suppose the width of the woven repeat to be two inches and the length of the repeat the same.

The boundary lines must, of course, first be drawn in pencil. These are represented by dotted lines, which form a square. In the centre of these construct the pattern as shown in Fig. 3. This will repeat upwards and onwards at intervals of two inches, and the same will be the result wherever the position of the figure is within the boundary lines. Another method is given in Fig. 4, which will show clearly the repetition of the pattern. In this case the ornament is drawn in one corner

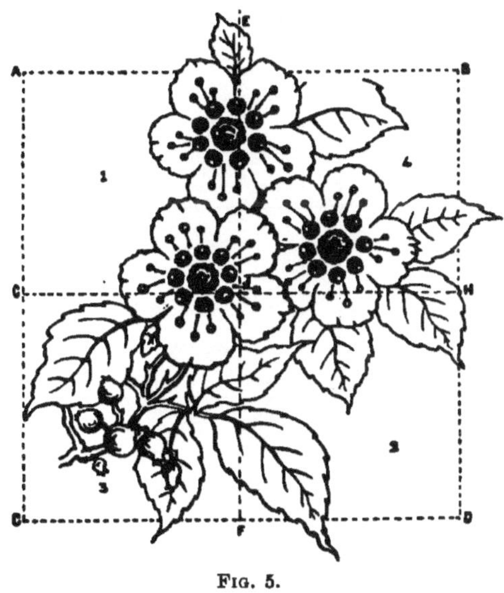

FIG. 5.

and repeated at the other three. It is not necessary to make any further remark beyond stating the fact that on the ruled or point paper a different quarter only of the ornament must appear, which will be found to join and repeat accurately when woven.

A MORE ELABORATE EXAMPLE.

Having given an elementary example, I will now come to one of a more difficult character, and here again I will take a small repeat, simply as an illustration, as the actual size of a pattern of this character would be much larger, in order to look effective, even in fine counts of yarn. The size of a repeat depends upon the requirements of the fabric for which it is intended, and of course varies for different classes of cloths. The method is the same no matter what the size of the design may be. The boundary lines having been indicated, commence drawing the chief object—a flower or figure

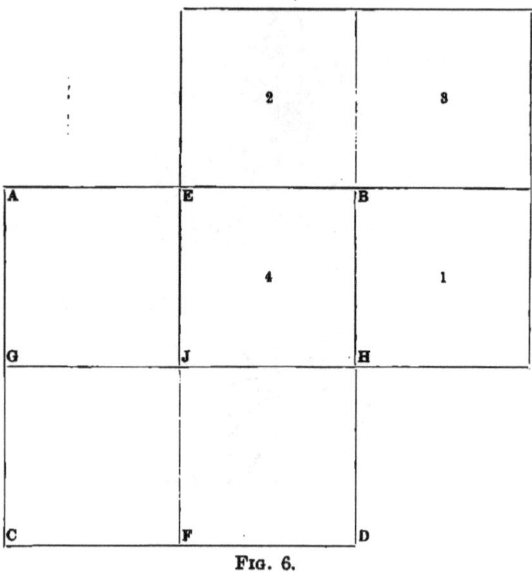

Fig. 6.

—as shown in Fig. 5. And here it is necessary to remember that the pattern must be repeated, and that as much as possible without producing a liney or stripey effect, consequent upon certain patches of the groundwork or prominent portions of the figure successively catching the eye in an upward, onward or diagonal direction. This is an error easily made, and should therefore be strictly guarded against. Having drawn a certain part of the pattern, the next step is to place it in its proper position, in order to secure the repeat, and this, in the case of a straight-over design, requires that the ornamentation shall join at each side and at the top and bottom of the boundary lines. To accomplish this, the part already drawn must be traced. Lines E F and G H must be drawn. They will serve as dividing lines, showing the parts to be transferred to their respective positions, in order that the design may be completed.

FIG. 7.

An experienced designer will do this with the least possible amount of trouble, as experience suggests, but, for the novice, it will be the easiest way to construct a square of the same dimensions as A B C D in Fig. 5, a right angle of which is already shown at E J H in the same figure. Having done this, continue the lines E B and H B as shown in Fig. 6. The portion of the pattern within the square 4 (Fig. 5) will not require transferring, but those parts within the squares 1, 2 and 3 must be transferred to the squares marked 1, 2 and 3 in Fig. 6. By referring to Fig. 7, it will be easily seen how this may be done and with what result. It will be noticed that an irregular space remains, which requires filling. The continuation of the pattern has been made as indicated by the dotted lines in Fig. 7. Now trace the remainder in the squares 2, 3, 1, and transfer to their proper positions at 1, 2, 3 (Fig. 5), and a complete design will result, as shown in Fig. 8. It may be asked, why not complete the pattern as shown in Fig. 7?

Fig. 8.

This may, of course, be done if preferred, but in Fig. 8 the main feature is clearly shown, whilst in the preceding figure it is divided. As a working pattern sufficient is shown, but the designer may complete a square of Fig. 6, filling in his pattern, when from the larger area covered a better idea of its effect may be obtained.

All this is understood and is extremely simple to those who have any knowledge at all of designing figured effects, but there are many who have not this knowledge, and therefore these hints are given for their benefit.

CHAPTER II.

A FEW HINTS ON DESIGNING ORNAMENTAL TEXTILE FABRICS (*continued*).

Reverse or turn-over designs are employed for certain classes of fabrics, the ornament of which is reversed or turned over, instead of being repeated straight across. If the student examines, say, a few pieces of silk damask, he will find this style of pattern much used, because the effect produced is that of a wider repeat than would be possible under other conditions. Of course, a particular tie-up or building of the Jacquard harness is required, but this is also the case with other designs, and the harness is good for any pattern of the same class and size as long as it bears the wear and tear. It is owing to the particular mode of tying up that the effect of a broader repeat is obtained. Supposing, by way of example, a fabric is taken the repeat of which is 12 inches. Begin by drawing the pattern in such a manner that the ornament will reverse or turn over at A B and at C D (Fig. 9), whilst it will repeat from B D to A C, as in any ordinary pattern. Thus the design has the appearance, not of a 12-inch, but of a 24-inch repeat, the harness being tied up so that a warp thread at A and E and two at C may be actuated at one and the same time respectively. By reference to the complete design shown in Fig. 10, it will be seen how the ornament reverses at A B and at C D, and also how the pattern joins or repeats from B D to A C, as explained at Fig. 9. It will, therefore, be understood that for some fabrics these patterns possess a great advantage over the ordinary styles. Silk damask has been mentioned as a case in point, but this is only one of the many kinds of textiles in which the adoption of this mode of arranging patterns proves advantageous. Suppose a dado curtain is drawn, the border, body and dado pattern may be taken and constructed, each one on the same lines, the body and dado reversing over and over, and the border reversing once from the centre. In such a case, the ruled or point paper pattern shows only half the full design, the reverse portion of border, body and dado not being required.

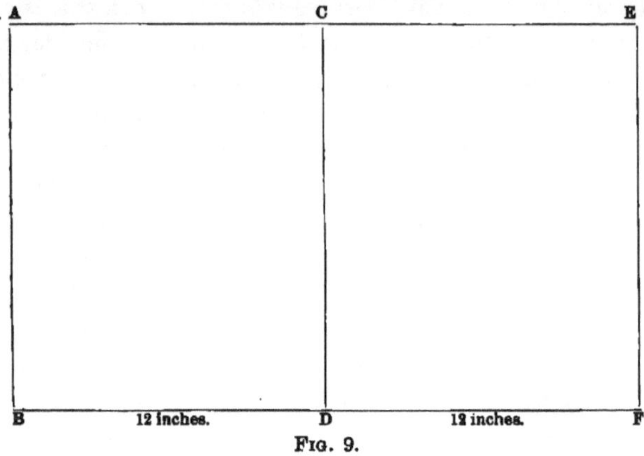

FIG. 9.

The effect produced on the curtain, as well as on all other fabrics treated in the same manner, is most satisfactory in comparison with the cost.

DROP PATTERNS.

The student, having mastered the few points required to be considered in the formation of patterns which repeat across or straight over, and in those which reverse or turn over, should next direct his attention to what is termed drop patterns. This class of design is much oftener used than the style first described, as the general effect gained is more pleasing. By noticing a piece of fabric hanging upon a wall, or a cover upon a table, it will be seen that the main feature of a straight-over pattern forms the four corners of a square, but, supposing the same fabric is ornamented with a drop pattern, the main feature will form the four corners of a diamond; then by comparing the two fabrics the student cannot fail to be impressed with the fact that the

FIG. 10.

latter has much the better appearance, the square formation looking *set* and formal. Given the required width, then the length of pattern to be designed must be decided. No matter what the length may be, the principle is the same. First draw the boundary lines and divide the space into four equal portions, as shown in Fig. 11. In drawing the pattern, whatever ornament appears in section A must be transferred to that marked B, and also that within section

C must be transferred to that marked D. Thus this result is arrived at—the pattern is the same in A and B and in C and D, and, finally, the two sides and the top and bottom of the design join accurately. Fig. 12 forms a complete illustration of a drop pattern—the dropping from A to B and from C to D being clearly noticeable. The method of drawing is very simple. The student may sketch away anywhere within his boundary lines, and the result will be the same. There will be certain portions to be traced into positions as above described. In Fig. 12 the principal

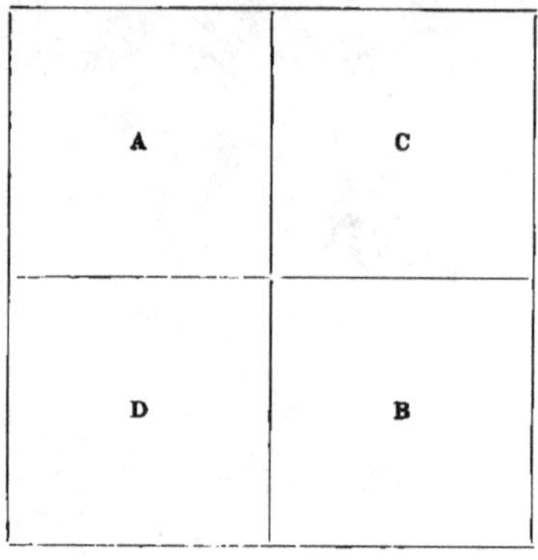

Fig. 11.

feature of the design is shown in the centre. If this is traced in the corners, there remains an irregular portion around the central feature which requires filling. The two portions of ornament within section A may now be joined by the introduction of connecting ornament. The same may be done within the section C. These last instalments must be traced in proper positions in B and D. There are now blank spaces at the terminations of the centre or dividing lines. If the pattern was cut across the centre and joined, the top to the bottom, the space which requires filling would be clearly shown. But a better method is to leave the design intact, simply tracing sufficient of the bottom portion of the design and transferring it to the top, to show the space still to be filled. Having completed the final portion, transfer to the proper position, and the whole design results.

FIG. 12.

A FURTHER EXAMPLE OF THE DROP PATTERN.

Having already alluded to the ordinary drop pattern, illustrations are given in Figs. 13 and 14 of a method of utilising this type, which is in use for certain classes of fabrics, and particularly for carpets, cretonnes, etc. In order the more easily to describe this mode, suppose a Brussels carpet is being designed, the full width of the fabric being 27 inches. It is quite a common practice to weave a carpet, the width repeat of which is double that, or 54 inches.

Now, as ordinary Brussels carpet has one standard width, *viz.*, 27 inches, it is obvious that to obtain a pattern of 54 inches in width, two separate widths of carpet must be used. To accomplish this the drop pattern is utilised, the length of which is generally equal to its width, *i.e.*, one and a half yards, but not necessarily so. The example given in Fig. 14 would be 27 inches long, which will answer every purpose for illustrating our remarks. In Fig. 13 A A represents the full width of the fabric, and A B the length. Rule the paper with the usual boundary lines, A A, B B. Next, draw one

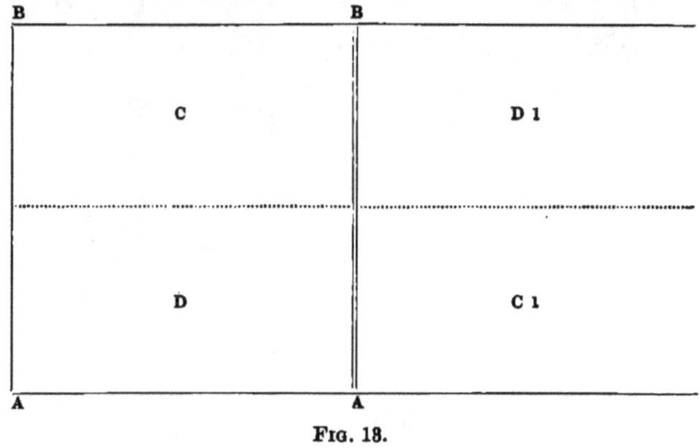

FIG. 13.

dividing line, as shown in this figure. More space will be required around the boundary lines than actually to fill, because each portion must be transferred to its proper position in order to complete the whole design. Thus it will be well to rule sections corresponding with D 1 and C 1, and sections similar to C and D 1, the base of the latter of which would be B B. In the actual drawing, the method of procedure is much the same as in the case of the drop pattern described in Figs. 11 and 12. In fact one half this pattern, taken lengthways, marked A D in Fig. 11, will furnish a full design for the purpose under notice, but the length will be double the width, *viz.*, one and a half yards, the width being three-quarters of a yard. The student is referred to the remarks describing Fig. 11, the instructions for constructing the pattern being similar to those given there. The diagrams Figs. 13 and 14 both show how the two widths of cloth join. That portion of ornament in section C comes again in C 1, and that in D repeats in D 1. The pattern joins top and bottom, from A to B, three-quarters of

FIG. 14.

a yard, and across in one and a half yards. Thus in carpets, in plush and in cretonne goods for hangings, etc., we are enabled to obtain designs which, for general conception and boldness of treatment, would be impossible, except under more expensive conditions.

REVERSE DROP PATTERNS.

Reference has been made above to the method of composing drop patterns; there are, however, varieties of this class of design, a very effective one being that in which the ornament drops and reverses at the same time. A skilful draughtsman will compose designs of this class which will somewhat bewilder the inexperienced observer, who may attempt to find the repetition of the ornament. The difference between this and the drop pattern, Fig. 12, already described, is trifling, being nothing more nor less than turning

Fig. 15.

the ornament completely round in dropping it into position. However, the student will probably find himself puzzled at times in doing this, but, after a little practice, the seeming intricacies of the style will disappear and he will have no more trouble in drawing one of these than he has in any of the other patterns. An illustration is given in Fig. 15. To briefly explain the points to be observed in drawing one of these designs, first rule the paper exactly as for the ordinary drop pattern, noted in Fig. 11; then sketch in a portion of the ornament, as in former cases. This now requires repeating in proper position; that portion in section A will come in section B, reversed, and that in section C will come in section D, also reversed. But what about the reversing of the ornament? This is easily accomplished. Trace the portion already sketched, and rule other lines upon the tracing paper, exactly as shown in Fig. 11, that is to say, trace the objects and the lines also. If the tracing is turned over a reverse of the ornament is shown through the tracing paper. Now take this, still face downwards, and place it upon the sketch, but let the lines surrounding section A in Fig. 11 come exactly over those surrounding section B on the sketch; then, by going over the tracing with a pencil, or rubbing carefully down with a paper knife, or such article, a reverse repetition of a portion of the ornament in proper position is got. Then portions in section B will require transferring to A, and so also from C to D, and from D to C, always turning the tracing face downwards, in order to reverse the ornament, until the design is completed, as in Fig. 15, which will now join straight at each side and at the top and bottom. In designing this type of pattern, much care is required in preventing a striped or lined appearance, because it will be found that certain figures or flowers in dropping and reversing come under each other. Now if there was a prominent spray of leaves tending upwards, say, somewhere near the centre dividing line, the same spray would appear underneath, the distance between the two being governed by the length of the whole design. Such a feature would at once be striking, and would, in the woven fabric, have a tendency to form an upward line throughout the piece. It is, therefore, particularly necessary to avoid anything which may tend to produce a lined or striped appearance. This applies to any design, but, in the present case, the caution cannot be too strongly impressed upon the student.

CHAPTER III.

A FEW HINTS ON DESIGNING ORNAMENTAL TEXTILE FABRICS (*continued*).

DIAPER PATTERNS.

PARTICULARS and illustrations of the various methods of constructing patterns for piece goods have been given. Designs for this purpose are usually known as body patterns, and of whatever class these piece goods may be, the instructions already given may be followed in all cases. Before concluding other remarks upon this part of the subject, some reference must be made to small repeating or "diaper" designs. From the simplicity of their construction, it may be considered that they should have been dealt with at the commencement of these pages, but they are not as largely used, on account of their set and formal appearance, as are those which take in a wider and a more varied range of ornamentation, such as the examples previously given. For table covers and such-like fabrics they are serviceable, and, as these are treated of later, the "diaper" patterns are introduced here.

Two illustrations, Figs. 16 and 17, are given. To draw these, and repeat for the full designs, construct a square and divide it into four equal parts, as in some of the examples already given. For Fig. 16, each of these four parts must be subdivided by lines running from corner to corner. Thus the square is cut into sixteen triangular divisions. Now sketch in one of these triangles some objects that will lend themselves readily to repetition. Taking Fig. 16 as an example, the objects given within one triangular division reverse or turn over sixteen times within the square. The second example, Fig. 17, differs from Fig. 16, by reason of its repeating or turning over only eight times within the larger square, the four smaller squares being subdivided once only, instead of twice, as in the former case. Now sketch an ornament in one subdivision. This will then reverse eight times, and the complete pattern will result. There are varieties of these patterns, but as they are the easiest form of ornamental designing, their further consideration may be left as variations will readily suggest themselves

Fig. 16.

Fig. 17.

by practice. Fig. 16 is utilised in treating upon bordered fabrics, such as table covers, carpets, etc., so that an illustration of the full pattern may be noticed.

DESIGNS FOR BORDERS.

The construction of border designs is a somewhat easy matter to those who have mastered the general principles governing the construction of ordinary body or piece goods patterns, but there are points to be observed which it will be well to mention here. These may be briefly enumerated. First, a border should usually consist of two or more bands —a narrow one and a wide one, or, as in the example given in Fig. 18, one wide and two narrow bands. The wider band may be considered as the border proper, the first narrow band serving to divide or form a distinct cut-off from whatever ornament the border may be placed against. The narrow band or bands should be either plain or formed of some pleasing object, frequently repeated. Commence with a plain line or lines, then form a band of balls, rings or scrolls, or other small objects, and finish off with another plain line; or a plain line succeeded by a repeated scroll running into the broad band or border proper will be satis-

FIG. 18.

factory—anything, in fact, which serves as a distinct dividing line may be utilised with good results. Next, the broad band or principal feature of the border must be constructed, and, for table covers, carpets and such-like fabrics, and for almost all such goods, a bolder treatment than that employed in the body pattern gives the best effect. Another narrow band may now be added—sometimes it is better to draw this a little wider than the first one—then finish off with a plain band, often called the heel, or have a repeated figure running down upon this plain band, but whichever is chosen it greatly adds to the appearance of the whole design.

The plain band or heel should usually be in the darkest colour used. Borders are also constructed consisting of, first, a narrow ornamental band or of even a simple dividing line, after which comes a broad band of ornament, drawn in such a manner as to produce a finished effect, by the simple addition of a half-inch or an inch of plain ground as a termination. Given the depth of the border, the wide and narrow bands should be drawn in such a manner that their relative proportions may have a pleasing effect to the eye, and that no top heaviness may be observable. The width of the border being decided upon, it is necessary to see that the pattern repeats within the given width. Fig. 18 forms a good illustration of these remarks.

There are various fabrics, too numerous to mention, which are not complete without the finish which a border gives to them, and I would therefore impress upon the student the desirability of paying some attention to their construction, for even though he may be employed in some branch where such modes of ornamentation have not hitherto been required, he never knows how soon a special call may be made upon him. Not long ago, fashion decreed the adoption of borders and panels (*i.e.*, very deep borders) for dress goods. How many designers, whose knowledge of ornamental designing consisted only in their ability to construct a simple sprig or other similar figure, found themselves nonplussed, it would be hard to tell.

STRIPED FABRICS.

In treating upon borders, a few remarks may be introduced upon the designing of striped fabrics—an important variety, including, as they do, dress goods of cotton, wool, silk, plush, wool and silk damask, tapestry and cotton hangings, mantle cloths, etc. There is such a varied scope in the drawing of these patterns that to give an example suitable for each of the above-named fabrics would take up too much space. A striped fabric, broadly speaking, consists in the repetition of a border, or borders, in a horizontal, vertical or diagonal direction, suitably divided by more or less plain ground, according to the nature of the fabric, or the exigencies of any particular case. A dress material may have a one-inch border effect to three inches of plain ground, whilst a tapestry fabric may have five inches of border to one of plain ground. In the former case, unless the plain was very greatly in excess of the ornamental effect, a most wretched fabric would result, whilst in the latter, if the plain ground was not sparingly used, a good appearance could not be produced. It may be generally regarded as a rule that, in all fabrics for wearing apparel, the ornamentation by striped effects should not be unduly crowded or pronounced, whilst, in those for hangings or similar purposes, ornamentation by stripes may be used to an unlimited extent. Now whether for a horizontal or vertical striped hanging, a good design may be produced from the border, Fig. 18, taking the design as it stands, and repeating top and bottom, a small portion of plain colour being given at the bottom, which will serve as a connection. Or a variation would be made by following the plain colour by a single line, and this line with the same width of plain ground as there appears above it, and then repeating the ornamental border; or there might be plain, then a line of colour; a line of ground, another of colour, and plain again, followed by repeating the ornamental border. A better effect, where the depth of the repeat would admit of it, could be gained as follows: Take the border as it stands, with the plain at the bottom; follow with a single line of colour; then plain, half the width of that above the single line; follow with an ornamental border, half the width of the first one; then a narrow band of plain; a line of colour, and then another narrower band of plain, and repeat the broad ornamental border. Taking Fig. 18 as the example, this would produce a horizontally striped fabric, and it does not require a great stretch of imagination to turn the same design on end, the ornament tending upwards, when an equally good vertically striped pattern would result. These remarks upon striped fabrics are amply sufficient for all purposes.

BORDERED FABRICS.

Having dealt with body, or all-over patterns, and given some information upon border designs, it is now necessary

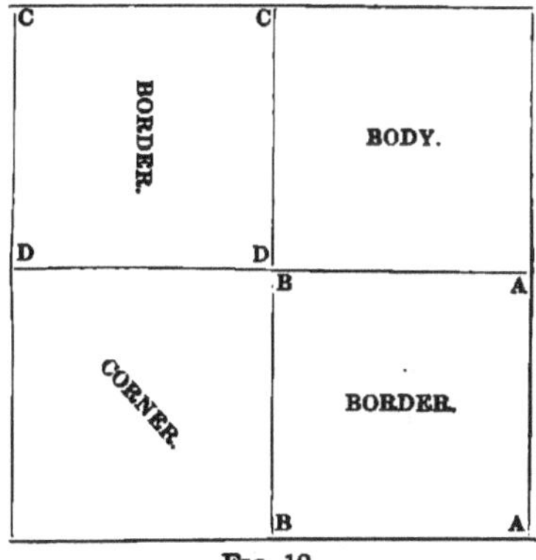

FIG. 19.

to deal with bordered fabrics. These comprise carpets, table covers, rugs, counterpanes, dress materials, etc. Very little information is needed, besides that already given, to enable the student to draw patterns for any of these fabrics, as the construction of the borders has only to be dealt with, and but few remarks are required to supplement those already made on borders given above. Having followed these instructions, it may be assumed that the student is able to construct a border design. Now in applying this to a body pattern, he will require to draw a corner piece, and, in order to thoroughly explain the usual methods employed, a diagram—Fig. 19—is given as the easiest way of illustrating these remarks. Assuming that the width of the border is equal to that of the body, construct a square of the exact dimensions required for the complete design. Divide this into four equal parts, and the result is one section for the body, and three for the border, that is to say, the body will have a border on two sides, with a corner connecting the two borders. It may be taken for granted that there are three ways of completing the border. The first is to draw the pattern within the square A A B B, and here may be remarked that this should always be done in this section, that is, below the body, for this reason—having the body pattern upright before us graceful ornament can be more easily constructed with good effect than when an opposite course is adopted. This seems peculiar, but it is, nevertheless, a fact. The old saying that "there is a right way to do everything" was never truer than in the case of designing fabrics. Let the student try for himself, and he will find that, in the wrong way, there is an awkwardness about his efforts, due to the fact that he sees his body pattern from a wrong view: now take the right way, and it is different. He constructs a pattern which, when repeated at the side, will not have any appreciably awkward effect. Having drawn in the border, which must repeat accurately from A A to B B, now repeat it at the side. There is still a square to form the corner. This may be done by running the first narrow band, surrounding the two sides of the body, across the border at each side and letting it join into the second narrow band, thus cutting off the corner. This gives a square, which can be filled in with any ornament to harmonise with the border. But a much better effect is gained by having the two sides and corner of the border continuous, as shown in Fig. 20.

In this case Fig. 16 has been utilised. By doing so, the complete pattern is shown worked out from the section given in this figure, which enables the student to judge of the effect produced by objects often repeated to form a whole design.

Fig. 20 forms the second illustration of the methods adopted for drawing borders. Between this and the third

FIG. 20.

method, there is only a slight difference; this consists solely in the manner of repeating the border from the bottom to the side. In the present case, it will be noticed that the bottom border has been traced so that, when transferred to the side, the portion coming at A A shall repeat at D D, and consequently that portion at B B must come at C C. Now to fill in the corner with the same style of ornament is an easy matter, and a continuous border results.

The third method, Fig. 21, produces a precisely similar effect to the preceding one. The difference in the two is simply this—when we have drawn the bottom border, we

FIG. 21.

trace it and, in transferring to the side, turn the tracing paper over, thus reversing the pattern, so that B B will come at D D and A A at C C. Thus a repetition of objects at B B and D D come close together, which is sometimes objectionable, as it tends to produce stiffness. Having drawn in the corner, there is again a continuous border around the body pattern. Taking everything into consideration, a decided preference may be given to the second method of designing bordered fabrics, as, in this case, there is less liability to stiffness, and consequently a better general effect may be reckoned upon. The examples given are particularly suitable for table covers, carpets and curtains of all descriptions.

CHAPTER IV.

A FEW HINTS ON DESIGNING ORNAMENTAL TEXTILE FABRICS (*continued*).

CENTRE PATTERNS.

THERE is a great variety of bordered fabrics which differ widely in body and border from those already treated upon. Instead of the body being composed of an often-repeated design, it consists solely of a large pattern in the middle, which reverses over and over—four, eight, sixteen or any number of times, in a circular direction, until the complete pattern results. This style is employed very largely for counterpanes of many descriptions, as well as for table covers of worsted and linen damask, printed cotton, etc., also for carpets, hearth rugs, sofa rugs, etc., etc.

Fig. 22 shows one quarter of a design. This would produce a square counterpane or other fabric. For most purposes, however, an oblong design is required, particularly for counterpanes, hearth rugs, sofa rugs, and, in the majority of cases, for table covers. But the illustration given will answer every purpose in aiding the student to master this style of designing. He must first draw a square or oblong of the size required for his pattern. If it be a square, a diagonal line must be drawn from the bottom left-hand corner to the top right-hand corner. This gives a centre line for the turn over of both body and border. For constructing the centre, the required space may be divided, by a simple geometrical problem, into as many sections as are desired, letting the lines converge to one central point at the top corner. In the case of an oblong design, a diagonal line cannot be drawn from corner to corner, but, by the same geometrical problem, the top right-hand corner may be divided for the reversing of the centre pattern, and so also the bottom left-hand corner, by one diagonal line for the

FIG. 22.

reversing of the border. In this figure one quarter of the centre is shown consisting of two sections, or a figure eight times reversed, to complete the whole centre. The border reverses from the bottom to the side; then both centre and border reverse each way, and so the full pattern is completed, thus producing a square fabric, with a centre pattern and a border all round. The oblong pattern is a little more difficult to design. The centre may be constructed exactly as for the square fabric, or it may be greater in length than in width, in order to cover some of the space which would otherwise remain vacant, consequent upon the pattern being oblong instead of square. This may be done by drawing a pattern similar to that shown in Fig. 22, which reverses equally from section to section, and, in order to fill up some of the vacant space, add to the pattern wherever required, by throwing out a piece of scroll work or a few flowers. Or the corner may be filled in with ornament, which will only reverse four times for the whole design. In this case, the space covered may gradually diminish in width, so that, when reversed, an oval formation will be produced. Or another way may be adopted. Suppose the corner is divided into four equal parts—in the top section, sketch in some ornament which would reverse to the next section. Now, instead of reversing it exactly, sketch an enlarged reversal of the ornament. Then treat this second section in the same manner, reversing on to the third section, and the same with the third, reversing on to the fourth section. There is thus a pattern consisting of four reversals of the same ornament, but, on account of each section being enlarged, an oval formation in the whole centre is produced.

In designing the borders, any class may be adopted for most fabrics, either those which have distinct dividing lines, or those which have no such lines, but run into the centre, as shown in Fig. 22. It is generally conceded that the latter class of border is the most effective. For a square fabric, no difficulty occurs, because the bottom border simply reverses to the side, the only other point to be observed being that the full quarter pattern must reverse at the right side and at the top, to complete the whole fabric. A corner should always be drawn, which should run up into the centre. For the oblong fabric, the same corner may be adopted, but when the border is reversed from the bottom to the side, there will still be a portion at the top of the side border to be filled in. This may easily be done by drawing a continuation of the same class of ornament. Another way is to trace and reverse as much of the bottom border only as may be desired, continuing the bordering by drawing in fresh ornament until completed, but, in any case, it must reverse at the top. Between the centre figure and the border, there will be a certain amount of plain ground. This may be either left plain or may be filled in with small repeating figures, such as small

FIG. 23.

diamonds, sprigs of leaves or flowers, or any diaper effect, not too large to take away from the pleasing appearance of the complete design.

STAIR CARPETS.

The remarks upon bordered fabrics would be incomplete without some reference to stair carpets, which consist of Brussels, tapestry, felt and such-like varieties. It will generally be found that where a body pattern is at all suitable, a stair carpet will be made to correspond with it. That is to say, the body pattern will be employed, suitable borders being drawn at each side. But, in many cases, a body pattern may be altogether too bold for such a purpose, but sometimes, in such circumstances, the nature of the design may allow of reduction. That is to say, the whole pattern is reduced proportionately, so that the same thing is on a smaller scale. Considering that a carpet is three-quarters of a yard wide, and that the full width is often taken for one repetition of the design, and that stair carpets for ordinary purposes vary from a half to one yard wide, and must include two borders in this width, it will be seen that, in many cases, the reduction of the pattern becomes necessary—particularly as the yard wide

FIG. 24.

stair carpets are an exceptional width. But it is often the practice, where the construction of a body pattern will, with good effect, lend itself to this, to copy in full size just as much of the most effective portion of it as may be required to fill in the space between the two borders. There is no repetition of the design in width necessary, and, therefore, this may be easily done, the only thing required being the repetition in length. It may be taken as a rule that large figures do not look well for this purpose. Imagine a staircase carpeted with a very bold design, and then another covered with an effective and neat pattern, and it will not require much judgment to pronounce upon them. A five-eighths stair carpet is a class commonly in use. Five-eighths, or twenty-two and a half inches, must be divided for the body and two borders. A good proportion is twelve and a half inches for the body and five inches for each border. For other sizes, similar proportions may be taken. It will be seen that there is not a great amount of space in which to draw a bold body pattern, even were such desirable. It may, therefore, be taken for granted that neat and effective ornament is best for the purpose. Moreover, the very nature of the use to which such fabrics are put demands that neatness should be considered. Particulars have been given for the construction of border and body patterns, which do not require enlarging upon, and, therefore, the illustration shown in Fig. 23 is sufficient to enable the student to construct a stair carpet pattern of this description without further instruction.

DESIGNS FOR RUGS.

In the designing of rugs, many styles may be adopted. There may be a centre pattern upon a plain or ornamental ground, this being surrounded by one repeated border, such as those shown in the table cover patterns, Figs. 20 and 21, or a centre pattern with a border similar to that shown in Fig. 22. The most effective rug patterns are those in which the ornamentation is most varied. But then, the entire rug pattern must be designed, which gives much scope for variety, both in borders and body. A good body pattern may be composed from trailing figures, such as those shown in Fig. 15, and to this might be added side borders both alike, but different end borders. In fact, where the whole rug pattern has to be designed, there is no limit to the scope for the production of effective patterns. A style which finds much favour is that shown in Fig. 24. The body pattern springs from one end; the side borders are alike; the two end borders, however, differ from the side, but are very similar

Fig. 25.

one to the other. Of course, this arrangement of borders is not necessary, but is left to the choice of the designer. It will be noticed that this pattern turns over from the centre, therefore one half requires to be designed.

DADO CURTAINS.

Curtains embrace many varieties, including tapestry, chenille, wool and silk damask, lace, Madras muslin, plush, printed cotton and muslin, etc. To give examples suitable for each would take up too much space, and therefore one only is given in Fig. 25, which will be effective for tapestry, wool and silk damask, plush and such-like goods. For printed cotton or muslin, this would make a good pattern, although it may be generally accepted as a rule that curtain patterns, without dado, are more successful. For chenille goods, an altogether bolder type of design is necessary, the coarse nature of the yarn not admitting of very finely ornamented patterns. For lace and Madras muslin curtains, dados are not much in favour. In the former case, stripes surrounded by the same border on three sides are effective and much used, whilst, for the latter, all-over patterns, such as those shown in Figs. 15 and 21, with a border on three sides, are in favour. In designing a curtain, the first point to be observed is to divide the given size into the necessary proportions for the body, border and dado, and a good division is to give the same space for the border as is to be covered by the body. In the example this has been done, but often the proportion allowed for the border is less. It will be noticed that the border does not appear as wide as the body. In designing the body and border, proceed exactly on the same lines as for the body and border patterns already described—in fact, in order to show the easy adaptation of a body pattern to the purposes of a curtain design, Fig. 15 has been introduced into the present pattern. This figure is a drop pattern, and, therefore, assuming that one of this description is being designed, rule the body section into four equal parts and proceed exactly as described in the remarks on drop patterns. As to the designing of the border, information is given under the head of designs for borders.

In designing the dado much scope is offered for variety, but, in all cases, it is necessary to commence with a band or such-like distinct feature, which will serve to cut off the dado from the body. In the present case, a broad band has been introduced which serves the purpose well and is a method much in use. But another effective way is to have a more ornamental and less formal "cut-off," formed so that the body pattern may run down into it in an irregular manner. For instance, suppose, instead of the broad straight band, one was drawn the top portion of which consisted of repeated semicircles, or of pointed work. It would be required to finish off the body and border patterns, sketching in a completion to each figure which comes against the semicircles or points. But in doing this, every bit of fresh ornament added to the body and border must come below the bottom boundary lines. This must be observed in order that the body and border patterns may repeat from top to bottom.

The space devoted to the dado must be divided in the length in exactly the same proportions as for the body and border, as it will be noticed that the whole of the dado repeats in exactly the same width as the body. In designing the present pattern, a deep panel running across the curtain has been introduced. This panel is a distinct and necessary feature in dados, except where cross stripes are introduced in its place. In some cases, instead of the panel running quite across the curtain, the border may be repeated down to the bottom of the dado, or, in place of this, a different border may be used, always providing for the border proper repeating top and bottom within the same limits as the body. Or instead of repeating the border, a narrow panel may be employed. In the example shown, the panel running entirely across the curtain requires a repetition within the same width as in the body, and, therefore, there is as much space to fill as corresponds with the width of the border. This is easily done, as reference to Fig. 25 will show. As a side boundary to the panel, the outer narrow border band has been used, and it is scarcely necessary to say that, in all cases, to produce a finish to the panel, some such feature must be added. As a termination to the dado, a broad bottom border may be drawn, finishing off with a repeated figure, running into a plain band; some form of ornamentation may be employed which may have a deep effect and which runs into the plain ground, as shown in Fig. 25. The little finishing touches given to this pattern come with practice. By these is meant the joining of one portion of the pattern to another, by little bits of ornament forming pleasing connections, as, for instance, the manner in which the scroll-work at the bottom of the dado terminates in the narrow band at the side of the panel.

As a curtain design without dado, this pattern may be easily employed. Take it—body and border—exactly as it now is; repeat the border across the bottom, and add a corner as for a table-cover pattern. Then, in order to give a finish to it, across the bottom place the scroll-work border shown at the bottom of the dado. Such a pattern would then form a good example of a curtain design, minus dado, and upon the construction of such patterns no further remarks are necessary.

Particulars for drawing all the most common classes of designs, with figures illustrating them, have now been given. It has been our endeavour to give the instructions as simply as possible, remembering that they are written for those who have no knowledge at all of designing ornamental fabrics, and it is hoped that our efforts may be of benefit to them.

CHAPTER V.

HINTS FOR RULED-PAPER DRAUGHTSMEN.

THE subject of ruled-paper drafting is one upon which a few words may be said in treating on the subject of Ornamental Textile Fabrics. . There is a wide difference between a designer and a ruled-paper draughtsman. The first is an inventor of patterns, the second occupies his time in working out these patterns upon ruled or point paper, from which the Jacquard cards are cut. In many establishments the two varieties of work are separated, the men of inventive capacity and artistic ability readily working themselves into the foremost position, whilst others have to be contented with inferior places and with a correspondingly less salary. Yet it is usual for the inventor of patterns to possess the fullest knowledge of ruled-paper drafting, without which he would not be considered in all respects a designer. In fact, in most branches of manufacture, it is absolutely necessary that his skill in this work should equal his inventive capacity. Take, for instance, Brussels carpet designing: it is quite the regular thing for a man to dispense entirely with a sketch—he will not go to the trouble of composing his pattern previously—he will, with a sheet of ruled paper before him, and by the aid of a pencil, brushes and a few pots of colours, straightway design and complete a pattern. This is not a difficult thing to accomplish, because the Brussels pattern is an exact *facsimile* of what the fabric will be when woven. But in the same department, others may be employed in drafting from small coloured or uncoloured sketches, which may have been purchased from outside artists. Much the same mode of procedure is adopted in tapestry carpets. In tapestry fabrics—those goods which are manufactured for curtains, table covers, and upholstery purposes—it is necessary for the designer to be well up in ruled-paper work, for he must fully understand how best any effects which he may introduce into a coloured sketch can be produced in the cloth. He knows for what particular grade of fabric he is designing, and fully understanding all technical details in the drafting for this, he can compose a design, well knowing that when this is handed on to the ruled-paper draughter, no mutilation of the pattern will be necessary in order to fit it for the purpose intended.

Now, where sketches are bought from outside artists, this mutilation is quite common. The writer has, scores of times, had patterns before him, the work of the best Frenchmen, which as artistic efforts were beautifully effective, but, when reduced to the cold, practical requirements of a particular fabric, were useless, because so much of their beauty was destroyed whilst being transferred to ruled paper. And such a state of things was absolutely unavoidable, because too much had been attempted in the sketch. The inventor was an artist, but had he shown more of the practical designer in his compositions, it would have been better, not only for the manufacturers who bought his sketches, but also for those who had the working out of them. In many establishments the designer is required to perform both offices—not only to invent the patterns, but, likewise, to work them out ready for the card-cutter. It may be concluded that it is necessary for all to be expert at ruled-paper drafting.

DESIGNERS' APPLIANCES.

All designing departments should be well supplied with the very best appliances required for the work which is carried on in them. The best advice that can be given to the student who reads these pages is: Let everything be of the best. There is nothing to be gained by inferior pencils or brushes—a man cannot do good work with bad tools. A common pencil may scratch the paper, or be constantly breaking, or may necessitate an undue use of india-rubber—these little things seem almost too trivial to be worthy of mention, but it is quite the contrary. Little annoyances cause the designer's attention to be unduly diverted, resulting in a break in the flow of his ideas, besides which, comfort in working must be reckoned as worth something. Even in the little question of the use of india-rubber a useful hint may be given. Much of that sold by stationers is of no value; a piece of india-rubber which will not even rub out a line, or, having erased it, leaves a dirty stain behind, is worse than useless. From long experience nothing has been found to equal a piece of grey india-rubber washer, such as can be purchased from any mill furnisher for a few pence, and which will last a generation. On the question of brushes a few words may be said. The cheaper kinds, such as camel's hair, are too soft and pliable for the production of satisfactory work. Every student should purchase a few good sable hair brushes, which, although costing a dozen times as much as camel's hair, will be found well worth the extra expense. With careful usage they will last a very long time, and when their points are worn away they are in their very best condition for ruled-paper work—indeed, it is a practice in some establishments, where large-squared design paper is used abundantly, to cut the sable brushes in order to give them a flat point, so that each square on the paper can be filled at one stroke. It would be impossible to prepare a camel's hair brush in this manner, and it would be equally impossible for the average hand to produce such beautifully fine work upon a sketch as is possible by the use of sables.

In selecting such brushes, buy those in which the hair is held in albata—a white metal—or in tin. They are more durable than those made from quills, because frequent soaking in water sooner or later softens the quills, which then often split at the brush end, when the hair falls out, and the brush is done.

COLOUR GRINDING.

Designers' colours cannot be too well ground. The more time spent in this operation the better and easier the colours will work upon the paper. The implements required are a slab of marble, or plate glass, a muller—a cup-shaped article, usually of marble, having a flat, smooth bottom—a steel pallet knife, and a similar one of bone. The bone pallet knife is always required for the grinding of carmine, in order that the pure brilliancy of the colour may be maintained, for use a steel knife and a black tone is at once the result—in fact, one might as well dispense with carmine and substitute one of the inferior colours as resort to the use of a steel pallet knife. For some classes of work the colours are mixed with size or Russian glue, whilst for others, the practice is to employ gum of good quality. In either case its value is obvious, being simply to produce adhesion to the paper. But, where gum is generally employed, an exception is made in the case of carmine, which should always be mixed with Russian glue, or the result will be similar to that produced by the steel knife—its brilliancy will be impaired. In grinding colours the method is to first dilute the colour upon the slab with water, to crush it well with the muller, then this article should be worked round and round the slab, keeping the liquid colour in the centre. In a few minutes the gum or size may be added—experience will teach how much to use—but it is never advisable to put the full quantity in at once, because even the experienced hand will at times overdo it. It is better to proceed with caution—to paint a little of the colour time after time on a slip of paper, which when dry should be rubbed on the back of the hand. If the colour rubs from the paper on to the hand more gum or size should be added, but when the contrary is the case no more is required. Each colour should be ground until every particle of grit is removed, and the student will find that the result quite justifies the time expended. Of all colours, carmine is the easiest to mix—in fact, it may be simply rubbed in a pot with the finger, when, with proper care, every particle will dissolve. Being a most expensive colour, this course may be recommended to students because, by its adoption, there is no waste. It is always well to give such colours as drabs and greys a good grinding, otherwise the tendency is for them to lie blotchy and uneven upon the paper, particularly where large patches of these colours are used. It will always be found advantageous to use gum for black.

VARNISHING PATTERNS.

In some classes of designing it is found of great advantage to have ruled-paper patterns well varnished. This is the case where such designs are subject to a great amount of wear and tear, as, for instance, in the case of those for tapestry carpets. To accomplish this a white spirit varnish must be used, and if carefully applied with a large hog's hair paint brush or a broad, flat, camel's hair brush, it will dry quickly, after which a second coat may be put on. But where patterns are to be varnished, the colours employed should always be mixed with gum, and a larger quantity of the latter must be used, or the former will have a tendency to smear when the varnish is applied. In grinding colours for varnishing it is, therefore, necessary to try each one on a slip of paper, but instead of being satisfied when they do not rub off on the back of the hand, it is well to subject the slip to a little rough treatment in order to make sure that the colour will not crack off. If it stands this test satisfactorily, the colour may be considered fit for varnishing. The mixing likewise is a little different, for the presence of an undue amount of gum has a tendency to produce dulness. It is found necessary, therefore, to allow for this in combining any particular colours in order to produce a required shade. For instance, carmine, being easily ruined, should never be used alone, but a colour, the basis of which is vermilion, would be found more suitable for the purpose. With attention to these few hints the student will find all else a matter of that practice which gives experience.

VARIETIES OF RULED PAPER.

The varieties of ruled paper employed throughout the textile industries are scarcely credible. Who would imagine that one printer alone has been in the habit of supplying no fewer than three hundred and fifty varieties, ranging from 3 × 4, 4 × 4, 4 × 4½, to 4 × 17, and 5 × 5, 5 × 5½, to 5 × 36, from 5½ × 6 to 5½ × 36, from 6 × 6 to 6 × 36, from 8 × 8 to 8 × 36, 9 × 9 to 9 × 36, 10 × 10 to 10 × 36, and so on, up to 16 × 40? These include the papers used in the dress goods, coating and suiting trades; for tapestry fabrics, damask and silk manufactures; for Brussels, tapestry, chenille and rug designs; for lace curtains and nets; for quilts and toilet covers, and, in fact, for every class of manufacture, a great number of them being for special purposes.

DRAFTING RULED PAPERS.

The process of copying sketches upon ruled or point paper is, in some branches of trade, called "putting on". In order to perform this properly, good drawing is absolutely necessary. It is the same with this as with all other classes of draughtsmanship—without skill in freehand drawing nothing can be successfully accomplished. Given a small sketch to work from, the first thing to be done is to draw an enlargement in pencil, to the size needed, according to the requirements of the cloth for which the ruled paper is intended. Some designers use charcoal. This can be purchased in sticks by the bundle, but it is by no means so cleanly as pencil, and, except in special cases, the latter is greatly to be preferred. But the proportionate enlargement

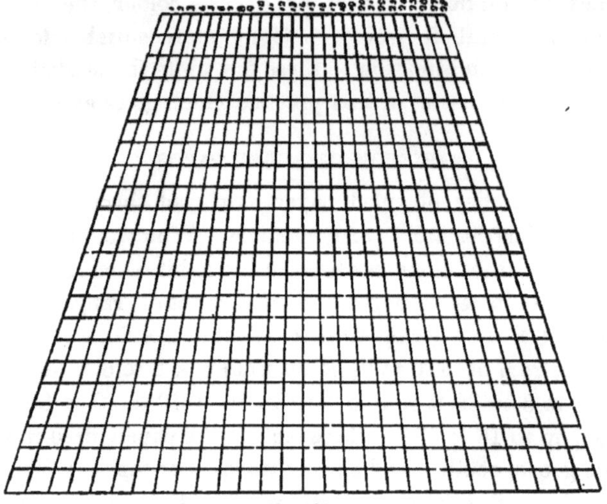

FIG. 26.

of a given sketch is not such an easy matter, unless the simplest means are adopted. Take a Brussels design as an example. Say the sketch is 6 inches square and the full size of our ruled paper is three-quarters of a yard, this being the actual size of a 10 × 10 large square Brussels paper. In this width, there are 256 small squares, called cords, 25 of the large black squares, called designs, and six cords over—that is 25 × 10 = 250 + 6 = 256. We have thus 25½ large squares. The easiest way to enlarge the sketch to this size is, therefore, to rule it into 25½ equal portions, both in a horizontal and an upright direction. This is quickly done by the use of a diverging scale, such as the reduced example shown in Fig. 26, and which any designer or student may rule for himself of the size most useful for his requirements. The method of procedure is as follows: Take a narrow strip of paper and upon this mark the width of the repeat of pattern. Place this upon the scale, so that the first mark upon the strip is immediately over the first diagonal line. Then with the eyes upon the space, between numbers

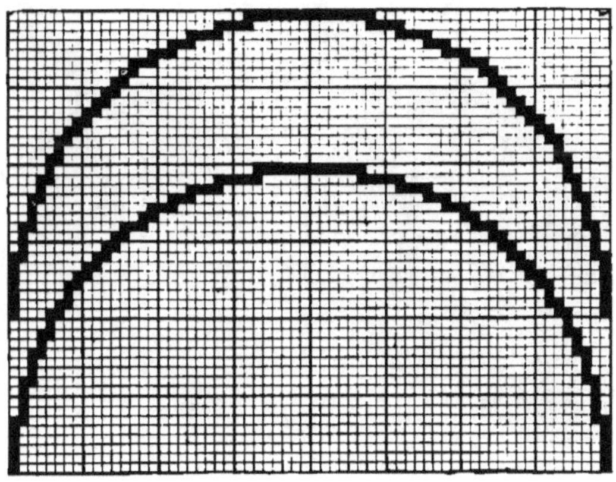

FIG. 27.

25 and 26, run the strip downwards until the second mark upon the latter comes midway between these two numbers. Now mark off the 25½ equal portions, and place the strip upon the sketch. Mark the latter, according to the strip, at the top and bottom, repeat the same at each side, and rule. Thus it becomes an easy matter to enlarge the sketch in the exact proportions. Of course, the same result may be accomplished by the aid of a pair of compasses or dividers, but the above is a much readier, more perfect and less tedious method. Where small square design paper is employed, it

will be sufficient to rule the sketch to correspond with every three or even every five "designs".

ERRORS IN DRAFTING.

Having made a correct proportionate drawing from the sketch, the next point is, of course, to paint it in. This requires the exercise of good freehand work, or an indifferent result will be produced. It is quite possible, and indeed not by any means unusual, for two men to be engaged upon similar work, when one will bring out a mass of broken-

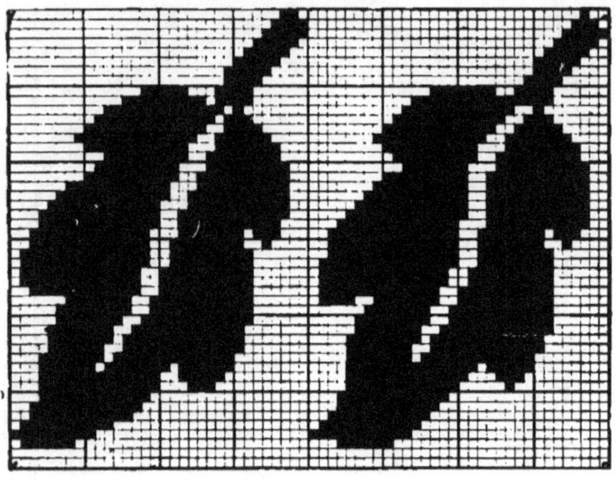

Fig. 28.

backed and altogether faulty ornament, whilst the other will produce a work, the drawing of which is full of spirit and life. Yet, in each case, the pencil lines may have been strictly followed. In the one, the man runs on as a mere machine, he follows his copy, without any idea of effect, the result being altogether displeasing. In the other case, skill in drawing, combined with general artistic ability, causes the artist to notice where errors are made, and to rectify them as he proceeds. The result is the best possible enlargement, which, when produced in the cloth, shows the design of the same size as the sketch, and which is just as perfectly and truly a copy of this as it is possible for a woven fabric to be like a hand-painted design. A couple of very simple examples are given in Figs. 27 and 28. In the first of these, two semicircles have been drawn, and, although the lines have been followed strictly in each case, the first one appears broken-backed, whilst the second shows a curve as graceful as it is possible to make it. In such objects as circles, long or short curves, stems of leaves or flowers, in scrolls, and so on, a system of careful graduation should be adopted; by this we mean such as is employed in the more perfect of the semicircles, shown in Fig. 27. Working from one of the bottom corners upwards, we paint the cords or small squares in this graduated order. Beginning with 6, this is followed by 4, 3, 2, 2, 1, 2, 1, 1, 1, from which point the curve turns over and repeats itself, thus, 1, 1, 2, 1, 2, 2, 3, 4 and 6 to the centre. Now mark the order of the other semicircle. Beginning with 7, it is followed by 3, which is too much of a drop in good drawing, then it goes on with 3, 2, 2, 2, 1, 1, 1, 1, to the turn-over point. This amply illustrates the meaning of careful graduation in drawing with the brush on ruled papers. The two leaves shown in Fig. 28 are each painted versions of the same pencil drawing, the actual lines being in each case closely followed. It is easily seen which of the two is the more perfect. Further examples might be made use of, but the above simple ones will probably be found sufficient, in order to point out common errors that a little skill and careful attention will overcome.

CHAPTER VI.

THE JACQUARD MACHINE.

Ornamental textile fabrics are of various classes, foremost amongst them being those in which the pattern is produced by the loom, those on which it is printed upon woven cloth, and those on which it is obtained by embossing. Amongst the former is an exceedingly wide range of fabrics in worsted, woollen, silk, linen, and the less important fibres; they include such fabrics as silk, worsted, woollen and cotton dress goods; worsted, silk, linen and cotton damasks; tapestry fabrics, composed of silk, wool and cotton; carpets, counterpanes, figured plushes, Utrecht velvets—in fact, a very numerous variety. Amongst the printed goods, the most important are cretonnes, blinds, muslins and cotton dress goods; druggets and such-like fabrics. Tapestry carpets are printed, but the printing takes place in the yarn, and, therefore, before the process of weaving. Embossed fabrics are those chiefly used for curtains and upholstery purposes.

The most important class of ornamental textile fabrics is that in which the pattern is produced during the process of weaving, and which fabrics require the use of the Jacquard machine and harness in their production. It will, therefore, be advantageous, before proceeding further, to give a few particulars of this machine. It would take a large volume to exhaust all that might be said upon this most important and ingenious mechanism, but the space at command will not admit of more than a brief reference to it.

Fig. 29.

Many of those for whom these pages are written will be thoroughly conversant with the class of machines called witches or dobbies. These are used in the production of fabrics in which the repeats are very limited, such, for instance, as coatings, suitings and small diaper effects for vestings and dress goods, etc. Nevertheless these machines are often called Jacquards, a mistake which it is difficult to understand. There is a great difference between a Jacquard and a dobby, as will be seen from the short description given of the former.

Fig. 30.

DESCRIPTION OF THE JACQUARD.

Jacquards are made in various sizes from 200's upwards. There are what are known as single and double-lift Jacquards. Briefly, these consist of an arrangement of upright and horizontal wires, inside the machine; of a harness suspended from the upright wires; of Jacquard cards, which are in reality another form of the design, and of the cylinder over which the cards pass, thus giving motion to the horizontal and upright wires, and raising the required harness threads or cords in order that a shed may be formed. The Jacquard machine has formed the subject of endless patents, both in this and the other manufacturing countries, and although there are various modes of construction, its distinguishing features are always the same—in fact, so perfect was its first inception that its general principles remain, to this day, as when introduced by Joseph Marie Jacquard. In giving a short description of the Jacquard, a 300's single-lift machine is taken, and one, the general construction of which is common in the Bradford trade. The Jacquard is mounted above the loom upon two gantrys, *i.e.*, horizontal bars or beams of iron or wood suitably supported. The distance between the machine and the loom is sufficient to allow for the proper accommodation of the harness. Fig. 29 gives a good illustration of a loom and a Jacquard. The machine first of all consists of a framework of iron, having four sides. Inside this framework are the upright and horizontal wires.

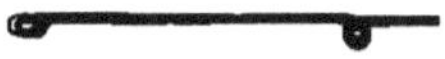

FIG. 31.

THE UPRIGHTS AND NEEDLES.—In the machine under notice there are 304 of each, divided into rows. First, taking the uprights, it will be noticed from Fig. 30 that they have a hook at the top and another at the bottom. The bottom hook is formed by bending the wire in such a manner that a portion of it turns upwards parallel with the main portion of the upright. Many of these wires are made with a simple turn at the bottom, similar in form to the letter U. Fig. 31 shows the horizontal wire called the needle. It will be noticed that at the end of the needle there is a loop, whilst upon the needle there is a twist or eye. Fig. 32 shows the upright and needle in proper position one to the other, as placed in the machine. The position of the eye upon the needle varies according to that of the upright to which it is attached in the machine. The illustration gives a view of one of the front uprights and needles. In the case of the second row of uprights, the eye upon the needle will be just as much farther back as the distance between the second and first rows of uprights, and so on for each row throughout the machine. Thus the eyes upon the first row of needles being one inch from the front, those upon the last row of needles are one inch from the back end.

FIG. 32.

THE BOTTOM BOARD.—The bottoms of the uprights rest upon a board usually called the bottom board. Every upright has a hole immediately under it in the bottom board. Just above this board is a grid or comb with stout wires running between the uprights from front to back. These wires simply prevent the uprights from twisting or otherwise getting out of position.

THE BLOCK AND KNIVES.—Towards the top of the machine and immediately below the top hooks of the uprights, the block is situated. This consists of an iron framework large enough to enclose the whole of the uprights in the machine. Across the block are situated rows of thin bars called knives. The number of knives corresponds with the number of rows of uprights. This is a most important feature in the mechanism, as the block rises and falls, causing the knives to come in contact with the hooks on the uprights, and, providing no card was in use, the whole of the uprights would rise and fall with the corresponding movement of the block. The knives are arranged across the machine with their faces at an oblique angle, in order that, upon the fall of the block, the knives may slide over the tops of those uprights that have not been raised according to the exigencies of the pattern being woven. But for this arrangement of the knives, they would, in falling, come down upon the uprights, the result being much damage to this important and most easily injured portion of the mechanism.

THE FACE BOARD AND SPRING BOX.—At the top, to the front of the machine, the face board is placed. This is perforated with holes corresponding to the number of needles, and consequently each needle has its own particular hole, through which its point passes, projecting sufficiently for the card to come in contact with it. Immediately opposite the face board, at the back of the machine, is the spring box. This is also perforated to correspond with the number of needles. In every perforation there is a small coiled spring. The loops at the back ends of the needles are so formed as to have the power of depressing these springs, every needle having its own spring.

THE CARD CYLINDER.—The card cylinder, illustrated in Fig. 33, has four flat faces or sides. Each side is perforated, the same number of holes, of course, being allowed on each side as there are needles in the machine and holes in the face board; in the present case this is 304. The cylinder is fixed towards the bottom of the cylinder frame in such a manner that the holes on any of the four sides come exactly opposite those in the face board. There are pegs upon each side of the cylinder which fit into corresponding holes in the face board. The cylinder frame has a swinging motion from its top, similar to a door upon its hinges. This movement allows of the cards being successively brought in and removed from contact with the needles. The card cylinder turns a quarter of a revolution at a time, a spring catch projecting from the side of the Jacquard to the cylinder in order to accomplish this. A spring hammer holds the cylinder in position until it requires another turn.

The machine has extra uprights for the edging or selvage, which are provided for in the bottom board, face board, spring box and card cylinder.

FIG. 33.

THE JACQUARD CARDS.—The cards consist of strips of pasteboard, having holes punched in them in accordance with the requirements of the design. Each card represents one pick in the pattern, and every hole punched means one warp thread to be raised. When the whole of the cards to complete a design have been cut, they are laced or sewn together to form an endless band. In the case of lacing, suitable holes are punched in each card, through which they are bound one to the other by the aid of string. Holes are punched corresponding with the pegs upon the cylinder.

THE HARNESS.

Such is a brief and simple description thus far of the mechanism of the Jacquard machine. How the various parts obtain their motion will be referred to later. There is still the harness to deal with, and this is treated of as shortly as possible. The operation of making the harness is called "tying up," and every particular composition of a harness is called a "tie-up". The harness is constructed of thin linen cords of great strength, and in order to add to their durability, they are subjected to treatment by a composition of litharge and other ingredients. As a simple example, suppose a design is being woven in a 300's single-lift machine, this would give 304 uprights to be utilised. If it is desired to have ten repetitions of the pattern in the full width of the cloth woven, there would be 3040 warp threads to operate upon. Therefore, ten harness cords would be operated upon at the same time by each upright in the machine. This would constitute a "ten pattern harness".

THE NECK BANDS.—The harness cords are connected with the uprights by means of neck bands, cords looped to each upright, and each neck band passes through a hole in the bottom board. Continuing the above example, there would be 304 sets of ten harness cords. Each of the sets of ten is stitched together and attached to its own neck band.

THE COMBER BOARD.—The comber board is a flat board stretching across and suitably supported upon the loom. This board is perforated, the closeness of the holes being guided by the number of warp threads per inch. The number of holes corresponds with the number of warp threads to be employed in the full width of the cloth to be woven. In the present example, this would be 3040. Now in the 300's single-lift machine (304 uprights), there are eight rows of uprights arranged in two nineteens, or thirty-eight to a row. As the same number of harness threads, *viz.*, 304, forms one pattern, the comber board is marked into ten divisions or patterns. In each division there are 304 holes. There are, therefore, 16 rows of 19 holes, or 8 double rows of 38 to the double row, or 3040 in the whole comber board. Then in the full width of the comber board there are 16 single complete rows, numbering 190 holes to each row, the same total, 3040, in the comber board. Taking a single upright and the harness thread attached to it, and showing the distribution of these harness threads across the comber board, a good idea of the formation of a harness is given. Taking the first upright to the left hand in the front row, and numbering from left to right, there would be the ten harness cords distributed, one in the first hole in each division or pattern, on the front row in the comber board, or, to put it another way, the 1st cord would be in the 1st hole, the 2nd in the 20th hole, the 3rd in the 39th, the 4th in the 48th, the 5th in the 67th, the 6th in the 86th, the 7th in the 105th, the 8th in the 124th, the 9th in the 143rd and the 10th in the 172nd hole. Now, taking the sets of ten harness cords which are attached to the remaining 303 uprights and distributing them in similar proper order through the holes in the comber board, the complete harness is produced. The particular upright above mentioned is taken as an example, because the harness cords come to the front row of the comber board, but the actual tying up of a pattern is done from right to left and from the back rows of uprights to the back rows in the comber board, so that the particular upright mentioned in the example would be the last to be operated upon in tying up a harness. Still, the distribution of the harness cords would be in the exact order given. The comber board is supplied at each end with holes for the accommodation of the harness cords for weaving the edging, or selvage.

THE HEALDS.—The harness cords having passed through the holes in the comber board have the healds or heddles attached to their ends. These are of two kinds, *viz.:* those of cord, containing a metal mail, as shown in Fig. 34A, and those composed of wire, as shown in Fig. 34B. In the case of those made of wire, the warp threads are passed through the loops or holes towards the centre. In those made of cord, the warp threads pass through the eyes in the centre of the mails. A harness weight or lingo is attached to the bottom of every heald, as shown in Fig. 35. The lingo is a long straight weight, a portion of it only being shown in this figure.

There are innumerable styles of tying up the harness, and to enter into these would be a very long task indeed. These pages are written for the benefit of those who possess no information on the subject, and, therefore, the remarks here made will be quite sufficient for this portion of the subject.

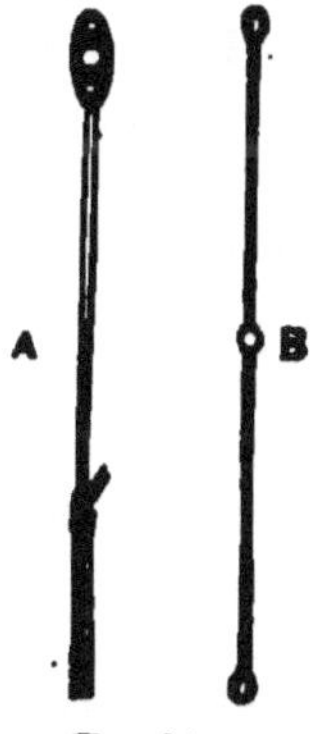

Fig. 34.

How the Jacquard obtains its Motion.—The Jacquard, of course, obtains its motion from the loom. Upon one end of the top shaft there is a sweep-plate, towards the edge of which a treading rod is attached. This treading rod is of a sufficient length to extend a little above the top of the Jacquard. To the top end of the treading rod, one end of the lever is attached, the other end of the latter, which is immediately above the centre of the Jacquard, being connected by means of a bar or rod to the block containing the knives. The lever is pivoted at a suitable point, and is also supported at this point. Now, upon the revolving of the top shaft, the sweep-plate revolves also. This causes the treading rod to ascend and descend. This in turn gives motion to the lever, and from this to the block. When that end of the lever which is connected with the treading rod descends, the reverse end attached to the block ascends, carrying the block with it, and *vice versâ*. The swinging motion of the cylinder frame is obtained from the opposite end of the loom. Upon the end of the top loom shaft there is an eccentric. From this eccentric a rod reaches upwards to the motion shaft, to the end of which it is attached by the aid of an iron arm. Upon the motion shaft there are smaller iron arms, placed in such positions that jack rods attached to them reach upwards, one to each side of the Jacquard. Side arms are fixed upon the cylinder frame, projecting along the sides of the machine, and to the ends of these the upper ends of the jack rods are connected. The swinging motion imparted to the motion shaft is transmitted by the aid of the jack rods and side arms to the cylinder frame, and thus is the cylinder alternately placed in, and removed from, contact with the needles projecting through the needle board.

THE ACTION OF THE JACQUARD.—How the Jacquard gets its motion from the loom has been shown. It only requires a few words upon its action. Given a set of cards: these are placed upon the cylinder, and the loom is set in motion. When a card comes in close contact with the needles, wherever there are holes, the needles penetrate them, and thus there is no movement of them, consequently the uprights remain in their proper positions to be raised. But all needles coming in contact with the blanks in the cards are pushed back, carrying their uprights with them. Thus, upon the blocks rising, the knives catch all the uprights which have not been pushed back, and raise them, and, therefore, the harness threads attached to these particular uprights are elevated, carrying their warp threads with them, and so form a shed with those warp threads not raised. Those needles which are pushed back by the blank spaces in the cards depress their own particular springs in the spring box, but immediately upon the cylinder turning for the accommodation of the next card, the needles are released and the springs push them back again to their proper position, ready for the next card to operate upon.

THE DOUBLE-LIFT JACQUARD.—The difference between a single and a double-lift machine is easily understood. Whereas, in the former, there is one block and one set of knives, in the latter, there are two blocks and two sets of knives. The arrangement of these parts is such that each set of knives is kept out of the way of others in rising and falling. There is a double set of uprights, but the needles are the same in number as in a single-lift machine. There are, however, two twists or eyes upon each needle, so that two uprights are operated by one needle. The uprights are longer than those in the single-lift Jacquard, and, instead of resting upon the bottom board, they come quite through this for some distance, but there is a bend at the end of each wire to which the neck bands are attached, and, following this bend, at the upward termination of the wire, there is a second hook. This hook, when not lifted, rests upon a grate. Each set of harness cords is attached by neck bands to two uprights, instead of to one, as in a single-lift machine, so that the harness is being operated upon by the two sets of uprights. The power is transmitted from the loom by means of a sweep-plate, fixed on the end of the bottom loom shaft, instead of on the top loom shaft, as in the single-lift machine. There are two treading rods fixed at opposite points on the sweep-plate. There are two levers, one for each block. The power actuating the cylinder frame is obtained precisely the same as for the single-lift machine.

By the use of a double-lift, a loom can be run much faster than with a single-lift Jacquard. Fig. 35 gives an illustration of a double-lift Jacquard.

Such is a brief description of the Jacquard machine, which has enabled manufacturers to produce much more beautiful fabrics on the power loom than would otherwise have been possible.

FIG. 35.

CHAPTER VII.

BRUSSELS AND WILTON CARPETS.

HAVING given a brief description of the Jacquard machine, which is used in some form in the manufacture of all ornamental fabrics made upon the power loom, I will now deal with the more important of those fabrics which are of a distinctly ornamental nature. Carpets are particularly of this class. Besides being amongst the most useful of articles, they are prominent in the adornment of the home, whether they be of Brussels, Tapestry, Axminster, or of the class known as "Scotch," "Kidderminster," or "Art Squares," or of the common varieties.

For the present the remarks on Brussels and Wilton carpets. Generally speaking, the two are really one fabric, there being little difference in the process of manufacture. In what this difference consists is briefly mentioned later. The manufacture of Brussels carpets has changed wonderfully. Twenty years or so ago, but one standard quality was made; now, so-called Brussels carpets can be bought at very low prices, but of the wearing qualities and taste exhibited in the design, it is best to say nothing. There have, however, been wonderful improvements made in machinery, as, for instance, in the looms for the manufacture of carpets in one piece up to four yards wide. The standard width of ordinary Brussels and Wilton carpets is three-quarters of a yard.

Fig. 36.

THE BRUSSELS LOOM.

The engraving—Fig. 36—gives a very good illustration of a Brussels carpet loom. This has been taken from a photograph supplied through the kindness of Messrs. John Crossley & Co., carpet machinery makers. The Jacquard, the card, the harness and the loom itself are all clearly visible. There is, however, one feature in the illustration which will not be understood by the general reader, *viz.*, the creels, shown at the back of the loom. These will be referred to later. As every one knows, the face of a Brussels carpet is composed entirely of small loops, the whole of it consisting of warp yarn.

Warp and Weft.—Brussels and Wilton carpets are woven upon the double shed principle. The wire forming the loops is inserted at the same revolution of the crank shaft of the loom, as when the shuttle is being picked or thrown. There are two chain warps and one stuffing warp, besides that which forms the face of the fabric. The last is, of course, operated by the Jacquard mechanism, but for the working of the chain and stuffing warps, three healds are employed. These warps are carried upon two beams placed at the back of the loom—the two chain warps upon one beam and the stuffing warp upon another. The face warp, only, consists of worsted yarn, the chain and stuffing warps being of cotton, linen or similar material, as is also the weft.

The Creels.—The warp forming the face of the fabric is wound upon bobbins, placed upon the creels, which are shown at the back of the loom. These creels vary in number according to the quality of the carpet. For what is known as a "five-frame," five creels are necessary; for a "four-frame," four creels, and for a "three-frame," three creels. Sometimes, however, a variation in the pattern causes the use of a sixth creel for the making of a five-frame fabric, a similar increase in the number of creels being necessary in the case of three- or four-frame fabrics. This, however, will be referred to later. Suppose "five-frame" carpet is being made. In the best quality, the standard pitch is 256 ends, showing upon the face in the width of the cloth, but, in reality, this number of ends must be multiplied by five, that is 1280 ends, representing the full number of ends of face warp employed. There are, therefore, 256 bobbins of yarn upon each of the five creels.

THE REED.—Through each dent in the reed, one end of each colour is drawn, and through the same dent, two chain warps and the stuffing warp are also drawn. There are thus no fewer than eight ends in each dent.

THE JACQUARD.—The Jacquard machine employed varies from that previously described, but still the principle of the machine is the same. The points of difference may be easily described. There are no wire uprights in this machine, their place being taken by cords, yet the result is the same, the necessary warp threads being raised as required. Still, machines have been made in which wire uprights were employed, but those in general use have cords, in place of uprights, worked by needles, precisely as in the ordinary Jacquard machine. There is the usual card cylinder, of course, but in this case it is hexagonal in shape instead of four-sided. There is a "lift board," situated towards the top of the Jacquard, perforated with holes, corresponding with the number of needles employed. This "lift board" raises the tail cords to which the harness threads are attached. The "lift board" is constructed so as to have a tilting movement, the object of which is to obtain a clean top shed, that is to say, that the warp threads may be exactly in line with each other. The comber board rises and falls by the aid of a lever, and by a cam is fixed to the bottom loom shaft. The object of this is that in weaving a five-frame carpet, four frames, according to the exigencies of the pattern, may be lifted out of the way, so that the shuttle may pass for the purpose of binding the fabric. There is no spring box, the needles being pushed back at every pick of the pattern by means of a back board, suitably actuated.

THE CARDS.—The ordinary Jacquard cards are employed, but, as will be seen from Fig. 36, three sets of cards are required for a three-quarters wide carpet. When carpets of a greater width are being woven, an extra set of cards is used for each quarter of a yard in the width of the fabric. Thus, for a yard wide, four sets of cards are necessary. Of course, the more sets of cards in use, the larger the Jacquard must be. The needles are increased in number, and the various parts of the machine are arranged accordingly.

THE HARNESS.—Little need be said upon the harness, which is of the usual character, with mails and lingoes complete. One point, however, may be mentioned—each pick of

FIG. 37.

the pattern brings 256 ends of warp to the face of the fabric. This means that in an ordinary fabric, such as dress goods, 256 harness cords would form one pattern of the harness, but, in the present case, this is not so. In weaving a five-frame design, there are five times 256 warp ends to provide for, therefore the harness contains 1280 ends.

THE WIRE MOTION.—The wire motion is a most important piece of mechanism, and is situated at one end of the loom. Its purpose is to actuate several long wires, upon which the loops of the fabric are formed. Figs. 37 and 38 are views of the two ends of a Brussels and a Wilton wire, Fig. 37 being the Brussels wire, which varies from 31 to 31½ inches in length, and Fig. 38 the Wilton wire, varying from 30½ to 31 inches in length. The number of wires in use varies, but, ordinarily, there are from 26 to 28, covering about three inches of fabric. Suppose a loom is working, and the first 27 of these wires have been operated upon, that is to say, 27 picks of the pattern have been formed. The twenty-eighth wire is being operated upon, the loops of the fabric are formed upon the wire, and the moment this has been done, the first wire in the set is drawn out of the fabric, and, when quite clear, passes forwards and is inserted in position, that is, taking the twenty-eighth position, and upon this wire the next pick of the pattern is formed. And so it goes on; as each wire is occupied another one is drawn from the fabric to take its place.

Fig. 38.

WILTON CARPET.

As before stated, there is not much difference between the manufacture of Brussels and Wilton carpets. There is, however, a slight difference in the binding of the latter, and the loops of the fabric are cut as the wires are drawn out after each pick, and for this purpose there is a small knife at the end of each wire, as shown in Fig. 38. After weaving, the fabric is passed through a cropping machine, which produces a smooth, even pile.

BRUSSELS CARPET.

The term "five-frame" carpet is commonly in use in all wholesale and retail warehouses, as well as in the factory, but outside the latter place, there are very few who understand anything as to the meaning of the term. They know that it is intended to convey the impression that the goods are of the best quality, but why, they cannot explain. I happened, a short time ago, to be in one of the largest wholesale carpet houses in this country, and, in conversation

Fig. 39.

with the salesmen, I discovered that not one of them knew what a five-, four-, or three-frame carpet was. I will endeavour, as briefly as possible, to give a few particulars upon this point. Upon reference to Fig. 36, it will be noticed that there is a series of frames called creels, at the back of the loom, placed in a slanting position, their near ends coming almost in close contact. In the weaving of a five-frame carpet, not fewer than five of these would be employed. Now, supposing there were five colours in one design—say, yellow, red, blue, green and black—there would be 256 bobbins of each colour. These bobbins would be placed upon the creels, each colour upon a separate creel. There would thus be five full creels of yarn, which would make a five-frame carpet. But there may be five, six, or any number of colours in a five-frame fabric, and here comes in the skill of the designer in arranging his design so that he may distribute his colours artistically, and yet within the recognised scope of the fabric for which he is designing.

A Five-Frame Design.—Fig. 39, a design for a Brussels or Wilton carpet, is given simply as an example to illustrate our explanations, and not as a specimen of a fashionable or good selling type of pattern. The design is on 128 ends and would therefore require repeating once to make up the full three-quarters, or 256 ends. Carpet designs have one distinguishing feature which is not at all common to designs for woven fabrics in general. The carpet pattern, when drawn upon the full-sized design or point paper, is the exact counterpart in size, colour, and in all other particulars of the fabric woven from it. Thus the designer sees, as it were, the actual thing growing under his brush, and therefore precisely what the fabric will be when woven. The point papers in use for the best quality carpets are 10 × 10 and 8 × 8. Returning to the explanation—the design shown in Fig. 39 is for a five-frame fabric, although six colours are employed. The use of the extra or sixth colour is made possible by what is known as "planting," that is, the arrangement of two colours on one frame. The simplest form of doing this is to have four full frames. Say, there are black, brown, gold, red, blue and green, which are good plain colours for illustration. The black, brown, gold and red could be full frames, that is, 256 bobbins of each colour would be used, and thus each would be employed throughout the full width of the fabric. But with the blue and green it would be different. These two colours must be "planted," which means that, throughout the length of the piece, wherever blue appears, no green may appear in line with it, and *vice versâ*. Fig. 39 shows this arrangement. If the reader carefully examines this design, he will notice

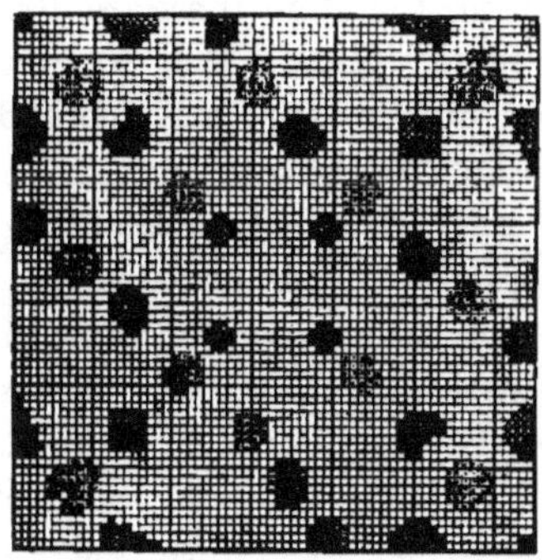

FIG. 40.

that the darkest and the second drabs (the lighter being employed for the ground) do not run in line, but are parallel with each other.

In order that this may be clearly understood, an illustration is given in Fig. 40, which shows how these two colours are planted. The crosses indicate the darker, and the dots the second drab. There is only one quarter of the design given, but this is sufficient, as the planted colours turn over each way.

In a "five-frame," as before stated, there are at least five colours which can be traced as spreading quite over the full width of the cloth. If there are more than five, it will be apparent that no more than an equivalent to the five colours will be used, and no fewer should be used, but that is another matter which is not always observed. Any salesman or buyer should, with a little attention, be able to "spot" precisely whether a carpet is three-, four-, or five-frame. It may be asked what particular virtue a five-frame has over a three- or four-frame. This is easily understood. There are 1280 ends of yarn used, and no more than 256 can come to the face of the fabric at one pick of the pattern, therefore there are 1024 ends forming the back of the fabric. It will thus be seen that the carpet is thicker, softer, and consequently more durable, besides which, better designs can be utilised.

The Plant or Gamut.—Immediately under the design is the plant or gamut. This indicates the arrangement of the colours in the design. In the present case it shows clearly that the first four colours are "full frames," that is, they are employed indiscriminately throughout the design, as may be required, 256 bobbins of each colour, of course, being used in weaving. The fifth and sixth colours are shown on the plant exactly as they are arranged in the design. There are 70 ends of dark drab and 58 ends of light drab, or 128 ends in all. When the pattern is repeated once there are 256 ends, or a full frame. Now, as the gamut is detached from the pattern, the designer, who places it in proper position under the portion of the design upon which he is working, is enabled to indicate upon it every fresh bit of colour that he uses; therefore, it effectually prevents the introduction of an excess of colour in the pattern. The bobbins are placed on the creels according to the arrangement of the colours on the gamut, and thus, in weaving, these colours appear in the carpet in their proper positions.

Manipulation of Colours.—In the designing of carpets,

by the careful manipulation of colours, wonderful effects may be obtained with many colours at precisely the same cost in yarn as if five only were employed upon the five creels. In the example only six are given on account of the difficulty of clearly showing more in a black and white engraving, but it would have been easy to have employed seven, eight, nine, or more in the same design, the only requirement being that all the extra colours should be planted. Now, suppose seven were employed instead of six colours in this design, say a salmon pink, there would then be one frame consisting of blue, green and salmon pink. The salmon pink could be placed at each corner of the four rosette figures, shown diagonally between the large centre figure and the same figure at each corner of the design. The gamut or plant would require to have the salmon pink indicated upon it. Counting from the left-hand side, this extra colour must be placed on the five ends from Nos. 20 to 24 inclusive, from Nos. 42 to 46, from Nos. 84 to 88, and from Nos. 106 to 110.

In the illustration one frame only is shown planted. It is, however, quite a common practice to plant the colours in more than one. Say there are three full frames. There could be changes of colour in the next two. There is scarcely an end to the planting of the colours, or to the general manipulation of them to which the designer may resort. He must, however, keep in view one or two important points—the planting of his colours must not be such as to produce a distinct striped effect—this must be entirely avoided, as also must a tendency to a blotchy appearance. It is quite possible for the designer to find that there is such a thing as too much scope for the production of effects of colour, which is apt to tend in the direction of vulgarity, instead of to neat and artistic excellence.

CHINTZ PATTERNS.—In the unlimited extent to which

planting of colours may be employed, probably a drab or green chintz pattern forms the best example. Taking a green chintz, which is a design in which floral effects are introduced, the designer gets as closely to nature as possible. He may employ a black, two greens and a yellow, which may be used for the ground, ornament and foliage—four full frames. The flowers will be in natural colours, but there would only be one frame remaining, on which these colours might be arranged. Here comes in the skill of the designer. He will arrange the flowers in such positions that only those immediately under each other shall be in the same colour. But dotted about in various positions across the width of his design he will have flowers in crimson, in scarlet, in blue, in grey and in other shades. But how does he get variety of shade in the *same* flowers? Simply by striping his flowers downwards. He commences at one side, say with deep crimson, and this is used from top to bottom of the flower, say for four ends, then on the next four ends he has a lighter crimson, and so on, until, at the opposite side of the flower, he has the palest pink or even a white. Each flower is treated in the same manner, and a very satisfactory result is obtained. Every change of shade must be indicated on the gamut, which may, in the end, show that on one frame there may be 20, 30, or more shades of colours, which means that on one creel alone there may be bobbins carrying 20, 30, or more different shades of colours.

USING EXTRA CREELS.—Occasionally a sixth creel will be employed for the making of a five-frame fabric, but this practice is by no means often resorted to. It is mentioned to show what may be done under certain conditions. For instance, the nature of the design may be such that only very small quantities of one or more colours are visible in some portions of the design. These small quantities of colour should be "stopped out" by substituting some of the other colours. There would, therefore, be a certain number of *ends* vacant, that is, a certain number of bobbins of yarn of one or more colours would be saved. The same number of bobbins might be placed upon the sixth creel, and thus an extra effect of colour would be obtained in the design. To make this clearer refer to Fig. 39. Looking straight up the centre of the design it will be noticed that between the small rosette at the top and bottom and the large figure in the centre there is only one pick of ground colour, but in line with this there are two or three picks of the same shade, within the large figure. This ground colour for, say, three ends could be "stopped out" with a little manipulation. The same is done in the dropped repetition of the pattern, and it gives us six bobbins of colour. If these six bobbins were utilised in some other portions of the design, by the introduction of small dots of a bright shade, a good effect would be produced. This "dodging" of colour is, however, oftener resorted to in three- and four-frame carpets, four or five creels thus being used. It is by no means an uncommon occurrence in a three-, four-, or five-frame fabric to "stop out" portions of colour in any one frame and to abstain from introducing a corresponding amount of colour in another place. The result of this is that a certain quantity of yarn is saved, and the general effect of the design is little, if any, the worse for the saving.

Sizes of Designs.—In the designing of Brussels and Wilton carpets, much scope is allowed to the designer, as will be evident from the foregoing particulars. In point of size of design also there is a good margin for the production of bold patterns. It will be understood that as 10 × 10 or 8 × 8 design or point paper is used, the ends of face warp equal the picks in a given area, as will be noticed from Fig. 39. A three-quarters design is 256 ends wide by 256 picks long. A yard and a half pattern is, of course, 256 by 512. Any length of design may be adopted up to the latter size, but it is not a usual thing to go beyond it. The yard and a half pattern is much used for bold effects, but one may go further than this by the adoption of the method described and illustrated previously in these pages. This method gives to a pattern the effect of a yard and a half wide repeat. For a description of this, it will be necessary to refer to "A Further Example of the Drop Pattern," and to Figs. 13 and 14 illustrating it. Hitherto body Brussels have only been dealt with, but there are borders and stair carpets, upon which we may be expected to say something. However, as most, if not all, that has already been said is applicable to the latter as well as to body Brussels, it is scarcely necessary to say much more. The sizes mostly in use for stair carpets are half-yard, five-eighths, three-quarters and four-quarters. The proportions for body and border of a stair carpet are important; the border may be too wide or too narrow. As instances of due proportions, we may mention that a five-eighths stair would have, say, 46 ends for each border and 126 ends for the body or filling, or 218 in all. A three-quarters would have, say, 54 for each border and 148 for the body or filling, or 256 in all. Borders vary in width—three-eighths, half-yard and five-eighths being sizes in use, although the most common are the two former. A three-eighths border would have, say, 126 ends, and a half-yard 172 ends. The planting of the colours and all other particulars are the same as for body Brussels.

CHAPTER VIII.

TAPESTRY CARPETS.

Tapestry carpets rank amongst the most important of ornamental textile fabrics, and we, therefore, propose to give a few particulars of their method of manufacture. The ordinary observer is quite unable, except from an examination of their backs, to distinguish between a tapestry and a Brussels carpet, and yet, in the processes of manufacture and in the cloths produced, there is a wonderful difference.

DIFFERENCE BETWEEN BRUSSELS AND TAPESTRY.

By placing the two side by side, a clearness and sharpness about the Brussels pattern is noticed which is absent from the tapestry. In the latter there is a mistiness about the colours, and the pattern lacks that sharpness and delicacy which characterises the former. This is due to the process of manufacture. A Brussels is a yarn dyed and a tapestry may be described as a printed fabric, but the printing is done upon the yarn before the process of weaving. The whole method of manufacture is most ingenious. In the making of a five-frame Brussels, to which the previous chapter was mainly devoted, no fewer than 1280 ends of face yarn are required for the weaving of one piece of standard quality—each frame consisting of 256 bobbins. It was pointed out that 256 ends only can come to the face at each pick of the pattern. Therefore, 1024 ends of yarn are hidden in the body of the fabric. There are many qualities of tapestry made, but these remarks will be confined to the standard quality. In the production of this only 216 ends of face yarn are required, instead of 1280, which shows at once that the Brussels carpet has the great advantage of being thicker, softer and altogether a more durable cloth, apart from other advantages which it possessès. There is a limitation in the

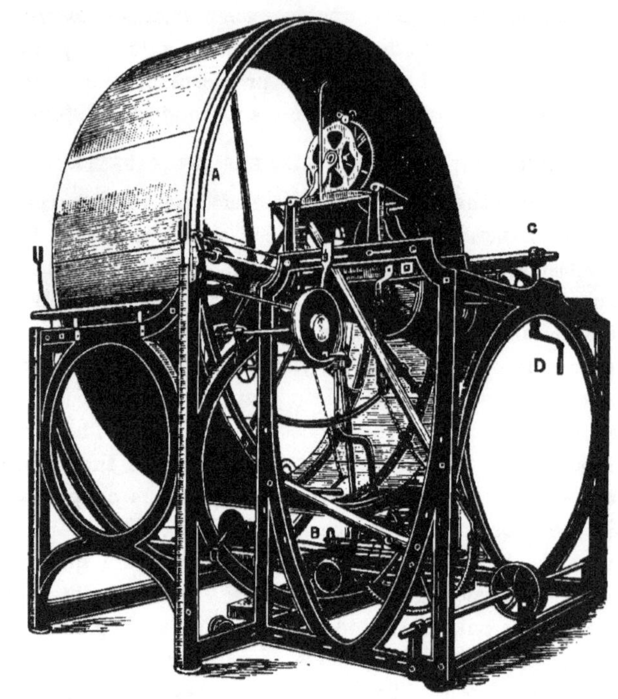

FIG. 41.

number of colours used in a Brussels as described in the last chapter. In tapestry there is no limit. In the Brussels the whole of the colours used show a more or less striped appearance at the back of the fabric. In a tapestry they do not show at the back at all. In passing, it may be said that this fact is made use of by householders in purchasing carpets, this being about the only way the average person can tell the difference between them. In order to pass off tapestry as Brussels, some ingenious makers have resorted to amongst other methods the striping in a regular manner of the backs of the former. The stripey effect in the latter is broken and irregular. A casual observation of the clearly defined character of a Brussels pattern should enable a buyer to distinguish between the two fabrics. There are three processes which call for special mention—those of printing, setting and weaving.

THE PRINTING PROCESS.

The illustration—Fig. 41—is that of a printing drum. It has been already stated that the yarns are printed before weaving. This operation is a most important one. The drums are of various sizes, the one shown being what is technically known as a "half print"—the precise meaning of which will be seen later. The dimensions of this are as follows: Circumference, 18 ft. 9 in., and width, 3 ft. First of all the drum is covered with thin oil-cloth of a special kind. The yarn is then wound upon the drum, from 6 or 8 bobbins, and, when full, the printing commences. One man, the printer, and a boy, the filler, are required for each drum. The printer stands upon a platform immediately in front of the drum.

THE PRINT BOARDS.—To the right hand of the printer is a narrow frame, not shown in our illustration, furnished with a cord and pulley. The print boards are attached to this cord, and the pulley enables them to be raised or lowered as required, in order that the operator may have any desired portion of the design within range of his eye. They consist of long, narrow boards, from which the precise manner in which the yarn must be printed is ascertained. The pattern to be printed from is cut into a certain number of strips, each of which is fixed upon a separate board. Every colour upon these bears a distinct number in white paint.

THE INDEX.—At the right-hand edge of the drum and running around its circumference are two indexes, A, one being for tapestry, numbered from 1 to 648, the other for tapestry velvet, numbered up to 432. The numbers upon the various colours on print boards correspond with those upon the index, and by reference to the two sets of numbers, the operator is enabled to print any colour exactly in proper position upon the yarn, as the drum revolves, either automatically or by hand as required, and to stop at any point desired.

THE COLOUR BOXES.—For each colour printed upon the yarn, a separate colour box is required, furnished with wheels, in order that they may pass under the print drums, a pair of *lines* being laid down for this purpose. Inside each box is a revolving disc. The colours are put into the boxes by the filler, whose duty it is also to place them upon the lines in the order called for by the printer. As the box runs along the lines forwards and backwards, the disc inside it revolves, bringing the colour with it. This disc is in close contact with the yarn, and, consequently, as the former revolves, the colour is printed in a straight line across the latter, the full width of the drum. This portion of the mechanism is situated under the drum at B. The filler stands at the right-hand side of the machine, at which point he has free access for the changing of the colour boxes.

PRINTING THE YARN.—Having briefly described the drum, the index, the print board, and the colour boxes, a few words will now be sufficient to show how the yarns are printed. The yarn being wound upon the drum and everything being in order, the printer refers to his print board. The colour, numbered 1, may be a red—his drum revolves to the corresponding number on the index; the word is given to the filler, and the required box is placed in position.

Away it runs forwards and backwards, leaving its impression upon the full width of the yarn upon the drum. All the red in the design is treated in a like manner, followed by other colours, the drum revolving and stopping as may be necessary until the yarn presents an array of stripes of varied hues—red, green, blue, black, brown, yellow, or any others that may appear in the design. It may be somewhat puzzling to understand how these yarns are made to compose a pattern, but this will be shown later.

REMOVING THE YARN FROM THE DRUMS.—When the whole of the yarn contained upon the drum has been printed, it is removed bodily, in order that more may be wound upon it, to be treated in like manner. Firstly, it will be seen that as the yarn is wound round and round the drum, it could not be bodily removed, and, secondly, as the lower portion of the drum is encased in a framework, the yarn could not be removed at all, except by the process of unwinding. In order to accomplish this, *three* contrivances are adopted. To produce a slackening of the yarn, a section of the drum (a "door"), at two opposite points, is let down. The yarn is, therefore, at once *loosened*. Then the upper portion of the framework, at the left-hand side, is also let down, which appears to produce this result, *viz.*, that as the shaft upon which the drum revolves is deprived of its means of support at the left side, it must inevitably topple over. But not so. Such a result is prevented by a little arrangement upon the right-hand end of the shaft. Upon this shaft there is an eye-bolt at C, by which, on tightening by the aid of the handle at D, the drum is held firmly in its proper position. The yarn and also the oil-cloth upon which it is wound are removed bodily, and all the parts are re-adjusted ready for the printer to operate upon a fresh lot of yarn. Such, briefly, is the process of printing yarns for the manufacture of tapestry carpets.

6

STEAMING THE YARNS.—Tapestry yarns after being printed are subjected to a steaming process, which fixes the colours. For this purpose, steaming chests are used, the shape of which varies, some being oblong, whilst others are cylindrical. The yarn is placed in these chests, stretched upon frames. There is little in this operation which calls for special description, neither is there in the process of washing—cold water only being used—nor in that of drying.

FIG. 42.

THE SETTING MACHINE.

When the printed yarn has been steamed and dried, it requires winding upon bobbins. It was mentioned that the yarn from 6 or 8 bobbins was wound upon the half-print drum at one time. This must now be re-wound upon the same number of bobbins. When the whole of the yarn, composing the full width of the carpet, has been printed and re-wound, it is sent to the "setter". The illustration—Fig. 42—is a view of a setting machine. This operation is usually undertaken by members of the female sex. The back portion of the view shows the creels, upon which the bobbins are placed. The ends of the yarns are then drawn through a pair of clasps, A, extending across the front of the creels. In front of the latter is the setting board, B. This is marked across its width with a series of parallel lines, the object of which is to enable the setter to arrange the various colours of the yarn in proper positions to form the pattern. The yarns next pass through clasps, shown at C, and from thence to the beam, which is placed upon the shaft, D. The large wooden roller at E presses against the beam, as the yarn is being wound upon it, and thus makes a hard, firm beam of yarn.

How the Setting is Done.—It will be understood that each end of yarn is printed in a variety of colours. There may be an inch of red, succeeded by six of blue, three of black, four of green, and so on, the colours ever varying throughout the whole length. As a large number of bobbins are being used it will be readily understood that by a proper arrangement of the various colours drawn from the whole of the bobbins some rough formation of a pattern is produced. It is the setter's duty to accomplish this. By a little manipulation with each end of yarn, using the lines upon the setting board as a guide, we ultimately arrive at an elongated representation of the desired pattern. Just to what extent this elongation appears will be understood when it is considered that a pile or looped fabric is to be woven, that the loop consists of two sides and the turn or top of the loop, and that, in the process of weaving, the two sides of the loop are practically hidden, the turn or top forming the face of the fabric. The creels are made to advance and recede for about the space of 12 ft., this being the length of yarn operated upon at one time. When this length has been properly set, the clasps, A, fix it until it has been wound on the beam. The same operation is repeated until the whole has been transferred to the beam, when it is ready for the weaver.

THE TAPESTRY LOOM.

The loom for weaving tapestry carpets is similar in some respects to the Brussels loom already described, and yet there are important points wherein it differs. A fabric is being woven consisting only of 216 ends, whereas the five-

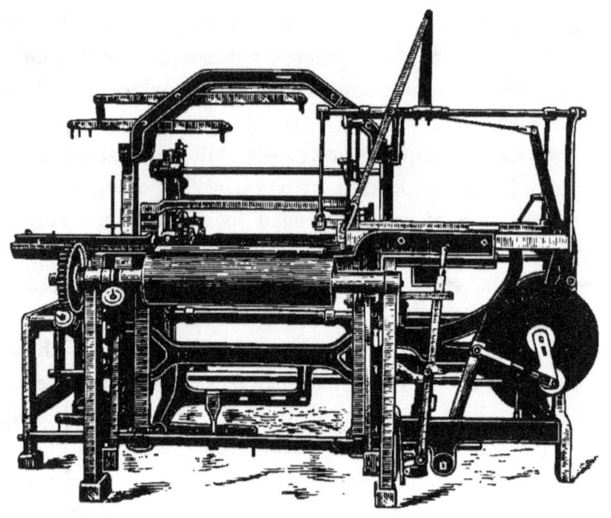

FIG. 43.

frame Brussels loom operates 1280. There is, therefore, no Jacquard, and consequently no cards or harness, neither are creels required. In other respects, the loom is much like that for the weaving of Brussels, as the following particulars will show.

WARP AND WEFT.—The warp forming the face of the fabric is wound upon a beam, as already stated. There are also two chain warps and a stuffing warp. The two chain warps are carried upon one beam, and the stuffing warp upon another. The double shed principle is adopted as in the Brussels loom. The chain and stuffing warps, and also the weft, are of cotton, linen or similar material, and are operated by four healds.

THE REED.—Through each dent in the reed, one end of face yarn, an end of each chain warp, and an end of stuffing warp are drawn. There are thus four ends through each dent.

THE WIRE MOTION.—The wire motion is almost identical with that on the Brussels loom, similar wires being employed to those shown in the previous chapter, the tapestry wire being like that in Fig. 42, and the tapestry velvet wire like that in Fig. 43. The motion operates in exactly the same manner as that already described. As the pick is formed upon one wire, another is inserted in its place. This wire motion is shown to the right of the loom, illustrated in Fig. 43. This is a view of a tapestry velvet loom. This is given because on the tapestry loom the wire motion being almost identical with that on the Brussels loom, a comparison between the tapestry and tapestry velvet motions may be made.

TAPESTRY DESIGNS.

There are various qualities of tapestry carpets, but the standard quality is 216 ends in width. For the designing of this quality, 8 + 7 ruled or point paper must be used. There are many points of difference in designs for Brussels and tapestry carpets. For instance, in the latter, there is no planting of colours to trouble one, as the method of manufacture is such that any number may be employed. Of course, the designer uses discretion in this matter. He will require just sufficient colours to produce a telling and tasteful effect. It is by no means an easy thing to draw a good tapestry design. Whilst in Brussels, every flower or ornament, in fact, every line or dot which appears in the design is reproduced in the carpet, in tapestry this is not the case. Certain colours run or spread into other colours, and the designer must thoroughly understand what will be the effect of the design when it is woven. Now suppose he draws a band in two colours, say a gold and a brown, with a row of balls in brown and white—he would have about double the thickness of gold lines compared with his brown lines. So

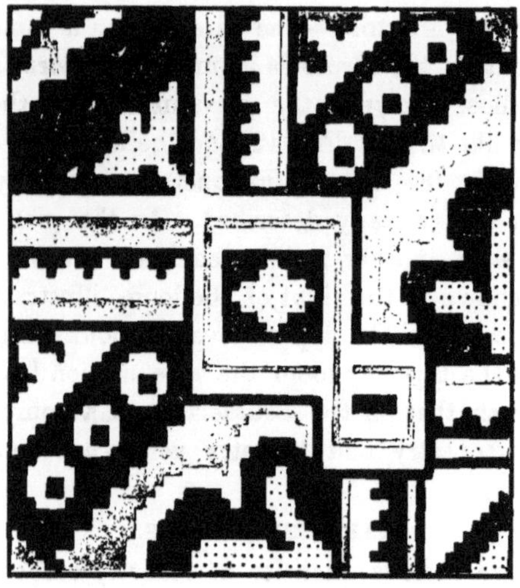

Fig. 44.

also, the balls would be mostly white, very little brown being sufficient to show up well when the pattern is woven. Thus, as the designer applies his colours to the paper, he must see in his mind's eye the result in the carpet, the lightest colours being made most prominent, but when woven, the light and dark will be pretty evenly balanced, owing to the *spreading* above mentioned. The result of this *spreading* of the colours is noticeable in any tapestry. It is to this that the pattern owes its ragged and misty appearance, which is entirely absent from Brussels. Fig. 44 is a section of a simple design for tapestry, which will serve the purpose of illustrating this manipulation of colours. Before leaving this part of the subject, it may be explained that, in certain cases, the balance of light and dark colours would be about even, that is, of course, if they were required to appear so in the woven fabric. Lines running upwards are treated in this manner, but diagonal lines, or those running across the width, would require more light than dark. The pattern, Fig. 44, has been drawn specially to illustrate these points.

The Sizes of Designs.—The designer is restricted to certain sizes of designs. The full width of the standard quality is, as before stated, 216 ends. It has been mentioned that the index upon the printing drum has divisions numbered from 1 to 648. Any division of 648 can be utilised for the length of a design. Thus—324, 216, 162, 108, and so on, can be used, but a good and useful size is 216. The illustration—Fig. 41—shows what is known as a half-print drum. There are also quarter-print and full-print drums. These terms denote the style of the design, and the style of design governs the particular drum upon which the yarn for that design is printed. A quarter-print pattern has four repetitions of the design in the width. A half-print has two repetitions in the width. These repetitions may be either straight across or "dropped". The full-print pattern is, of course, one in which one repeat occupies the full width, *viz.*, 216.

Borders and stair carpets are, of course, made in tapestry. The borders mostly in use are woven two in the width of a piece. In stair carpets, half-yard, or, as they are technically termed, two-quarters, five-eighths, and three-quarters are mostly used.

Designer's Colours.—The tapestry designer is furnished

with a full range of all the colours he ever requires, and these are legion. They are, of course, mixed by himself, or by one of his assistants, by the aid of a glass or marble slab, a muller and a pallet knife. In the mixing of tapestry colours, a large quantity of gum is used, because the designs are all coated, when finished, with spirit varnish, to prevent the latter from smearing or otherwise spoiling the design. In Brussels designing, colours are usually mixed to shade for each separate design. In tapestry, as above stated, the designer has a range of colours of every conceivable shade, that he is continually using, and as they are finished, others exactly like them are mixed to take their places. The colours set hard in the saucers in which they are placed, but a little water is all that is required to make them usable again.

CHAPTER IX.

INGRAIN CARPETS.

THE fabric commonly known as "Scotch," "Kidderminster," and "Art Squares" is properly called "Ingrain Carpet". This differs widely from the two fabrics already described, as it is not a looped fabric. Many readers are conversant with double cloths for wearing apparel, and the ingrain carpet is a perfect type of a double cloth, for the decoration of the home, which may be worn on either side, with equal satisfaction from either a wearing or an ornamental point of view.

The fabric in an artistic sense does not compare in its effectiveness with the more expensive Brussels carpet, its clearness and beauty in design and its great adaptability for tasteful colour effects giving the latter the pre-eminence, but its wearing qualities are considered to surpass those of tapestry carpets. Being a double cloth, it is reversible, for whereas there may be upon one side light ornament on a dark ground, on the other there would be dark ornament on a light ground. There are varieties of the fabric made, and to touch upon all these would take up too much space, but in order to give sufficient particulars to enable the reader to learn something of the method of manufacture, attention is called to the extra super two-ply ingrain carpet, which is the standard quality made.

INGRAIN CARPET LOOM.

The illustration—Fig. 45—shows a loom for the manufacture of ingrain carpets, engraved from a photograph supplied by Messrs. John Crossley & Sons. This loom in its general features partakes more of the character of a Jacquard loom for the weaving of fabrics for wearing

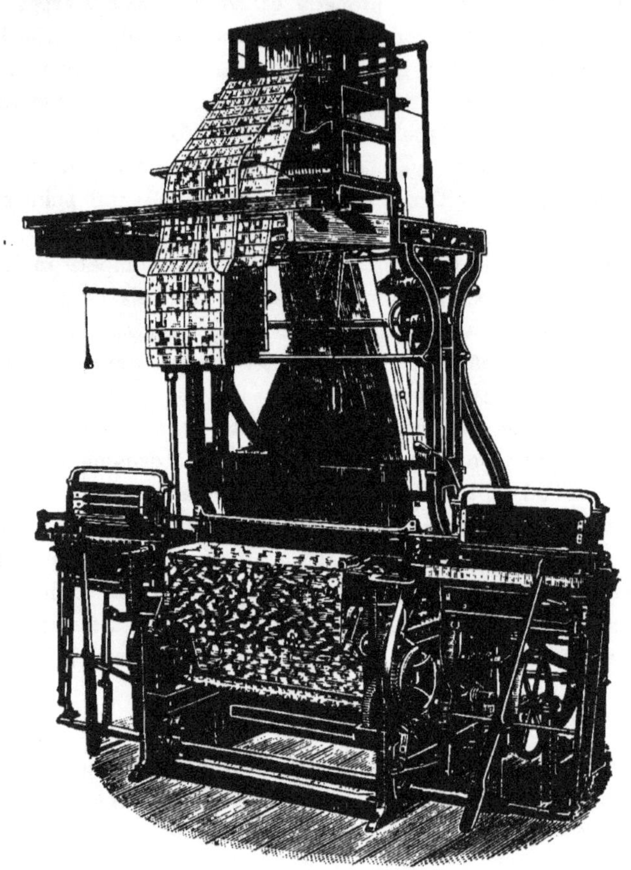

FIG. 45.

apparel than of the two previously described, *viz.*, the Brussels and the tapestry looms. The ingrain looms are generally of the kind known as vertical box-looms. They are made up to six boxes. The illustration shows the Murkland type, which is an American invention, but has been improved in various particulars in this country. This loom is made with upright or circular boxes, the former being shown in the illustration.

WARP AND WEFT.—For the manufacture of extra super two-ply ingrain, four warps are required, which, however, really work as two. These are wound upon one beam. They are solely controlled by the Jacquard mechanism—no healds being required, as in the case of Brussels carpet. Through each dent in the reed, four warp ends are drawn. In any ordinary case, four wefts are employed, but in some, extra colour effects are produced, and, therefore, more shuttles are used.

THE JACQUARD.—The Jacquard machine employed is similar to that for the manufacture of Brussels carpets, but differs in important points from the machines ordinarily in use for the generality of fabrics. For the weaving of a piece of ingrain carpet, a Jacquard of 272 needles is employed; this produces one repeat of a design half a yard in width. Like the Brussels Jacquard, the majority of machines have cords worked by the needles instead of by wire uprights, as in the ordinary Jacquard. In some cases, wire uprights are in use, but the cords appear to be in greater favour. For weaving an art square, which is a most popular form of ingrain carpet, there would be of course a Jacquard of double capacity, *viz.*, 544 needles or two machines of 272 needles each. The needles in one of the single machines, or half the number of those in the double machine, would be utilised for the weaving of the body, the border and corner being controlled by the remainder of the needles. With the remark that the Jacquard is very similar to that used in the Brussels loom previously described, this portion of the subject may be dismissed.

THE HARNESS.—The harness is constructed upon the principle generally in vogue. There are 272 needles, which would weave a repeat of half a yard. The full width of a piece of ingrain carpet is one yard. Therefore every needle is controlling two repeats of the fabric. The harness is, however, much more extensive when weaving an "Art Square," because it would be required to control the warp threads for the borders and corners at each side of the carpet, and also a number of repeats of the body according to the width of the "square" being manufactured. But one point may be mentioned. There are four warps, really working as two, and, consequently, instead of 272 harness threads being required for each repeat of a pattern, there are 544 or 272 for each side of the double cloth.

THE CARDS.—In the manufacture of these fabrics, the Jacquard cards are an expensive item. The ordinary cards are employed, and in the making of an "Art Square" some idea of the cost may be obtained. For *piece goods*, of course, one set of cards only is required, but for the "square," a set is necessary for the body, one for each of the two borders, and one for the corner, or four sets in all. For each change of the cards, the loom must be stopped, and the change effected by hand.

THE INGRAIN CARPET.

In the manufacture of ingrain carpets, four warps and four wefts are employed, as previously stated—two warp threads and two weft threads for the figure, and the same number of each for the ground. Extra effects of colour may be obtained, first, by ordinary means, and, second, by special means. By the ordinary method, a striped warp is employed, the proportion of the various colours being guided by the ruled paper design. The planting of colours has been described in the particulars given on Brussels carpets. This planting is all done in the warp. In ingrain, extra effects may be got by planting or striping the warp, and, further, by employing extra shuttles. The result is not, however, perfection, as a fabric is obtained more or less one mass of stripes. The colours show up plainly in all places where they are intended to show, and, to produce this result, what are termed half-tone effects of the same colours show between, which cause the fabric to be stripey, and far from pleasing from

Fig. 46.

an artistic point of view. The special means adopted for producing extra colour effects are due to enterprising manufacturers, one of whom, in the Leeds district, shows some really beautiful specimens of ingrain carpets. By these special means, extra colours are placed in required positions, according to the nature of the design, without the objectional feature above referred to. By way of example, notice the design given in Fig. 46. In the upper right-hand corner are three flowers. By the ordinary method of striping the warp, the centres of the three flowers could be got in different colours, but there would be a subdued stripe effect of the same colours running down the design, until same flowers appear again, and if it was required to bring up these colours in the small flowers which intervene, the largest of them striped would be in the two colours used for the centres of the large flowers immediately above. Here comes in a little lesson in designing. This design does not lend itself readily to this method of striped warps, as, in order to produce the best possible results, the designer must either refrain from bringing up extra colours again, that is, they would not appear again until the same flowers were struck in the next repeat, or he must alter his design in order to more effectively make full use of his extra colours. These remarks apply to all classes of textile fabrics, where planting of colours is an important feature. Under such conditions, the designer will generally see that flowers, leaves or portions of ornament, which can be utilised for the introduction of extra colours, are placed in relation one to another, so that the object to be attained shall be effected with the best possible results. The design—Fig. 46—would not be objectionable if special means were adopted for using extra colour effect. Manufacturers have been ready to recognise the objection to the striped effects in ingrain carpets, and, to avoid this, have hit upon the plan of a neutral shade of warp, or some union of warp threads which will harmonise with the weft colours introduced to give a pleasing variety to the design, the warp being of one shade for the figure and one for the ground only, throughout the fabric. In Brussels, almost any number of colours can be used, because they only show just where required on the face of the fabric, and, when not required, are hidden away at the back. In ingrain it is different—the stripes show on both sides of the cloth, and hence the great improvement resulting from the efforts made by various manufacturers to overcome what were, to any one with taste and artistic feeling, objectionable fabrics. Where these striped fabrics are manufactured, the objection to them is not so forcible as was formerly the case, where large geometrical designs were employed, and stripes of from four to six inches of one colour were displayed throughout the length of a piece. Truly, the taste displayed in the manufacture of ingrain carpets has made vast strides during the last generation.

INGRAIN DESIGNS.—In designing for ingrain carpets, there is much scope for the skilful draughtsman, who should always bear in mind the nature of the fabric for which he is designing. In other words, he should endeavour to have the fabric growing in his mind's eye as he proceeds with his work. He should be ready to fully estimate what the effect of any portion of the work upon which he may be engaged will be upon both sides of the fabric. The illustration given in Fig. 46 shows a good specimen of a design for an ingrain carpet. The bordered designs which were given earlier would also adapt themselves readily for this purpose. Referring to Fig. 46, the large figure lends itself readily for the introduction of extra colour, which might be placed in its centre portion. The same colour could come in the three small flowers at the edge of the scroll above. Then the centres of the three flowers at the top, to the right hand, could be in the same colour, which might be also utilised for the smaller flowers below. Floral or ornamental designs are very popular, but large geometrical figures of the class already named are out of date. The patterns should not be too crowded nor too much cut up, as a mass of detail is objectionable. When it is considered that the full repeat of a design is half a yard, it is seen that the designer has much scope for his powers. The same size is allowed for a border and for a corner, and thus the designer, with a ready conception, can produce effective and artistic patterns. But here an observation may be made which is applicable to any form of border designing, *viz.*, whilst a border should harmonise with the body, it should not partake too closely of the *motif* of the body pattern. Let the border be bold—if possible, bolder than the body, and whilst in full harmony with it, let the ornamentation be different. In the majority of cases, the result will be most satisfactory, as variety is thereby obtained, and variety is pleasing. The width of a repeat has been mentioned. The most suitable length for a design is the same, *viz.*, half a yard, because it enables the manufacturer the more easily to utilise a design, either for piece goods or for a "square". The length of the repeat being equal to the width enables the same ornamentation of the border to be used at the sides of a fabric that appears at the top and bottom, this being a desirable feature, producing a full carpet square of the most harmonious character. It may be taken for granted that a manufacturer having an eye to his interests will be ready to supply any pattern, either in piece goods or in the form of the "Art Square," so popular in ingrain carpets.

Ruled or Point-paper Patterns.—In order to show the method employed for drafting designs upon ruled paper, a portion of Fig. 46 has been worked out as an example, Fig. 47. This takes in one of the flowers shown at the top, to the right hand, in Fig. 46, with portions of the ornament immediately surrounding it. The design—Fig. 47—shows four colours, two for the figure and two for the ground. The first figure thread, which is white, mates with the first ground thread, black. So that in weaving, white figure appears on the face, and black figure on the back. The same occurs with the next thread, and so on throughout the pattern. A further colour effect might be obtained by shading a design, where possible. By shading a design, the introduction of a half-tone is meant. This might be produced by indicating upon the ruled paper alternate picks of the figure and ground, as shown in the centre of the flower in Fig. 47. This is useful, not only in this case but also in the shading of large leaves or scrolls; in fact, it may be employed where it is not desired to use extra colours, or even in conjunction

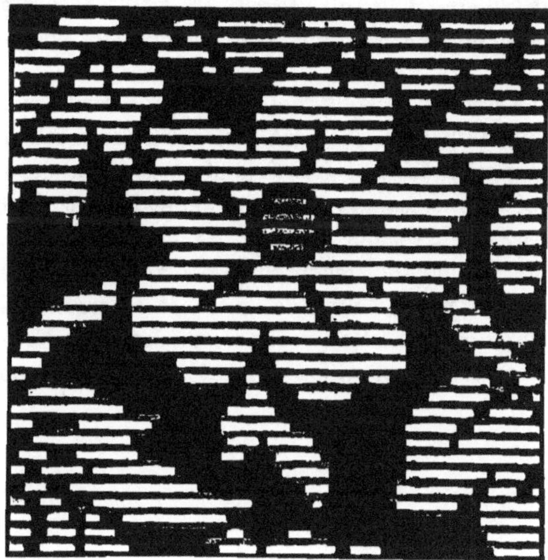

Fig. 47.

with them. Taking Fig. 46, this half-tone would be used in the centre portion of the large or principal figure and in one or two other places, which might be found suitable by the designer, as he worked out the pattern upon ruled paper. Where extra colours are used, they would be placed in similar positions to those indicated for the half-tone effect. The example given in Fig. 47 should supply any additional information upon ruled-paper drafting required by those interested, and we, therefore, consider further particulars unnecessary—beyond the fact that design paper, having an equal number of *cords* or squares each way, is used for the drafting of extra super two-ply ingrains; thus 8 × 8 paper may be used. The full repeat of a ruled paper is 272 *cords* or squares in width, this being the standard for the cloth here described. In the drafting of patterns for ingrain or "Art Square," four ruled papers are required—one for the body, two for the end and side borders, and one for the corner.

If the student carefully notes the particulars here given, he should, with practice, be able to work out a design suitable for ingrain fabrics, granting, of course, that he is possessed of the necessary inventive power and the skill required in the way of freehand drawing. A good technical knowledge of the loom and Jacquard is not absolutely necessary, even to the most skilful designers of a large variety of ornamental fabrics. Many very clever designers have little knowledge of looms, whilst a great number have none at all.

CHAPTER X.

AXMINSTER CARPETS.

INFORMATION has been given on Brussels, tapestry and ingrain carpets; a most important variety, namely, Axminster, must now be dealt with, as these chapters would not be complete without some notice being taken of this really beautiful fabric. It is with no little difficulty that this portion of the subject is taken up, as there are many varieties of Axminster, and to treat upon all would be almost an impossibility; therefore, those particular cloths which will, from their importance, prove the most interesting and instructive will be considered.

THE AXMINSTER CARPET.

The fabric is constructed of hank-dyed yarns, as in the case of Brussels and Wilton carpets, but they differ widely in the process of manufacture. The Wilton is really a Brussels with the pile cut. An Axminster is also a cut-pile fabric, but the pile is formed in a totally different manner from that of the Wilton, besides which, it is much thicker. The Wilton is woven on wires—the Axminster is not. It will be seen later how this is done. In the former, there are certain limitations to the use of colours, as described in a previous chapter. All colours used above a certain number require to be planted—that is to say, in the weaving of a "five-frame" there may be ten colours (any reasonable number may be used), and, if there are four full frames, six colours would be planted in the fifth frame. These six colours would run in rows, lengthwise of the piece. In Axminster, there is no limitation to the number of colours employed, but the means by which this is accomplished will be mentioned in proper order. As before remarked, there are many varieties of the fabric; for instance, "hand-made," "patent or chenille," "royal" and "aristo," the two latter being the same fabric, differing only in "pitch".

One of the main difficulties in the treatment of such a subject as the present is its proper illustration. Firstly, as to illustration by designs—no good service would be done by giving a "ruled-paper pattern" of each class, therefore only one has been drawn, and, even in this case, an imperfect result is obtained, consequent upon the inability to show in a black and white engraving a necessary number of colours. Notwithstanding this drawback, the pattern will be found useful for the proper elucidation of one or two points. This design is for a three-quarter yard fabric, only half this width being shown. It is a reverse or centre pattern of the same type as that explained in Figs. 9 and 10 in the chapters given earlier upon "Hints on Designing Fabrics". The "royal" is a cloth which has attained much prominence in the trade, because it is woven upon a power loom of unique construction, the original patent for which lapsed some time ago. The illustrations given in the patent specification are of too complicated a nature to be of service in a treatise written in the simplest manner possible.

Axminster carpets are continually gaining in popularity. The fabric is beautifully effective—is thick, and at the same time soft to the tread, whilst it is also durable, and, what is most important to the purchaser, it has come down greatly in price.

HAND-MADE AXMINSTER.—Briefly, this is made without a loom, and something after the following manner: Two wood rods run parallel with each other. In the manufacture of a three-quarter yard fabric, these rods would be such a distance apart as to accommodate that width of cloth. The pile is constructed of tufts of yarns, each one of which is separately tied into the warp, and, when a full row has been fixed, the weft is introduced, and thus the process proceeds until a complete piece results, which then requires to be cropped and finished. In the case of a "square," the procedure is much the same.

THE PATENT AXMINSTER.—There is a great difference between the making of the "patent" and the "royal" Axminster carpet, but, at the same time, if these carpets in their finished state were laid side by side, it would, in some cases, be difficult for an inexperienced person to distinguish between them. There is also a very wide difference between the making of the patent Axminster and the tapestry or Brussels, and while one might be deceived with the patent and the royal, no one, not even the most inexperienced, could fail to discover the difference between these two and the tapestry or Brussels. There are two processes of weaving in the patent Axminster, while in the others, there is only one, and, moreover, in the former, there is really no limit to the number of colours or shades that may be used, and, what is of more consequence, carpets may be woven in one piece, without seam or join, to fit any room, hall, landing or stair. The advantages of this are very apparent to all, even to those who know little or nothing about carpets, inasmuch as users know well that all joined carpets wear at the seams, and at the mitres at the corners. Of course, some Brussels are now made to do away with the mitres at the corners, and tapestries and Brussels are also being manufactured in squares without seam, but the fact remains that, for beauty, and, what is infinitely of greater value, durability, there is nothing to excel the Axminster. As a proof of the favour in which Axminsters are held by the community, it is only necessary to mention such names as Richard Smith & Sons (The Carpet Manufacturing Co., Limited), Tomkinson & Adam, James Templeton & Co., and John Lyle & Co., who are so closely identified with this particular make of carpet, and when the thousands of workers they employ are considered, some idea of the demand for the fabric can be formed.

In making a patent Axminster carpet, the first thing a manufacturer has to consider is the quality wanted, and the qualities that can be made are legion. Having determined this, he then proceeds to put the design on point or ruled paper, according to the quality determined upon. These papers are then cut into strips or shots, and from them, the weft cloth is woven, according to the design, in looms specially built for the purpose. From the weft loom the cloth passes on to the cutting machines. These machines cut the webs of cloth, which are woven on what may be termed skeleton warps, into strips, which, on being closed or twisted, as the case may be, form the chenille fur shots, which go to make the surface of the carpet. The next process of manufacture is the making of the back of the carpet and the setting of the face thereon. This also is done on an elaborately and intricately built loom. The warps having been set in the loom—in some cases there are four or five warps—the formation of the back begins, either with a fine jute thread or with a heavy woollen one, as desired, and on this the chenille fur, which has previously been prepared, is set, while the back is being made. It will be readily conceived that as each consecutive chenille fur shot, which is woven in the necessary colours to the previously painted papers, is set, it will form and produce a pattern in the cloth, the same in every respect as that originally painted on the paper. From the setting loom, the carpet passes to the cropping machine, where the surface is cropped of all the loose fibre or fluff, and, finally, it is steamed and finished, from whence it issues a beautiful and durable article, ready to adorn our homes.

ROYAL AXMINSTER LOOM.

Amongst the several inventions for the manufacture of

FIG. 48.

this cloth there are two which contain so many points of similarity that we shall endeavour to treat upon both, showing the reader in what manner one differs from the other, but, in the end, accomplishes the same result. The first of these is an invention by A. Smith and H. Skinner, and the second by C. E. Skinner and E. Tymeson, all four of whom have their homes in the United States of America.

Reference has been made to the hand-made cloth and how each tuft in a row requires to be tied separately into the warp. The object of these inventions is to perform this process by mechanical means, and, at the same time, to bind them into a perfect and durable fabric. There is no necessity to enter fully into the subject of the whole loom, as certain parts, which are in reality the essence of the inventions, are only necessary to give the reader a good idea of the method of manufacture. Briefly, there are a breast beam and cloth roll in front of the loom and also warp beams as in any other carpet loom. There are healds too for forming the shed, constructed and operated in the usual manner, and means are provided for beating up the warp threads. In Brussels and ingrain carpet looms the Jacquard machine is an essential portion of the mechanism, but in the present case this is entirely dispensed with, the various colours of yarns, or tufting materials as they are called, being arranged upon spools, each of which is operated as desired. This is a most important point, the means for effecting it being similar in the two inventions.

The Spools and Tubes.—The spools upon which the tufting material is wound are of a length sufficient to hold the yarn required to form a row of tufts across the width of the fabric. Attached to the spool and running parallel with it is a bar fitted with as many short tubes or nozzles as there are tufts in a row across the fabric. Each spool turns upon journals held in a spool frame. A separate spool is required for each row of tufts in the whole pattern, thus in weaving a pattern of 100 rows, that number of spools is required, each one being brought into its proper position to form the necessary row of tufts.

Four illustrations are given. Fig. 49 shows an elevation of the spool and tubes. Fig. 50 is a plan view of the same, and Fig. 51 an end elevation. In Fig. 52 we give a tube in

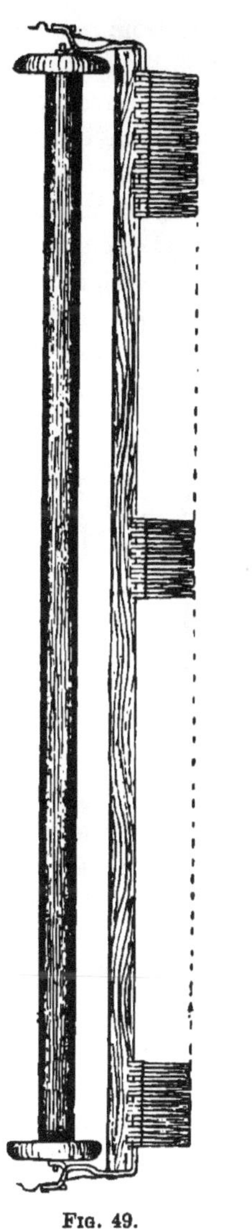

FIG. 49.

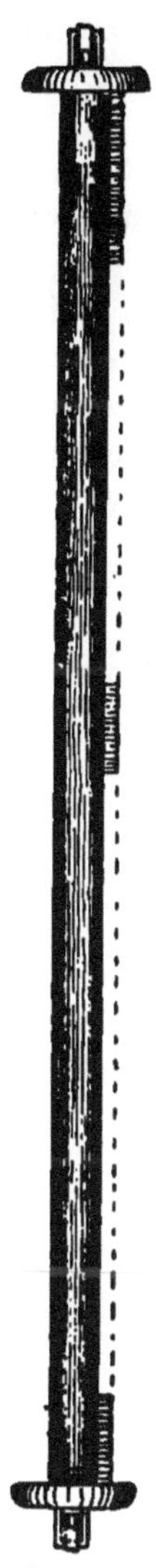

FIG. 50.

its actual size. Of course the tubes reach from end to end of the spool, although they are not shown in the drawings.

The material for each tuft is wound on the spool in a belt or zone. By referring to the design given in Fig. 48, and taking the bottom row of the pattern, sufficient of each of these colours should be arranged on a spool, in the exact order here given, and these colours would come up in the carpet in positions exactly as shown on the design.

Fig. 53 is a rough drawing, representing a portion of a spool with different coloured yarns upon it ready for use. This shows clearly the manner of "setting" the yarns. Sup-

Fig. 51.

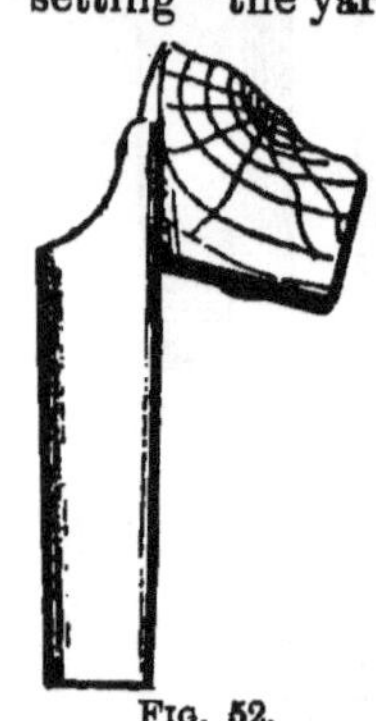

Fig. 52.

posing that in a single row of design there are four brown, succeeded by four black, six blue, three black, six red, two white, two green and so on; these yarns are wound upon the spool, as shown in the illustration, the four brown being represented at A, the four black at B, the blue at C, the black at D, the red at E, the white at F, and the green at G, to be followed by other colours to the end of the row, as indicated upon the design.

The use of spools gives much the same effect as that produced by a Jacquard, but whereas the Jacquard can manipulate only a certain number of colours running in line with each other by the system of spools, each succeeding tuft in the length of the pattern might be of varying shades. The absence of restriction in the manipulation of colours forms a distinct advantage over Brussels and Wiltons, enabling colour effects to be easily produced, which in these cases could only be attained with imperfect results, even after the exercise of great care and ingenuity on the part of the designer.

When tubes are prepared for use, the ends of the tufting materials from the spools are passed through and protrude sufficiently from the tubes, H, as indicated by the dotted lines in Fig. 53, usually for about an inch—ready to be engaged by the warp of the fabric.

THE SPOOL CHAINS.—In order that the spools may be

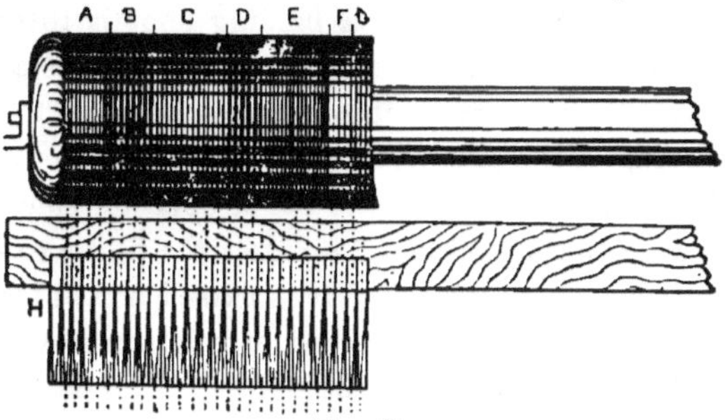

FIG. 53.

held and presented in their proper order to the mechanism which takes them and introduces the ends of the tufting materials between the warp threads, two parallel chains are provided. These chains are endless, and pass round sprocket wheels, secured to a shaft supported by the frame of the loom. These chains are long enough to hold as many spools as are required in the weaving of any particular pattern. Each spool is taken from the chain in succession by the aid of transferring arms, and placed in position over the warps, and, after use, is returned to its original place upon the chains.

WARP AND WEFT.—The spools are presented to the

warps with, in the case of the first invention, their tubes in horizontal position, and are then rocked so as to turn the ends of the tufting yarn down between the warp threads. After the ends of this tufting yarn have been introduced between the warp threads, a shot of fine filling is introduced into the shed to secure and fasten the ends of the tufting materials, after which these ends are turned backwards and upwards by means of a comb, previous to the introduction of a shot of coarse filling. In the case of the second invention the spools take a slight sideway movement, which lays the tufts across the spaces between the warp yarns; hooks then protrude through the warp from underneath and draw the tufts down through it, when a binding shot is introduced. The tufts are next turned upwards by the aid of a brush, and another binding shot is introduced.

Returning to the first invention, the filling is wound upon two bobbins or cops. These are set at opposite sides of the loom, in convenient positions, to permit the filling to pass to the devices which act upon it. It is passed across the loom through the open shed by means of a reciprocating weft carrier. Two loops of weft or filling, one from each side of the loom, are passed through each shed that is opened. Thus both selvages are made secure, although the weft is introduced in the form of a loop. The same weft carrier passes the weft from both sides of the loom. There are two warps —one fine and one coarse—and, by a suitable arrangement, these are presented to the weft carrier in the order required. There are fine and coarse fillings—the former being used after the insertion of the tufting material, so as to fasten it, and the latter at other times. In order that the weft thread introduced by the weft carrier, while moving in one direction across the shed, may not move back with the carrier when it moves in an opposite direction, a spring weft finger is provided at each end of the lay to hold the end of the loop (warp).

When the lay retrogrades after beating up the filling, the weft fingers withdraw from the loop.

CUTTING THE TUFTS.—In the "Smith and Skinner" invention, the cutting of the tufts is performed by a disc-cutter, which turns upon its central axis as it moves backwards and forwards across the loom. This disc-cutter operates in connection with a fixed blade, having a long cutting edge, so that it may perform the double object of cutting and supporting the tufting material for the action of the disc-cutter. The latter and the fixed blade are so arranged as to enable them to be moved out of the way of the spool frame at the time the latter is moved to the warp, and to be returned into position again after the spool frame has been moved back. The fixed blade and disc-cutter are so connected with the loom frame as to have a reciprocating movement towards and from each other, and the position of the tufting yarns is intermediate between the positions of the two cutting implements, when they are farthest apart.

In the "Skinner and Tymeson" invention, a different method of cutting the tufts is employed. The cutters consist of two shear blades arranged crosswise of the loom above the warp. The front or upper cutter has a straight edge and is arranged at right angles to the warp. It has a simple backward and forward movement. The back cutter, which has preferably a curved edge, has a peculiar movement, having the effect of causing a small portion of each one to be in action at any time.

AXMINSTER DESIGNS.—The principal features of the royal Axminster carpet loom have now been described with the spools, the tubes, the spool chains, the warp and weft, and the cutting of the tufts; with the shearing and finishing of the fabric, the carpet is complete. In reference to the arrangement of colours nothing can be said more than has been already stated. There is much scope for the skilful designer with a taste for colour effects, to produce really beautiful patterns, as is evidenced by the tasteful fabrics one sees exhibited in the windows of carpet stores. The design given in Fig. 48 is defective, from inability to introduce more colours in a black and white engraving.

The particulars as to the "pitch" or size of patterns vary greatly, as patent Axminsters are made with four, five, six, seven and even up to twelve shots to the inch, in both three-quarters wide carpeting and bordered squares. Royal Axminster is woven with five and seven shots to the inch, and with seven reeds to the inch in both qualities, the latter quality being known as the "aristo". The example—Fig. 48—is designed for this fabric.

CHAPTER XI.

DAMASK AND TAPESTRY FABRICS.

In preceding chapters, various classes of carpets, namely, Brussels, tapestry, ingrain and Axminster, have been dealt with; the consideration of other fabrics of an ornamental nature now claims attention. Equally as important as those already treated upon is a variety of beautiful cloths for upholstery and general decorative purposes. In this class, first worthy of notice are damasks and tapestry fabrics. Worsted damasks were at one time much used for hangings, table covers and furniture upholstery, but they have been superseded by what are considered more effective fabrics, although there is still an extensive trade done in them. Linen damasks for table linen, towels, etc., have not, so far, encountered a rival, neither have the beautiful and delicate silk damasks, which will always meet with a steady demand, their extremely rich appearance and general excellence for hangings and upholstery purposes ensuring them favour with those able to afford high-priced fabrics. There are also damasks of low quality, such as those composed entirely of cotton.

Worsted damasks appear to have given way in popular favour to the more effective cloths known as tapestry, in which, owing to the fondness of the public for colours, a large trade is done in window curtains, table covers, furniture coverings, etc. The skilful use of colours assists the designer in his work, and, by their aid, he is able to produce patterns of a striking character, and, in this particular class of fabric, every possible means is adopted in order to utilise them to their fullest extent. In Brussels carpets, the designer is restricted to the planting of colours in the warp, but in tapestry

FIG. 54.

fabrics both warp and weft are often so treated for this purpose. These fabrics have held the field for a great number of years, but have, of course, been subject to the fluctuations of fashion and to competition with other cloths. When the popularity of Paisley shawls became a thing of the past, many manufacturers turned their attention to tapestry fabrics, large quantities of which were manufactured in the Paisley factories. But, in time, the same manufacturers deemed it advisable to make another change. It is not intended, however, to give the history of the trade in these cloths, but to deal with them as occupying a prominent position amongst ornamental textile fabrics, and for which there is and always will be, from their high decorative character, more or less of a demand.

Linen damasks, as every one is aware, are prominent fabrics for household use. It is impossible to conceive anything more suitably adapted for the purposes for which they are employed. Their purity of appearance, combined with their durability, renders them indispensable for table use, and the possibility of their being superseded by any other fabrics in the estimation of the million is remote.

In this chapter, a few particulars of use to the designer and student will be given, first, upon damasks, and, secondly, upon tapestry fabrics, illustrating the remarks in a suitable manner, as in previous chapters.

DAMASKS.

In treating upon damasks, it is not necessary to enter fully into the subject of the loom and Jacquard, as this has already been done in the chapter upon the "Jacquard Machine". The remarks will therefore be confined to the fabrics themselves, and illustrations will be given so that the learner will be able to thoroughly understand the observations.

Some seven centuries ago, fabrics were extensively manufactured in Damascus, and were in great demand in all countries. But these textures were composed of silk, and ultimately the trade came to recognise any silken fabric as a damask. In the present day, the name is applied not only to those of silk, but also to those of worsted, linen, cotton, etc. The design given in Fig. 54 is specially suited for a damask, but more particularly for those of linen and worsted. In the chapters on "Hints on Designing Fabrics," the patterns Figs. 10, 14 and 15, are specially suitable for silk damasks.

DAMASK DESIGNS.

In working out the design given in Fig. 54, the first consideration is, of course, the size which it must assume when woven, this being regulated by the fineness of the reed, etc. Having decided this question, sketch the design upon ruled paper and carefully paint it in, after which, bind the figure and ground in a suitable manner. This might be done by means of a twill, such as the one given in Fig. 55, wherein

Fig. 55.

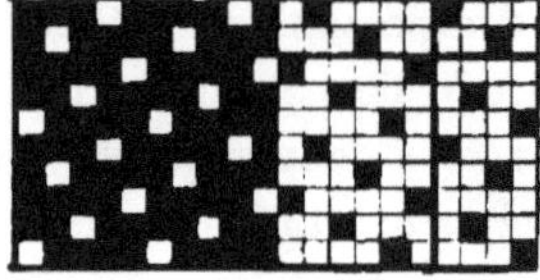

Fig. 56.

the weft intersects the warp at every fifth thread. But twills produce a diagonally lined appearance of the cloth, more or less minute according to the coarseness of the twill, it is true, but sufficiently noticeable to be objectionable for regular use. Hence recourse is had to the use of broken twills or satins. In these, the warp threads intersect the weft threads in irregular succession, thus producing the smooth, even face so admired in satin and damask fabrics. Those most commonly in use are from five to eight shafts, shown in Figs. 56 and 57. When weaving the pattern given in Fig. 54 in a common quality, the figure and ground should be dotted with a five shaft (Fig. 56), but if for a good quality the eight shaft would be used (Fig. 57), because, the yarns being much finer, a closer dotting is not necessary. In these figures, the white dots represent the figure and the black dots the ground. The next consideration is the prevention of floats in the veins of the leaves and flowers and in the fine lines in the ornament. This may be done wherever required by a special dotting, which will fit in nicely with the figure and ground satin.

FANCY EFFECTS.—Having briefly referred to the most simple method of drafting a ruled paper, this in combination with fancy effects must be considered. In Fig. 58 is a

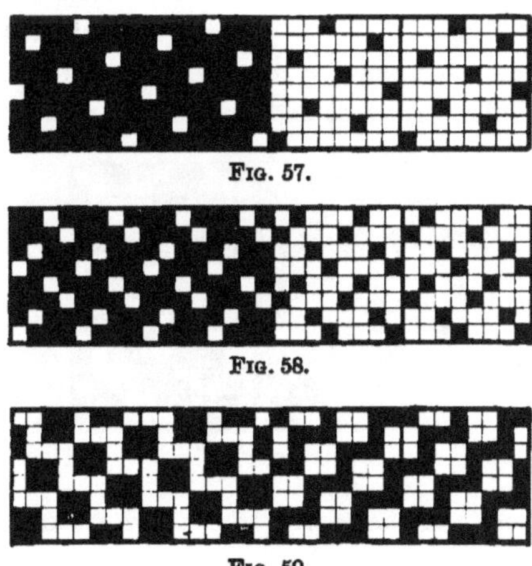

FIG. 57.

FIG. 58.

FIG. 59.

weave known as a Swansdown crêpe, which might be used independently for figure and ground, or in combination with a satin effect—for instance, a five shaft satin figure and a crêpe ground, or *vice versâ*. Taking Fig. 54, the crêpe dotting could be introduced within the scroll, which comes between the flowers.

In Fig. 59, another fancy weave is given, which might be employed alone for figure and ground, or in combination with one of the others. The weave shown in Fig. 60 produces a very pretty fabric, when used with a satin. Supposing a designing for a linen damask was claiming attention, and a scroll pattern was employed such as that given in Fig. 14 ("Hints on Designing Fabrics"), a five shaft satin might be used for the scroll, and this fancy weave (Fig. 60) for the ground. In this case the scroll must be edged completely round, that is, must have an outline. This forms a cut-off between figure and ground, and at the same time adds to the effectiveness of the fabric. This weave could be suitably employed within the scroll between the flowers in Fig. 54. Should another pattern consist of a large leaf within a circle, this being, of course, repeated at intervals to form the full design, we could have the fancy weave, Fig. 60,

Fig. 60.

for the ground, and the leaf dotted a five shaft satin, whilst the ground of the circle would also be dotted a five shaft satin, the leaf and ground being treated as ordinary figure and ground dotting. To be more explicit—the leaf should be painted in colour, the ground of the circle being left white, and the fancy ground weave in the colour used for the leaf.

There is an almost endless number of combinations which may be used in designing for linen, worsted and silk damasks, but they must be left for the consideration of the intelligent student. One point that may be mentioned relates to the manner of drafting, so as to produce the best possible effects, apart from combinations of weaves. If there is a scroll pattern, in which one portion of the scroll crosses over another, in some cases it would be advisable to run in a close dotting on the under portion, immediately against that which crosses it. This would have the effect of sinking the under and raising the upper portion, which would produce clearness in the formation of the pattern. The same idea might be adopted with leaves over-wrapping each other, or with leaves partly covered by flowers, but the numerous cases in which this or some similar plan might be carried out with advantage will be readily understood.

Silk damasks offer more complications than either worsted or linen, because more is done in the way of colour. For instance, if the pattern given in Fig. 10 ("Hints on Designing Fabrics") is used, the figure would be in brown satin, and the ground in gold. The figure would be made with a silk warp, and the ground, end and end weaving, that is, alternate shuttles, of gold and brown, the former only showing on the surface. The yarns being much finer than those employed for other damasks would probably necessitate the use of about 250 ends per inch, and dottings up to sixteen shafts or so could be used. Besides, there are fabrics in which the figure is woven in various colours, and many fancy effects are introduced—diamond, basket, lozenge, etc., such as those figured later in tapestry fabrics, being employed with good results.

This subject has not been fully dealt with, but enough has been said to enable the intelligent student to grasp the methods employed in the making of damask fabrics.

TAPESTRY FABRICS.

THE LOOM AND JACQUARD.

The chief feature of the manufacture of tapestry fabrics consists of the application of the Jacquard machine, together with the box loom. This loom is familiar to all having the slightest knowledge of weaving, and, for that reason, it will be enough to mention the fact that the boxes are arranged upon a rising and falling or upon a circular principle, each one receiving a shuttle containing a different coloured yarn, which the manufacturer or colourist may wish to use in the production of a pattern. This may be said to be the first principle in procuring the varied and beautiful colour effects which lend so much charm to the better qualities of tapestry fabrics. But the box loom permits a manufacturer to go so far and no farther in the attainment of his object, and therefore many and varied are the means employed to satisfactorily overcome difficulties in the arrangement of colours, and it is only after repeated trials that certain desired effects are produced. The frequent changing of shuttles, beyond those which the boxes themselves will effect, is often resorted to, but this, in many cases, necessitates extensive alteration to a design, and the consequent re-stamping of cards, in order to attain the end at which he aimed. Extra colours may cause a design to assume a liney or stripey effect, and whenever this defect is apparent means must be employed to obviate it.

In the case of complicated patterns, where the changing of the shuttles does not give a satisfactory result, the manipulation of the warp must be resorted to. This may be done by single, double, and triple warp arrangements, and also by what is known as "end and end" effects, which we shall mention later.

TAPESTRY DESIGNS.

The first consideration in designing for tapestry fabrics is the size of the design required. The usual width of woven tapestry is six-quarters and eight-quarters, that is, 54 in. and 72 in. For weaving a 54 in. cloth, the harnesses are tied up in divisions for weaving patterns of 6½, 9, 10½, 13 and 26 inches, respectively. When tied up for centre patterns, such as Fig. 10, in "Hints on Designing Fabrics," a 6½ division will produce a 13 in. pattern; the same will apply to the other widths, *viz.*, 9, 10½, 13 and 26 inches. There are cases in which other sizes of patterns are used, but these are to meet some special demand, when the manufacturer and designer must work in unison, the former having his harness tied up in a suitable manner, and the latter adapting his design upon ruled paper to suit this tie-up.

In drawing a sketch for a pattern for a 54 in. cloth, the designer must, therefore, conform to one of the sizes; in other words, he must make the width of his repeat 6½, 9, 10½, 13 or 26 inches, as may be required. In the length of repeat there is no restriction, providing it be kept within reasonable bounds. The sketch, previous to being drafted upon ruled paper, is highly coloured, in order to be an exact representation of what the cloth must be when woven. The shuttling and warping arrangements are all indicated, and considered from a weaving point of view. The sketch is then passed to the drafting designer, whose business it is to work out the pattern upon the ruled paper, from which the cards for the Jacquard machine are stamped.

The successful tapestry designer must be possessed of much originality of idea, combined with skilful powers in the use of his pencil and brush. As a colourist, his imagination must be of no mean order. A well-formed pattern may be ruined by indifferent colouring, and the most artistic colour effect may be equally spoiled by defective drawing. And thus, the best designer is he who possesses a combination of these necessary qualifications. The student who desires to enter upon the study of designing for tapestry fabrics will find much in "Hints" given in the earlier chapters that will be of service to him, as many of the patterns described and figured there might fittingly be introduced into this chapter. The straight-over repeat, the drop pattern, the centre or reverse pattern, the reverse drop pattern, the border, table cover, and dado curtain designs are all examples of those in daily use in the tapestry fabric trade.

Construction of Cloths.—In the manufacture of tapestry fabrics an almost endless amount of information might be written, but this would only lead to such complications as none but experienced minds could be capable of understanding, and thus the object in view would be defeated, *viz.*, the rendering of these chapters as simple as possible.

Plain Pick and Pick.—Probably the simplest formation of a tapestry is a cloth similar to an ordinary damask, but with an extra shuttle thrown in, that is, two wefts and a warp. The design shown in Fig. 61, consisting of flowers and leaves, will form an example for the better understanding of our observations. Supposing the two wefts were maroon and green, the maroon shuttle would be utilised wherever required to make the flowers, whilst the green would go to the back, by the lifting of the warp, which would be arranged for upon the Jacquard cards. The maroon and green run alternately, and that which is intended to float on the face must not have the warp threads lifted. It will thus clearly be seen that when the maroon shuttle runs, the warp must lift on the leaves, and where the green shuttle runs, the warp must lift on the flowers. In this case the warp would make the ground, which would probably be dotted five or eight shaft satin, or a fancy effect could be used, as would be found most suitable, according to the tightness of the cloth required, which would also have the effect of fastening up the two wefts floating on the ground at the back of the cloth.

This may be described as the rudimentary principle of the construction of a tapestry fabric. Having grasped this, it will be easily seen how it may be further employed for the utilisation of three or more shuttles. It is, however, seldom that manufacturers go so far without resorting to the use of two or more warps, as these being upon the beam do not take up time, as is the case in the travelling and picking of shuttles.

End and End with Pick and Pick.—It will be seen what effect may be produced in the design shown in Fig. 61, by using three warps of red, citron and maroon cotton. The ground should be made with a shuttle of maroon worsted,

Fig. 61.

and the leaves with a shuttle of green worsted. The red would be used for the flowers, and the citron to light up these and the leaves. The maroon warp should be used with the object of tying down the maroon worsted ground, say, with a five shaft satin. By this means a spotty appearance would be avoided, such as would result from the use of a lighter shade, and a worsted weft ground of a good solid colour, bound by a thin cotton warp of the same shade, would be produced.

In the ruled-paper drafting of this it is necessary to consider how these ends of warp are tied up, and design for them accordingly. Supposing a 600 Jacquard is in use, and the harness is tied up for a 10½ in. repeat, the warp would be divided into three parts of 200 ends of each colour, as follows: 200 ends red, 200 ends citron and 200 maroon. This is the "end and end" principle before mentioned. In order that the card stamper may know how to cut his Jacquard cards, it would be needful to show upon the ruled-paper design three distinct colours, worked according to the sketch, but these colours would be on different ends, thus—the red for the flowers, and the citron for the lighting up of the flowers and leaves by upright lines, the former on the first, fourth, seventh and tenth ends, and the latter on the second, fifth, eighth and eleventh ends, and so on across the width of the pattern, whilst we should use the third, sixth, ninth and twelfth ends for the binding of the ground in maroon, and also for the green weft. *See the examples given in Figs.* 62, 63 *and* 64.

It must be understood that, in following these diagrams, two shuttles are represented by one square. The diagrams, simply for illustration, show 12 ends and 12 picks. The 12 picks really mean 12 of maroon and 12 of green, each of the shuttles picking 12 times. This observation is necessary in order to understand how the combinations are formed. To get the utmost value out of a cloth and to show how far these combinations may be carried—and are carried in many of the cheaper continental cloths—the method may be pointed out of combining the wefts with the warps, so as to produce what cretonne manufacturers understand as *super-position*, but which in tapestry fabrics scarcely approaches the same satisfactory results. This arrangement is known as a "tabby," that is a half-and-half effect, or equal portions of warp and weft up and down. Therefore, if the red flowers were to be shaded (warp) on the under and darker side, the lines one, four, seven and ten should be dotted every other pick, alternately, in the colour representing the maroon shuttle, as shown in Fig. 65 by the ×, the first and seventh ends, with the fourth and tenth ends. This would produce a shaded sunken effect for the shadows of the flowers, *i.e.*, a shade between the red and the maroon.

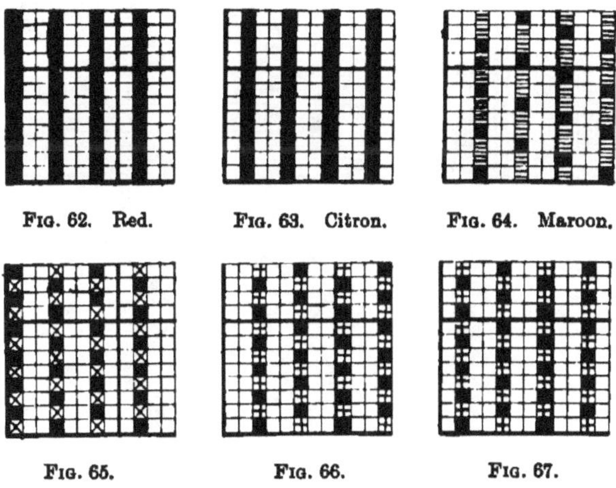

Fig. 62. Red. Fig. 63. Citron. Fig. 64. Maroon.

Fig. 65. Fig. 66. Fig. 67.

Now apply the same idea in the shading of the darker side of the leaves, reversing the warp and weft. As in the case of the flowers, the red is the warp, and consequently a mixture of two colours is obtained by adding the maroon weft for binding purposes, for the making of good cloth. As the foundation of the leaves is green weft, the maroon warp is added, which means that each pick marked + is dotted alternately on the third and the ninth, and the sixth and the twelfth ends, as in Fig. 66. Whilst engaged upon the green weft of the leaves and as the warp is light citron, which is in shade lighter than the green, it readily suggests itself for the lighting up of the green leaves. This would be worked in the same way, bringing up the ends occupied by the citron, *viz.*, the second, fifth, eighth and eleventh, in Fig. 67.

So far, effects produced by the combination of warps tied by wefts have been dealt with, but other combinations are adopted by mixtures of the two warps floating down the first, third, fifth and seventh picks, as may be considered necessary, in order to produce a particular appearance or handle of

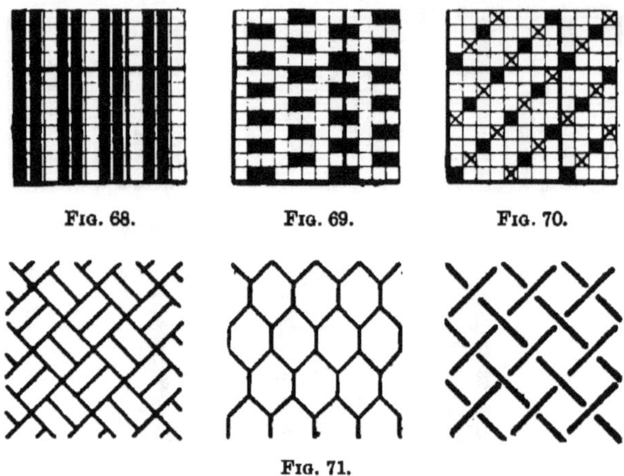

FIG. 68. FIG. 69. FIG. 70.

FIG. 71.

the cloth. This is a point which must always be considered in the application of various methods.

In the foregoing diagrams, we have illustrated the use of the warp separately. Now let us use the double ends, as such has become the invariable treatment in low and medium quality tapestries, by which means, many very happy arrangements of colours can be produced. Thus the citron and the red running together on the first, second, fourth, fifth, seventh, eighth, tenth and eleventh ends, as shown in Fig. 68, would vary the flatness of a field of one colour, and would tend to lighten the flowers in the opposite direction to the shadows produced by the maroon—pick and pick with the end and end, whilst working on the second, third, fifth, sixth, eighth, ninth, eleventh and twelfth ends, as in Fig. 69, a darker shade of citron.

These combinations must always be considered with special reference to the most appropriate manner of binding, and this should be regulated by the type of figures in the design and by the space to be covered. If this latter be fairly large, many fancy effects may be adopted, such, for instance, as the diamond, lozenge, basket, etc., examples of which are given in Fig. 71. But we must always remember that these forms must, in all cases, be subservient to the length of float required for the making of a good fabric.

BINDING THE BACK.—The next consideration is the binding of the fabrics, in order to prevent long ends of warp floating. The usual method of accomplishing this is to run a special dotting on the face, an intermediate one running between those already in use, as shown in Fig. 70. This should be indicated in the opposite colour to that which is used for the dotting of the warp upon the face, the dotting, of course, covering every square or end downwards, excepting the one which is immediately up, whilst in dealing with the ground colour, this particular end would be used for the face, and a twill or intermediate dotting would be employed on the other two ends, with the opposite shuttle to that working where the ground comes.

STRIPED WARPS.—In tapestry fabrics, many very artistic effects are produced by striping or planting colours in one of the warps. For instance, taking the design given in Fig. 61, we might bring up the two large flowers—which are placed side by side—in different colours, shading each flower inwards, which would enable us to get some touches of another shade for the smaller flowers immediately under the larger ones.

By a careful manipulation of a planted warp, a good colour effect could be produced throughout the design, which would be further enhanced by the changing of the shuttles.

The principles treated upon in this chapter are all open to variation, and the intelligent manufacturer and manager are continually studying to extend upon them, in order to produce novel and good selling effects. Much of the success of tapestry manufacturers depends upon the manipulation and extension of these principles, which can only be accomplished through the possession of a thorough knowledge of the capabilities of the looms at their service.

CHAPTER XII.

SCARF SILKS AND RIBBONS.

As it is intended in these chapters to give information upon all classes of ornamental textile fabrics, it is proposed now to deal with the manufacture of silk, treating upon neckties, scarfs, ribbons and dress fabrics in the order here given. But on entering the last-named branch of the subject, it will be hardly possible to separate it from dress fabrics made from other varieties of yarns, so closely do the methods employed in the designing of the cloths resemble each other, therefore these tissues will be considered in a separate chapter.

The silk industry is one of great antiquity, the rearing of silkworms and the reeling of silk having been practised as far back as 2640 B.C. It was, however, owing to the revocation of the edict of Nantes, about 1680, that a great number of French artisans settled in Spitalfields commenced hand-loom weaving, which flourished, and has continued with more or less varying fortune down to the present day. The silk trade extended to other places, notably, to Coventry, Macclesfield, Leek and Congleton, and, although power-loom weaving has superseded hand-loom, yet with the Spitalfields' weavers the latter holds the field. The majority have looms in their own homes, and may be seen any morning, with bags upon their shoulders, bringing their finished pieces to the city or returning with a fresh supply of warp and weft. But it is a declining industry, and, ere long, may be a thing of the past, and yet some lovely fabrics are made in the district, and one or two London firms are noted throughout the whole range of the trade for the artistic beauty of their productions.

Simpler in design, but not less perfect as fabrics, are the scarf and necktie silks, which these Spitalfields' weavers produce, and which form the first item for treatment in this chapter.

SCARF AND NECKTIE SILKS.

The silks most popular for scarfs and neckties are the satin, the matt and the ottoman, in each of which is much scope for pretty effects, and in dealing with them, such drafts and particulars as may be necessary to effect our purpose will be given. Before doing so, however, it is necessary to say a few words on the machinery used by the Spitalfields' weavers, passing over the loom, the Jacquard, and the harness, about which there is nothing special to be stated, yet there is one machine in use in this and in some other branches of the silk trade which, from its antiquity, requires mentioning—this is the reading-in machine.

THE READING-IN MACHINE.—The machines commonly used for the purpose of preparing the Jacquard cards are well known, but there is one of which, probably, very few of our readers know anything, as it has long ago been superseded by much superior inventions: it is now thoroughly out of date. Roughly speaking, this machine consists of a stout, upright framework of wood. To the front are two side-posts or uprights. Now imagine an endless warp of thin but strong cords suspended between the uprights and running under two rollers, placed at the bottom of the machine. These cords then pass up the back of the machine and across the top, where lingoes are hung, similar to those used in a Jacquard. Running down each side-post is a stronger cord, which, for description, may be called the selvage cords. The selvage cord to the left hand of the operator has strung upon it a quantity of cords knotted together in lots of eight—that is, supposing the design paper most commonly used is 8 × 8. These cords may be called the weft. There are thus warp and weft cords. Then there are needles, as in a Jacquard machine, as many of these being employed as there are warp strings. The latter are suitably connected with the needles. A punch box is perforated on its face—the number of holes corresponding to the number of needles. Each of the holes contains a punch, all of which work in unison with the needles. At each side of the box is a peg upon which the punch-plate slides, face forwards, into close contact with the box. The warp threads are divided by a comb into lots of eight each, and, to further facilitate matters, two rods are inserted crosswise of the warp threads.

The operator sits in front of the machine, his ruled paper suspended before him, a movable straight edge indicating the particular point upon which he is working.

As he reads the pattern off, he picks out the required warp strings with the fingers of his right hand, passing them on to his left, where they are held until divided from the remaining strings by cross or weft cords. When eight rows have been read in, the whole eight are knotted together upon the selvage string to the right hand. In this manner, all the design is read in by the interlacing of the strings representing warp and weft. In the next step certain adjustments of the machine are required, and the cutting of the cards commences. Each of the weft strings is operated upon separately. Taking up the first string, we insert a roller in its place, which, in its turn, operates in connection with a lever arrangement, and upon depressing which, we draw the warp strings tight: this has the effect of shooting the required punches into the plate fitted against the punch box. The plate is then operated upon by any ordinary cutting-machine, after which it is replaced against the box into which the punches are returned by the aid of a board, studded with pins, corresponding to the holes in the plate. This operation is repeated upon every weft string until the cards for the whole pattern have been cut. For the repeating of cards, there is a machine constructed upon similar lines, but there is no need to enter upon it here. That there are variations of this reading machine

FIG. 72.

there is no doubt, but the one described has been used largely for a long time. A well-known machine maker states that he ceased making this apparatus twenty-five years ago, and yet it is largely used in the silk trade at the present day.

FIGURED SATINS.

Of all the varieties of weaves in use in the manufacture of scarfs and neckties, perhaps the most popular is the satin. They are to be seen in every hosier's window. The matt or the ottoman may be conspicuous by its absence, but never the satin. From the small spot or ball to the all-over method of ornamentation, nothing is more saleable than this class of fabric, when offered for the personal adornment of the male sex. Fig. 72 is a design for a small figured satin, in which two wefts and a warp are employed in weaving. In designing these small effects, in which the figures are dotted over the surface at regular intervals, it is necessary to observe one point, for the demonstration of which we have inserted this pattern. The figure should be so constructed that it may be clearly divided in shuttling so as to produce an extra colour effect, without additional expense in weft. In Fig. 72 the rosette is kept quite clear of and does not overlap the two leaves under it. This pattern with the leaves may be produced in, say, pale blue and the rosette in pink, or some such combination, or the figure may be woven entirely in one shade of colour. In drawing the pretty all-over figures often seen in scarfs, the same principle may be adopted, if proper care is taken in the composition of the pattern. In these days especially, anything which can reduce the cost of an article, whilst maintaining its quality intact, should receive due attention. And really, in the present instance, a waste of weft is not necessary, because, in the majority of cases, good and effective all-over patterns can be produced, where changing of shuttles can be accomplished with the best results.

In showing the drafting of a figured satin, where two wefts are employed, take the example, Fig. 73, which is a small ball pattern, and here, again, it may be observed that the two balls are quite clear of each other, so that each may be in a separate colour. This figure shows the open style of drafting, *i.e.*, pick and pick, the light dots giving the satin and the black dots the figure weft binding. It will be observed that the latter binding comes exactly in the same position as the satin, or, to use a technical term understood in the trade, the two dottings are on the same "foot". This is necessary, as, otherwise, the satin face would have a broken appearance. This is the principle adopted in drafting a pattern of this nature, whether it be a spot, a small figure, or an all-over effect. But in actual practice, a more

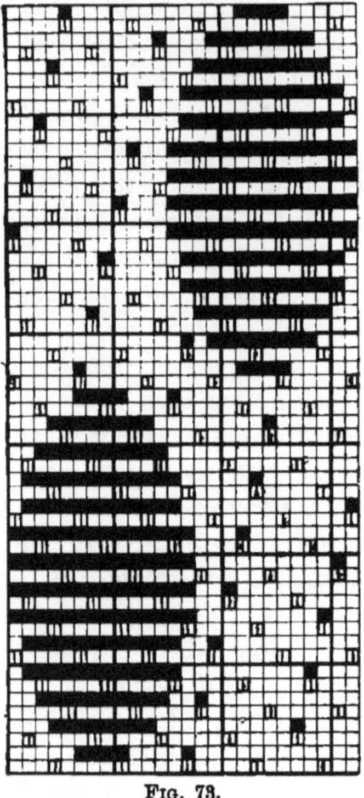

FIG. 73.

ready method would be employed. That is, the pattern would be drawn on every pick, and only the figure binding would be indicated upon the ruled paper, the ground satin being understood. In cutting the cards, all that would be necessary would be to cut five cards for the ground satin and to repeat them as many times as required for the full design, the cards being laced alternately ground satin and figure. In some branches of weaving, floating of the weft on the face is specially guarded against, but, in the present instance, floating often improves the beauty of the face. In Fig. 73 the float is over fourteen ends, and this is not too long.

A satin composed of a warp and two wefts has been dealt with, but in some instances there is a ground warp as well as a satin warp, in which case the figure weft should be bound with the former and not with the satin warp. This has the effect of keeping the satin clear of the figure weft. The broad principles upon which figured satins for scarfs and neckties are designed have been given, but it will be obvious

FIG. 74.

that these principles may be applied to the drafting of any satin fabrics, irrespective of the scope of the design.

MATT PATTERNS.

This class of weave is much in vogue for the fabrics under notice, as some very pretty effects can be produced by the use of warp and weft of different shades of colour. Fig. 74 is an example of a matt weave, which produces a tissue exactly alike on both sides. Of course, in this pattern, the number of warp and weft threads may vary according to the quality of the material to be woven. With 200 ends per inch and 100 picks per inch, it would be necessary to draft double the number of warp ends in comparison to the weft, thus requiring the use of 8 × 4 ruled paper. The same weave could be drawn on a greater number of ends and picks than is shown in our example, with good results.

Fig. 75 is another weave for a matt. This is a fairly good specimen, and would make a saleable cloth for any purpose where both sides are not required to be exactly the same. Fig. 76 would also make a matt, but in this case the pattern would be the same on both sides. The beauty of a good matt lies in the floating of the warp and weft being unbroken, and also in its being a perfect reversible fabric, and we therefore give preference to the example in Fig. 74, but, at the same time, the others will be found useful.

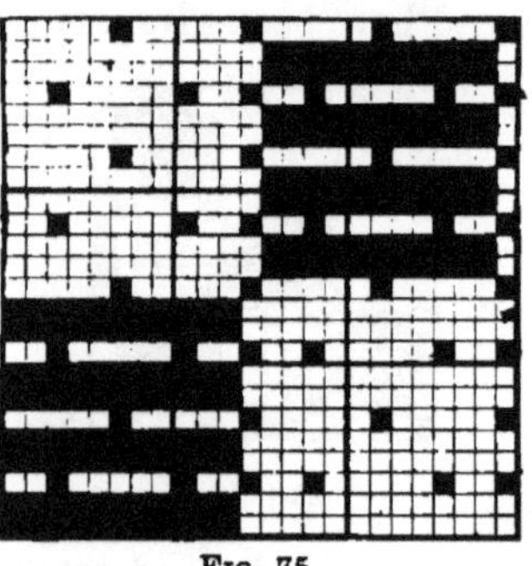

FIG. 75.

This class of weave has been dealt with as far as the ground fabric is concerned, but many very good effects are produced by introducing figures dotted about at intervals, keeping, however, within the matt formation. For instance, by using an extra shuttle, a diamond or a zig-zag, or other small figures can be introduced which can be varied in colour by a change of shuttle. Take, as an example, black and steel blue for warp and weft, and a small figure with the extra weft of rose pink changing to white. Further good effects are obtained by the use of striped warps, bringing up the squares of the matt in different colours by the aid of a change in shuttles. Take, for instance, Fig. 74, and stripe the warp alternately with five ends of tan and five of white, then, in the weft, give ten picks of white and ten of steel blue alternately, and a very pretty cloth is produced. The same method might be employed in the production of large checks or tartans, of course more colours being employed. Some such weave as that given in Fig. 76 could be used with a satin effect, that is a satin ground and figure in navy blue, surrounded by a matt check of white and navy blue. In this case the warp of navy blue would be striped by white—say about 264 blue and 96 white. There would then be a change of blue and white shuttles in similar proportion, resulting in

FIG. 76.

navy blue satin figure and ground, surrounded by blue and white matt check, with white matt corners.

OTTOMAN PATTERNS.

To produce a perfect ottoman pattern, the rib should be the same on both sides, and the weave—Fig. 77—possesses this qualification. Of course, the same weave could be used to produce a heavier rib, by introducing more picks. The example given is known in the trade as a "four and four shoot". The dotting shown by the × indicates the use of a ground warp, which is necessary in order to keep the fabric flat. This ground warp may be of cotton, without in any way injuring the appearance of the face of the fabric. A second weave is given in Fig. 78, which is useful for fabrics to be made into ties, because it is only a one-faced ottoman, whereas Fig. 77, being both sides alike, can be used for loose scarfs, that is, scarfs which the wearer folds and ties himself.

Striping and dotting are favourite methods of ornamenting ottomans. As to the former of these, weave, say, twenty ribs of the ottoman in black weft, of course having a black warp, then change the shuttle and throw in about twenty picks of cardinal, say, a satin effect; then a few more ribs

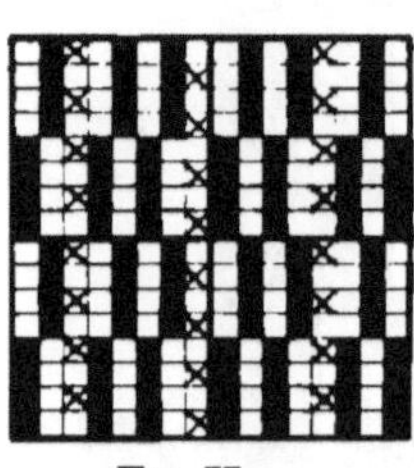

Fig. 77.

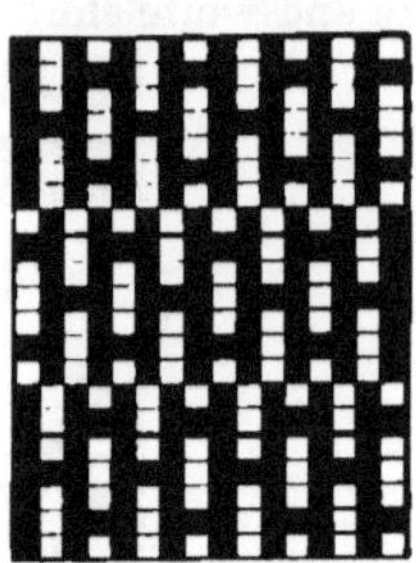

Fig. 78.

succeeded by another twenty picks of cardinal; then repeat the order. By this means a good striped fabric is obtained.

More might be said on the subject of scarf and necktie silk designing, but this would require much more space than we can devote to this branch of our subject, besides which, we should be introducing complications that are best avoided in a plain, straightforward explanation of the subject.

FANCY RIBBONS.

The home of the British ribbon industry is situated in Coventry, where the power-loom is mainly used for the production of the beautiful tissues which come from that quaint and pretty city. The bulk of the weaving is done in the operatives' own homes. But if power-looms are used, how can this be? say some. The houses are built in rows, as is the case with most working men's homes. The weaving "shops" are usually at the tops of the dwellings, a line of

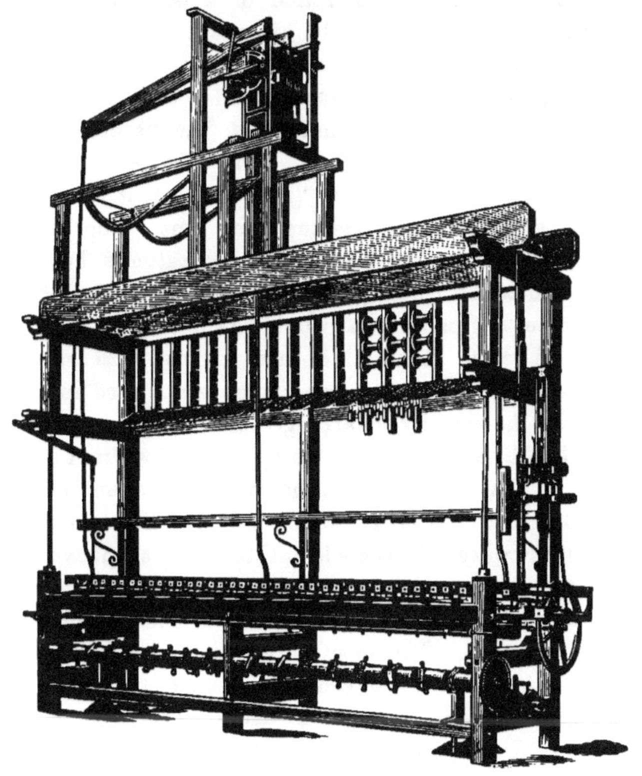

FIG. 79.

shafting running the full length of a row, and the same gas or steam power turns the whole. Of course, there are hand-looms in use, but these are for the making of narrow goods, and never for fancy fabrics. The proportion of power-looms compared with those worked by hand and treadle, is 50 to 1 in favour of the former.

THE RIBBON POWER-LOOM.

In Fig. 79 is an illustration of a power-loom made by Mr. T. Wilkinson. The Jacquard used upon this loom is an ordinary 300 machine, no special features being introduced in its construction. Neither is there anything unusual in the nature of the harness, which is omitted from the illustration. The loom is of the type known as an "eighteen space," that is to say, it will weave eighteen ribbons at one and the same time. The harness would therefore be tied up for eighteen patterns, but each pattern would be complete with selvages instead of being closely repeating patterns, as would be the case for any ordinary broad goods. For each of these ribbons there are separate sets of shuttles. The box motion is not used in these looms, but the shuttles are arranged in tiers, run in slots, and are worked by a rack and pinion motion. The front of the batten, *i.e.*, that which carries the shuttles, rises and falls as required to place the latter in the desired position to be engaged in the warp. In some looms, there are as many as ten shuttles in a tier, and besides the use of these, changes are often resorted to when a great number of colours are being used in a design. The loom shown in the engraving, as already stated, weaves eighteen ribbons at one time, but other looms are made to produce from ten to twenty-four at one operation. In the present instance, the fronts of the shuttles are removable, to allow of other colours being placed therein. It is likewise fitted with an automatic marionette, for the working of the shuttles. Not only are ordinary figured ribbons woven on these looms, but also book markers, hat bands, coat and skirt bands, etc. A machine for reading-in the patterns for the card cutting, constructed in a similar manner to the one described already, is used in the Coventry trade.

FANCY RIBBON DESIGNS.

In entering into particulars on the subject of fancy ribbon designs, a few serviceable drafts will be necessary to show the methods adopted in the trade for procuring various effects. The weaves and instructions already given for scarfs

FIG. 80.

and neckties are equally applicable to this branch of the silk industry. There is scarcely any need to state that there are the satin, the matt and the ottoman ribbons, and, moreover, the information given upon tapestry and damask fabrics in another chapter, might well be repeated here. There are tapestry and damask ribbons, and the end and end and pick and pick principles are extensively used in the trade. Warp as well as weft figuring is employed, and the striping of the warp is adopted in some varieties with good results. Some floral designs show no fewer than ten changes of colour in the warp in about 2¼ inches. In special cases, portraits and pictorial effects are produced with remarkable results. In a portrait, for instance, the lights and shadows are procured with a delicacy of toning which is almost surprising. To

FIG. 81.

design a thing of this description is a matter of skill and experience. It is quite necessary to understand the value of every dot put upon ruled paper, as, for example, in a black and white portrait, single grey dots representing black weft would go through with white ground weft, thus producing a

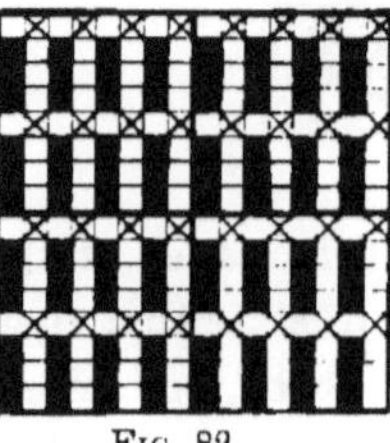

FIG. 82.

FIG. 83.

soft shade. Single black dots would be black weft only, the warp not rising for the white ground weft. This gives a darker shade. When two or more brocade shuttles are used, very beautiful shading and toning effects are procured, by "mixing" or passing two or more colours through the same *shed* or lift.

SOME USEFUL WEAVES.

The illustration, Fig. 80, represents a pretty style and is shown in the actual size when woven. In Fig. 81 the method of working the ruled paper is given. There are two

FIG. 84.

shuttles and a warp, one shuttle being used for the flowers and the other for the leaves. As the draft explains, it is designed on the pick and pick principle, with a satin ground.

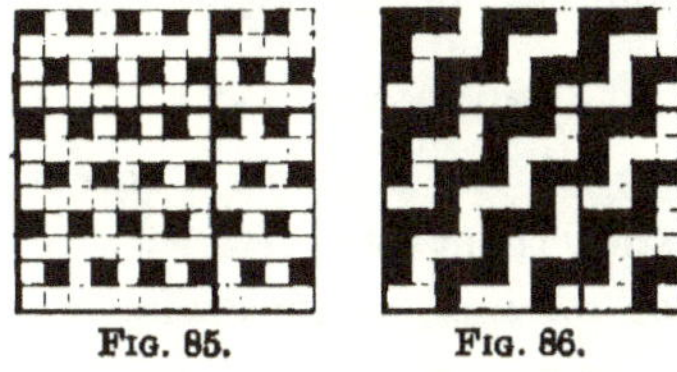

FIG. 85. FIG. 86.

Some very pretty effects can be gained in this class of ribbon, and shading can be obtained in the leaves and flowers by bringing up a warp dotting, carefully manipulated. A delicate

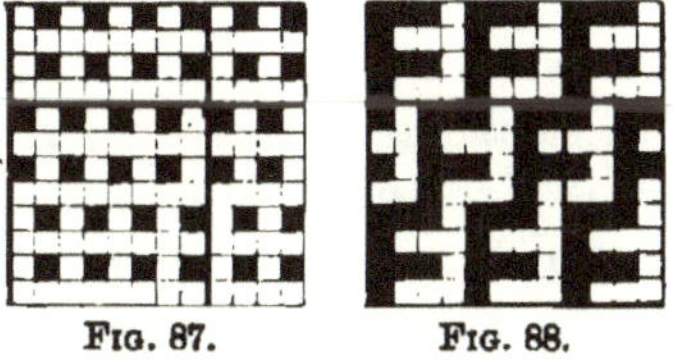

FIG. 87. FIG. 88.

fabric would result from the employment of a white warp ground, the leaves in a yellowish green, and the flowers in a salmon pink. A more serviceable result would ensue from the use of a black ground, with the leaves in tan and the flowers in steel blue.

In Fig. 82 is shown a weave for a terry or ribbed fabric. This is usually made with two shuttles, a fine weft being used for the single pick (×) and a coarser one for the remaining three picks. This could be employed in combination with many fancy effects, with good results. Fig. 83 gives a double satin weave on sixteen shafts. This weave, as its name implies, produces a satin effect, both sides of the cloth being the same. Fig. 84 is for a satinette, also reversible. There are many other weaves used in the ribbon trade, but those already noticed will be found sufficient, as they represent the most common. It must be understood that the satin, the matt and the ottoman, illustrating the remarks on scarfs and neckties, are, as previously stated, included in the list of those given for and used in the ribbon trade.

EDGING WEAVES.

As no treatise on the methods of constructing ribbons would be complete without some reference to the composition of the edgings or selvages, a few drafts are given showing the principal styles in use. Fig. 85 is what is known as a two-cord, or pull-over edge, and is generally adopted in one-sided fabrics, that is, tissues which are not reversible. The warp floats on the face only, but is partly pulled over by the weft on returning, which is done when the whole of the warp in the edge lies down. Fig. 86 is a four-cord edge, and is the same on both sides. It is, therefore, used for reversible ribbons. Fig. 87 is a one-sided bead edge, and is much the same as Fig. 85, but looks richer, on account of the warp floating longer. Fig. 88 is also a bead edge, but two-sided, that is, the same on both sides of the fabric.

CHAPTER XIII.

SILK HANDKERCHIEFS.

In the last chapter necktie silks and ribbons were dealt with; silk handkerchiefs come next. As most people of average intelligence are aware, Macclesfield is a centre of the silk industry, some eighty firms being engaged in the manufacture in that town. An immense quantity of handkerchiefs are made there, and many beautiful patterns and delicate textures owe their origin to the designers and workers in that Cheshire town.

SILK HANDKERCHIEFS.

Much of the information already given on scarfs and ribbons is applicable in discussing the subject of silk handkerchief designing. It is exceedingly difficult to separate one particular class of silk fabric from another, as the various methods of obtaining desired effects, the weaves employed, etc., etc., are commonly used in every case. Hence, much of the substance of the last chapter might be repeated here. Indeed, to be complete, it would be necessary to begin with the twill and satin weaves, introduced in the chapter on "Damask Fabrics," continuing with the figured satins, the matts, the ottomans, the terry or rib, and the edgings, given in the remarks upon scarfs and ribbons. All such weaves are useful in the designing of silk handkerchiefs, and combinations of them tend to the production of very effective fabrics. Examples of handkerchief designs are given next with ruled-paper diagrams, showing the method of drafting most suitable for the production of good and effective tissues.

A HANDKERCHIEF DESIGN.

The first example, Fig. 89, is offered as a suitable design for a one-coloured handkerchief of white, cream, pale blue, pale salmon, or of any delicate shade. The main portions of the figuring would be best produced in a satin weave and the ground in a four-shaft twill. The various fancy effects introduced in

Fig. 89.

the figuring tend to add to the effectiveness of the pattern, but it is impossible to show these upon the ruled-paper example in Fig. 90, as to give the whole would occupy too much space. The design, Fig. 89, is, however, carefully worked out, and the student who desires to make the attempt should not have much difficulty in drafting the full pattern upon ruled paper with advantage to himself. In this task, the particulars given in these pages upon silk designing will be of considerable help to him. So much for the centre portion of the pattern. A comparatively plain border enhances the

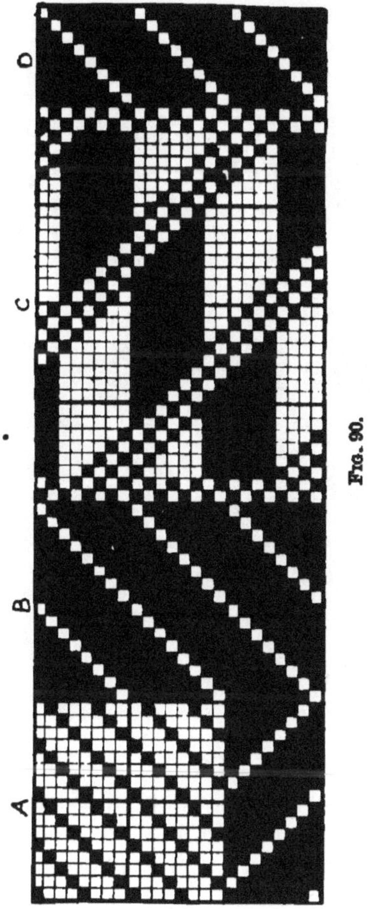

FIG. 90.

effect produced by the ornamental centre; an ornamental border, however, might be employed in the present case with good results, but what, for purposes of distinction, we have termed a "comparatively plain border" has a remarkably rich effect if drafted as shown in Fig. 90, in which a bold twill band is succeeded by a fancy diamond effect, these being again followed by the twill. Attention must now be given to working out the draft for the complete border. In the first place, a small portion of the bold twill and diamond

Fig. 91.

weave only is shown. The number of ends per inch would be 120, and the picks per inch, 100; thus the pattern would be more correct if drafted on 12 × 10 paper. The twill, A, represents a portion of the body. In drafting the border, about 60 ends should be allowed for the twill, B, or about half an inch when woven. The fancy diamond weave, C, should be drafted on, say, 90 ends, or about three-quarters of an inch in the cloth. For the twill, D, this should be continued for about one and three-eighths inches of cloth. This is for the side border. For the bottom, repeat the side

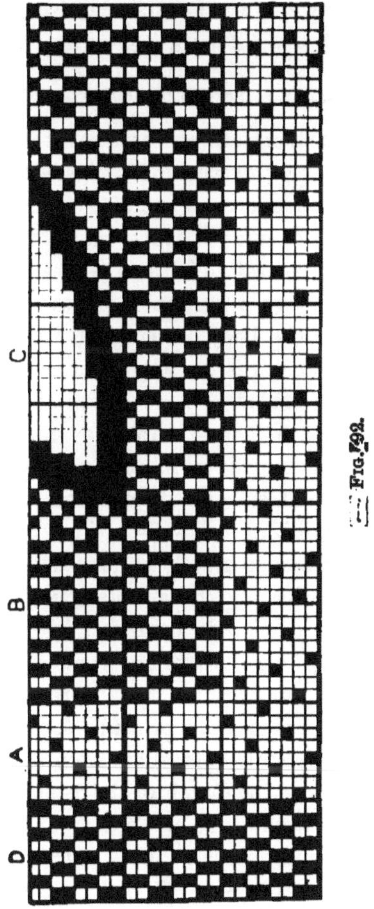

Fig. 792.

border, allowing the same proportions for the twills and diamond weave. Thus for the inner twill band allow 50 picks, for the diamond 75 picks, and for the outer twill band continue for the same width as that running up the side. The corner would consist of a continuation of the diamond bands crossing the outer twill band. A variation in the border might be made by having the different bands narrower and finishing off with a broad satin weave.

ANOTHER HANDKERCHIEF DESIGN.

Fig. 91 is a small pattern, repeated at intervals upon a fancy ground. The method of working is illustrated in Fig. 92, but again it is not possible to show the whole ruled-paper drafting, on account of the amount of space which would be required. The figure should be drafted in satin, and a plain satin border given. Thus A shows a portion of the satin border, B is the ground weave for the body or centre, C is a small portion of the satin figure, and D is the edging or selvage which goes up each side of the ruled paper. A variation could be made by the use of an ornamental border, or one such as that in Fig. 91 could be employed with good results. For instance, there might be half an inch of satin and the same width of ground weave, finishing off with satin. The effect of some handkerchief patterns is greatly enhanced without the use of extra colour shuttles, by the simple expedient of printing upon the figured portion in some bright colour. Thus, in Fig. 91, the balls show that which would be printed. Supposing we made our cloth in a delicate blue, a charming effect might be produced by printing the balls in crimson. Although the designer would show both the woven and the printed portion upon his sketch of the design, it goes without saying that he would take no notice of the latter when working out his ruled paper. This pattern would produce the best result if woven with 312 ends and 80 picks per inch, and would, therefore, be more correctly drafted if 4 × 16 ruled paper were used, instead of that we have employed to simply illustrate the method of working out the pattern.

CHAPTER XIV.

DRESS FABRICS.

In the remarks upon damask fabrics, it was stated that some seven centuries ago these materials were extensively manufactured in Damascus, but they were composed of silk, and the trade came to recognise any silken texture as a damask. In treating upon this class of goods, various drafts were given which are all equally used in the manufacture of dress fabrics. The twill, the satin and the fancy weaves are of equal importance in the present case. It is necessary to mention this fact in order to render this chapter complete in itself. In the course of the observations made designs and drafts will be given, and, although these have been drawn specially for silk fabrics, the general scope of the chapter will be equally applicable to fabrics manufactured of other yarns.

SATIN EFFECTS.

There are many beautiful designs for silk goods, particularly those for high-class fabrics for evening wear, which are manufactured in a simple satin weave. Many of these patterns are somewhat extensive, consisting of long sprays of flowers and leaves, in some cases, executed in their natural size. The drafting of a pattern of this character would be the same as that given in Fig. 90, in the last chapter. Suppose two colours are employed for the figure, the pattern would be drafted as shown in Fig. 81 (Fancy Ribbons), and if it was desired to introduce a third, then proceed in the same manner, employing a third shuttle wherever required—this would be bound on the back on the satin foot. Considering all that has been said in the two previous chapters applicable to the drafting of designs with the satin weave, there is no necessity to enter further into this part of the subject here.

Fig. 93.

A SIMPLE DESIGN.

The matt, the ottoman and such-like weaves, of which examples have been given before, are much used in the production of a variety of dress fabrics, not only in silk, but also in cotton, wool, etc., and, when used in combination with ornamental figuring, some really good results ensue. Many very pretty fabrics are woven by the simple expedient of utilising two or three ordinary weaves in one pattern. As an instance of this see Fig. 93. This consists of a design in outline, four of the most elementary effects being included in its composition. Yet a texture of this description, if woven in silk, say 112 picks and 136 ends per inch, has a remarkably tasteful appearance.

As no treatise upon the subject of dress fabrics would be complete without some reference to the subject of swivel weaving, this matter must be dealt with briefly here.

FIG. 94.

SWIVEL WEAVING.

This consists of introducing extra colour effects into fabrics in such a manner that the yarn runs on the back of the fabric at intervals only—that is to say, it is employed only in the formation of the figure, spot, or whatever may be the character of the ornamentation, and does not, therefore, as in the ordinary form of shuttling, run across the whole width of the piece. The arrangement is used to a great extent upon hand-looms and also upon power-looms. There have been a great number of inventions during the past few years for various forms of mechanism for swivel weaving, but all are more or less upon similar lines. In the last chapter, a ribbon-loom was described. This was constructed to weave eighteen ribbons at one and the same time. In this case, there are, of course, eighteen shuttles running at once. Swivel weaving is the application of the principle

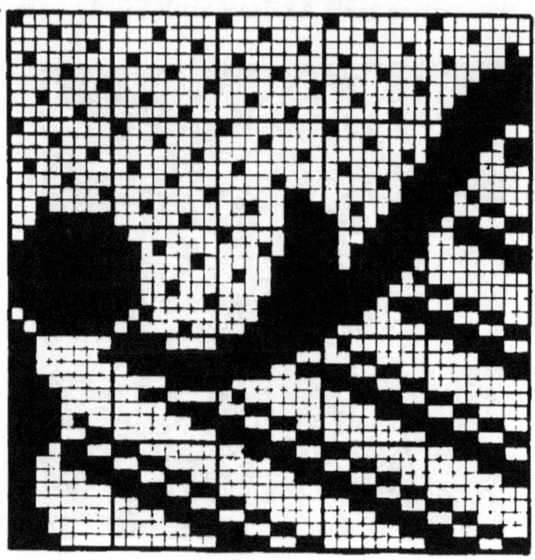

FIG. 95.

of a number of ribbon shuttles to an ordinary loom, the ribbon shuttles working in unison with the ordinary loom shuttles. The small shuttles are arranged at intervals, across the loom, in a frame attached to the front of the slay. This frame is so arranged that, through the action of the Jacquard, it may be raised or lowered as required. The frame may thus remain up or down as long as may be necessary for the weaving of any particular pattern, according as the cards which govern it are plain or punched.

Suitable mechanism is provided for the running of the small shuttles, and means are also afforded for throwing the ordinary picking motion out of gear when necessary. One great drawback to swivel weaving lies in the fact of the prescribed limits to its use. For instance, there must be a specified distance, crosswise of the loom, between each leaf, figure or spot, where extra colour is to be inserted, and, although the frame for the next row of spots or figures may be moved, so that they appear in the fabric midway between the previous

Fig. 96.

row, this does not tend much to obliterating the set and formal appearance often noticeable in fabrics made on the swivel loom.

A variation of the swivel motion is provided by what are known as circles, which accomplish the same purpose as the swivel, but the yarn enters the shed with a circular motion, and by this method, a greater number of spots or figures can be woven in a row than is the case with the swivel motion. The shortest possible descriptions of these mechanisms have been given; they are, however, sufficient to give a general idea of their method of working. They are by no means

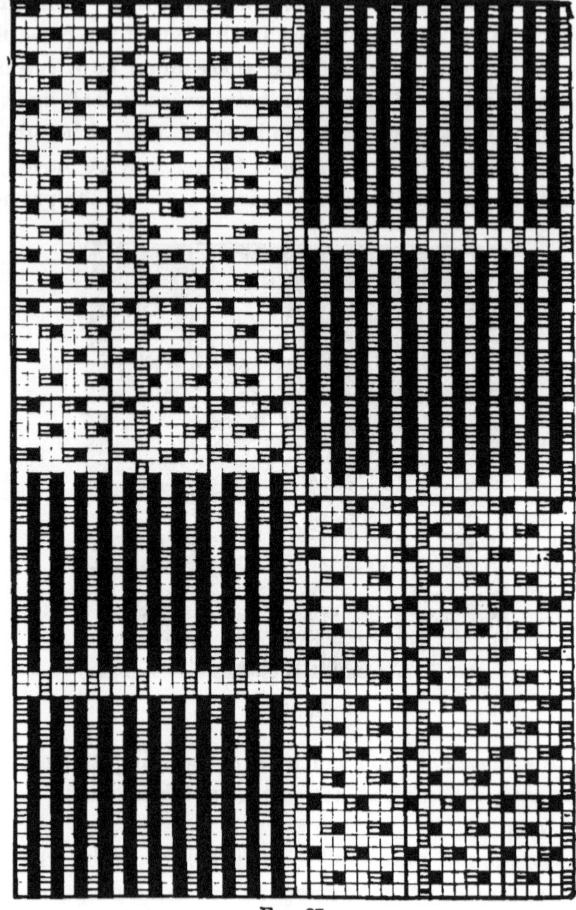

Fig. 97.

universally regarded as successfully accomplishing their object; for one reason they are too slow in their action, and therefore a sufficient quantity of work in a given time cannot be got by their use. A prominent loom-maker says that he does not make them, as he considers them out of date when compared with embroidering machines. It is quite true that some beautiful effects are produced upon silks and other varieties of fabrics by the aid of embroidery machines, but the subject being dealt with is swivel weaving, and therefore it may not be out of place to give one or two designs which may be produced by this method.

EFFECTS BY SWIVEL WEAVING.

The design illustrated in Fig. 94 has been specially drawn for silk dress goods. It is intended to be woven with a black warp and a coloured weft, such as a pale sage green. The small portion of ruled-paper drafting, Fig. 95, explains the method of treating the design throughout. The figure portion is clearly distinguishable, as likewise is the diagonal ground. The half-tone dotted portion of the design, Fig. 94, is the satin. If the pattern is worked out to these instructions, a very good and rich effect will result, say a sage green figure, black satin panel, and a diagonal ground of sage green and black, in weaving which, allow 290 ends and 100 picks per inch. It has already been stated that in swivel weaving colours can only be introduced at intervals; in Fig. 94 this point is illustrated. In this design the flower is shaded by lines, and would be woven by the swivel mechanism. The design being arranged on the drop principle causes the second row of flowers to come midway between the first row, and thus tends to lessen the set appearance inseparable from the system of introducing colour into a fabric by the aid of swivel weaving. This flower should be in salmon pink, which will harmonise nicely with the black and sage green of which the fabric is woven.

The next illustration of a dress goods design, Fig. 96, shows a ground of the matt or basket character, an old and valuable formation in many classes of designing. In the present instance it forms a good pattern for our purpose, and is given in the exact cloth size. The scrolls and balls are intended to be produced by the aid of the swivel. A full repeat of the matt draft is given in Fig. 97. The light dots in the draft indicate ground warp and weft. The black is figure weft and the white the warp. In weaving it will be found expedient to have the ground weft on a separate beam. With reference to colour, black warp and weft, with the swivel figure in any delicate shade—blue, mauve, rose pink, etc.—may be used, which would produce a good useful class of silk fabric, as would also be the case if navy blue for warp and weft, and gold for scroll were employed. Another effective colouring would be ground myrtle green and figure pink. Other colours that harmonise well are brown and pale blue, and maroon and gold. The weave given herewith would be found serviceable if used alone, the basket formation giving to the surface of the fabric a beautiful lustrous appearance. In fact, the designs—Figs. 94 and 96—form examples of good useful styles when employed without the aid of the swivel, but, as it is necessary to deal with this portion of the subject, it would be difficult to show two patterns which more clearly illustrate our remarks upon this class of figure weaving.

DRESS GOODS.

Having briefly described the process of swivel weaving, one or two other designs for dress goods may be considered. The designer may obtain an almost endless number of effects by the exercise of a skilful arrangement in the drafting of a pattern, and in this respect much can be done by the use of fancy ground weaves, some of which have been previously given, but it will be advantageous to show a further specimen of this variety of design.

A DIAGONAL WEAVE.

In Fig. 98 a sketch of a design is given in the actual size it would appear when woven. This should preferably be in delicate shades of colour—a pale blue ground being very suitable. The figuring of the design shown in white should be in pale salmon pink, the dotted portion representing the blue weft floating. The pattern is drafted on the pick and pick principle, the figure being treated exactly as in the examples previously given, notably the one for drafting the figured

FIG. 98.

satin. Thus the main portions of the ornamentation would come up in pink, the small spray of leaves being blue, with a pink outline. The floating of the blue imparts to the pattern a rich appearance. As this has been drawn with the special view to the utilisation of a fancy ground, it becomes a question as to the form this should assume, in order to produce the very best result. Many styles will readily occur to the mind of the practical designer, and, amongst these, small diaper effects, such as the diamond and the lozenge, would stand prominently forward as serviceable *motifs* for employment. But for the production of a remarkably rich and pretty fabric, it would be difficult to find a better weave than the diagonal, given in Fig. 99. We have already mentioned that the pick and pick principle of drafting is used, a further illustration of which is given in this figure, which requires little in the way of explanation. The black represents the blue weft, the white is the floating blue warp, and the

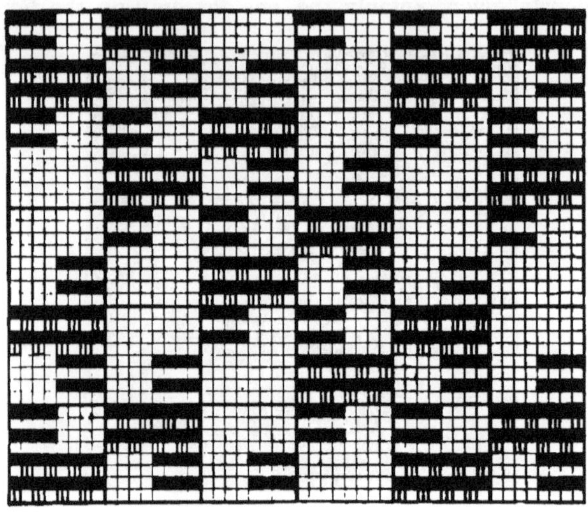

Fig. 99.

light dots show the binding of the pink weft on the back. The best result will be obtained by allowing about 360 ends and 96 picks of each shuttle per inch.

REVERSIBLE WEAVES.

Many neat and taking fabrics may be woven by the expedient of drafting minute figures in such a manner that they produce a reversible pattern. In accomplishing this, it is necessary to so construct the pattern as to produce an exact equality in warp and weft on each side of the fabric. The double satin and two of the three matt weaves, etc., show this feature. Although it may appear simple, it is by no means an easy thing to construct a good ornamental weave of this description, such as the one illustrated in Fig. 100. Here we make use of one figure, repeating it upon the drop principle, and, at the same time, reversing the order of

Fig. 100.

the warp and weft—that is, the weft in the one figure becomes the warp in the other, and *vice versâ*, and thus we have equal portions of warp and weft up and down in the whole pattern. In the production of this, suppose a white warp and a lavender weft are employed, or a delicate pea-green for the warp and a gold for the weft, or, say, pale blue and pink—the colours should only be a few shades removed from white—we should procure a neat and good result, the general appearance being greatly enhanced by the effect of the light and shade which play upon the figures. Much of the admiration bestowed upon silk, as well as upon many other fabrics, is in no small degree due to effects produced by light and shade. For instance, the floating of silk is so much resorted to because the light striking it gives it a beautiful, lustrous appearance, which would not be the case, at all events to so great a degree, if floating were avoided.

Much may be done with this small pattern by a judicious combination with other weaves. It can be seen how the idea works out, using this figure in combination with the first of the matt weaves and the double satin given in the chapter on "Scarf Silks and Ribbons". Supposing a stripe is to be attempted with warp and weft of the same shade, allow two inches of figure, then half an inch of double satin, the figure and satin being divided by a few ends woven plain. The double satin might then be succeeded by a similar width of the matt weave, followed by satin, and finally repeating the figure. The pattern would require about 200 ends per inch, but, where the double satin comes, about 400 ends per inch would be required.

This type is useful as a groundwork for further ornamental effects, and much may be done in this direction by the aid of one shuttle only, the designs most suitable being those of a trailing or open character, that is, patterns which do not cover the ground too much. But in preparing ruled papers for these, it is advisable to entirely surround the ornamentation by a little plain drafting, in order to throw it clearly out from the ground effect. The figure upon the face would be formed by the weft, that upon the back by the warp, and thus the reversible character of the pattern would still be maintained.

END AND END WITH PICK AND PICK.

Many very good fabrics are produced upon the end and end and pick and pick principle, but as this was fully dealt with in the chapter on "Damask and Tapestry Fabrics" there is no need for repetition here. Not only is the principle adopted in the manufacture of silk fabrics, but also in those composed of cotton and worsted yarns, etc. The designs usually employed are such as cover the ground well, and there is therefore much scope for the skilful designer in the production of good ornamental patterns, such as those illustrated in Figs. 12 and 15, in one of the chapter on "Hints on Designing Fabrics," and, for the purpose under notice, no better examples

Fig. 101.

Fig. 102.

could be given, as they furnish precisely the class of pattern usually adopted. With these observations, the end and end and pick and pick principle of drafting fabrics may be left.

TWEED DRESS GOODS.

Upon the subject of tweed and the heavier makes of dress fabrics, little needs to be said. Where ornamentation is employed, it usually partakes of the simplest character, being, in fact, seldom more than a leaf, ball, cube, diamond, lozenge, basket, zig-zag, crescent, or some such elementary device, repeated at intervals. Even where patterns of a more ornamental character are made use of, they are generally of the simplest description, such, for instance, as those given in

Figs. 101 and 102, which are very fair examples. Patterns such as these give the best effect when woven in bold repeats, six inches not being too wide for either design. The weaves employed call for no special mention, much being possible with the most rudimentary of them. An important object in many tweed dress fabrics appears to be the production of good ground effects, such as those known as heather mixtures. Camel hair yarns are used to some extent, being often introduced in the ornamental portions of the fabric, thus giving the figures a shaggy and extremely ugly appearance. Knop and curl yarns have been and will, no doubt, continue to be used largely, and grounds, figures and stripes of these materials have by no means a bad effect. Flocked yarns are also much employed, producing the irregular spots or splashes of colour often seen distributed over the surface of a tweed dress fabric. But in this make of goods, as in many others, fashion rules, and it is not always that ornamentation in them is generally acceptable.

LENO OR GAUZE FABRICS.

The subject of dress goods could not be left without some reference to the class of cloths known as leno or gauze fabrics; but only a passing reference to them will be made in closing this chapter. The few observations will be found equally applicable to fabrics woven from silk, cotton or worsted, and the design and section of ruled paper given are likewise suitable for all these fabrics. Any one who has taken the trouble to inspect a sample of leno or gauze cloth will have noticed that the warp threads do not lie parallel, but are twisted round each other in such a manner as to form, along with the weft, open work in the ground or figure. This twisting is accomplished by the aid of doups, forming a portion of the Jacquard harness. To be more explicit, there is employed what is generally known as the douping warp, in addition to the ordinary or ground warp, and the intertwining of the two, in conjunction with weft threads, forms the leno or gauze.

In tying up a harness, a certain proportion of the Jacquard uprights or wires is required for the doup harness cords, the exact proportion differing in various cases, although a common division is one-third for doup and two-thirds for the remainder of the harness. The doup leashes consist of ordinary harness cords, furnished with the usual mails. A loop or slip is employed, one end of which is drawn through an eye in the mail, the douping warp passing through that part of the slip or loop which protrudes through the mail and not through the mail itself. Should an end of douping warp break, the corresponding slip falls from the mail, and, in order to obviate this, the slip is, in some cases, passed through two holes in the mail, and thus it is impossible for it to fall out. But this causes extra friction, with consequent wear and tear, and, therefore, the remedy is not regarded favourably. The doup harness is attached to the front rows of uprights, the back rows being, of course, occupied by the remainder of the harness. The use of a slackening arrangement is necessary in order to properly operate the doup warp. This may take the form of a back harness, worked by levers, arranged a short distance behind the harness proper, and through this the doup warp is drawn. But there are other methods employed—one by a Lancashire maker. In this case, the levers are dispensed with and the back harness is attached to the hooks of the Jacquard machine.

Leno weaving has formed the subject of innumerable patented inventions, some dealing with one portion of the mechanism and some with another, and to treat this process fully and quite up to date would require the consideration of many of them.

Leno weaving can, of course, be done by the use of healds

in place of the Jacquard, and some very pretty effects in small figures, checks, stripes, etc., can be produced, but then the designer has the trouble of constructing the douping plans, which are not necessary when the Jacquard is used. In any case, and particularly by the aid of the Jacquard, the designer has a wide scope for the exercise of his powers; take, for instance, alternate checks of gauze and plain, the latter having a small figure upon it. In stripes, some pretty combinations are possible. Examples are common of neat floral effect in coloured warp upon plain stripes, connected by stripes of

Fig. 103.

gauze. Twills and satins may be employed—in fact, there is scarcely a limit to the variety of effects which may be obtained.

A LENO DESIGN.

In Fig. 103 a sketch of a simple figure is given as an example, and in Fig. 104 a small portion of the ruled-paper drafting is shown, but the whole pattern may be completed upon 144 ends. In cutting the cards, the black and the light dots are required to lift. In this type of patterns, two ends cross two ends. In the weaving, it is necessary that the doup should be raised first and immediately before the figure begins, if only for a single pick, as, otherwise, a float and an imperfect gauze crossing will result. The doup is shown on the ruled paper, Fig. 104, in a half-tone dotting. Although the figure is given as plain weaving, a fancy figuring may be employed, having a small portion of plain around. A further variation may be given to this design by making the ground plain and the figure gauze, a remark which may

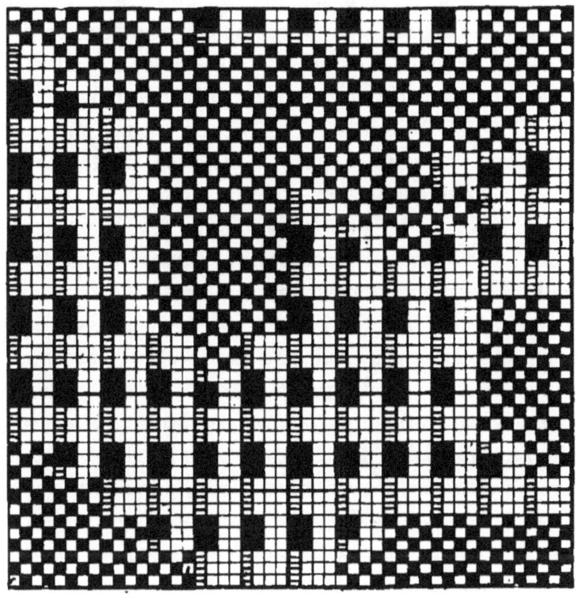

Fig. 104.

be generally accepted, as gauze figures on plain or fancy grounds are often quite as effective as are those composed in the contrary manner. For a worsted leno, this design would come out well in 2/80's yarn for warp and weft; 15's reed; 4 ends in a reed; 60 ends per inch, and 54 picks per inch. For a cotton leno, the following particulars may be taken as a guide: 1/50's yarn for warp and weft; 20's reed; 4 ends in a reed; 80 ends per inch, and 70 picks per inch.

CHAPTER XV.

MANTLE CLOTHS.

In dealing with the subject of mantle cloths, one great drawback presents itself, *viz.:* much, if not all, that has been said in the last three chapters might, with advantage, be stated here, and, therefore, it is difficult to separate handkerchiefs, dress goods, mantle cloths, and such-like fabrics one from the other, in order to treat upon each as complete in itself. A designer may select any of the weaves already given, and, from it, construct a pattern for a mantle cloth; for instance, the satin weave is very often employed for some classes of these fabrics, notably broché satins, and some of those woven in worsted yarns. Figured tissues are, however, not always admissible—they are subject to the fluctuations of fashion, at one season only the plainest cloths meeting with general acceptance, whilst at another the desire for ornamentation amounts almost to a craze, during which period one may, at times, see some startling novelties, such as an elephant's head and trunk closely repeated as a drop pattern. Dragons and serpents and such-like atrocities have also been employed, whilst birds, butterflies and insects have furnished the designer with good ideas for pretty patterns. Flowers, leaves, scrolls, etc., down to the simplest formations, are extensively used in the figuring of these cloths. In connection with the fabrics which, for distinction, are here called plain cloths may be mentioned twills, diagonals, hopsacks and similar weaves. In reversible cloths, some good things in tweeds are often to be noticed, such as those formed by showing upon one side a diagonal of black and white and upon the reverse side the same yarns worked up in the form of a plaid. Black and grey, brown and fawn, and such combinations of colour, form pretty effects in checks. As a further example, a cloth may be constructed showing alternate diagonal lines in brown and

Fig. 105.

silver grey upon both sides. An extra effect is then produced upon one side by means of a skeleton check, in red or blue, say, two inches square, this being crossed by the same size of check in a black and grey twisted yarn. More showy examples are such as have tartans of red, black and green, or some similar combination of colours, upon the reverse side, whilst the face has, say, a flocked effect, or one woven in two colours neatly blended by the aid of some simple fancy weave. But such cloths as these are not ornamental ones, in the sense in which fabrics are being treated in these pages, but, nevertheless, they are of sufficient importance to merit a brief reference here.

Ornamental fabrics for personal adornment assert themselves at recurring periods. They come and go; at times their reign is brief, at others they maintain their popularity until the highest and the humblest wearer are satiated, and fashion declares in favour of plainer cloths. They make

FIG. 106.

their début in the form of silk, satin, plush and other expensive varieties, and, by gradual stages, appear in inferior and still lower goods. In manufacture and design the scale is descended until the lowest point is reached, and they become a thing of the past. Such is the fate, to a greater or lesser extent, of all fabrics that are subject to the claims of fashion, and in no case is it more apparent than in that of mantle cloths. If the statement requires any qualification it is due to the fact that there is always a proportion of the population that prefers ornamental fabrics for personal adornment, and, therefore, there is a certain amount of trade constantly done in them. For instance, good figured worsteds, broché silks and satins, and broché velvets and plushes may be had at all times, and, consequently, it is advisable to deal with some of these here.

A WORSTED MANTLE CLOTH.

A very neat and effective mantle cloth may be produced

FIG. 107.

by the use of the satin weave, a design for which is given in Fig. 105—a most suitable pattern for this class of cloth. It will be noticed that in this figure the whole of the ornamentation has been drawn with a special view to avoid binding of the figure, as a much clearer and better appearance is produced by allowing the whole of the latter to float.

The method of drafting is shown in Fig. 106. The main difference between this and the one given in the chapter on "Silk Scarfs and Ribbons" is that a three and one twill is used behind the figure in place of the plain ground weave. This weave could, however, be used so as to produce two colours in the figure, by following the method shown in the chapter just quoted. This design would be effective in a repeat of from 3½ to 5 inches in width, the larger size being preferable.

A BROCHÉ SATIN.

The design, Fig. 107, is a good example of those used for broché or brocaded satins. In drafting ruled papers for this class of tissue, many simple expedients may be adopted in order to produce light and shade, to add variety, and generally to promote effectiveness in the fabric. How this desirable state of things is arrived at may be best described by considering what may be done with the pattern under notice. The ground is, of course, satin, but the whole of the figure would be in a ribbed weave. Over this latter, the large flower should be allowed to float as much as possible, but, where this would not be satisfactory, shading, by means of a tabby or twill, or the bringing up of the rib, should be resorted to. It will be noticed that this flower has been cut up by means of lines, in order to ensure floating to a large extent, but shading may be adopted in various portions; for instance, some of the petals, particularly the two largest, may be so treated, the latter at their inner terminations. This would give them a sunken effect, thereby throwing up the main portion of the flower. The stem of this flower, and those of the leaves, would come out best in the rib, and the few larger leaves should also be shown in this effect, but floating on the outlines on one side of the leaves, and also of the veins, should be allowed. The various sprays of small leaves should be shaded by means of a tabby or twill, the portions not shaded floating. The wreath of small flowers may also be treated in the same way, but, in this case, very little shading should be adopted, as the more floating is re-

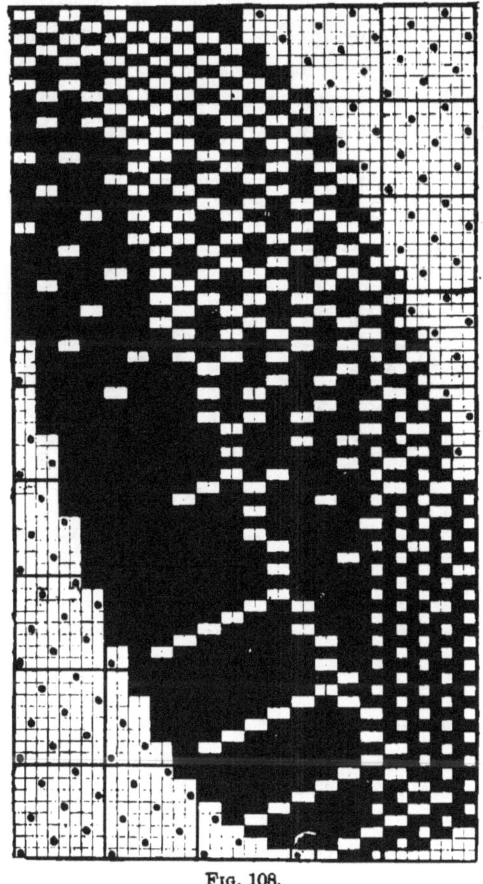

Fig. 108.

sorted to here, the better will be the result. The festoon of beads may also be floated or shown in the ribbed effect. In using the various weaves for the purpose of shading, they may be employed simply or in combination one with another. A tabby may come first and then a twill, and the latter may run first in one direction and then in another.

In the limited space available it is impossible to give an illustration showing the many and varied means employed in drafting in order to obtain the utmost perfection of effect, but the small example given in Fig. 108 will exemplify the general method of working. This is drafted pick and

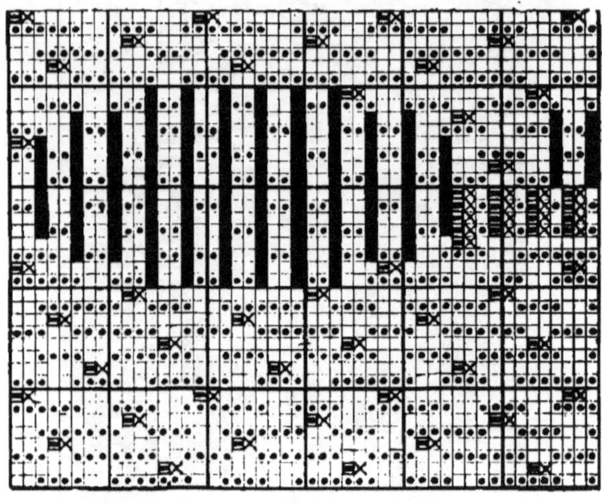

FIG. 109.

pick. In the first place, the whole design must be drafted, so that every two picks are exactly alike. Upon every odd pick the rib must be shown throughout the whole figuring of the pattern. In the illustration it is only shown on the first five odd picks. In actual practice the designer would not put this rib dotting on at all, because the card stamper takes it as understood, and cuts his cards accordingly. The floating figure, and likewise any shading of the design, are worked upon the even picks.

ANOTHER WORSTED MANTLE CLOTH.

Some very good cloths for mantlings may be woven upon the end and end and pick and pick principle, and curled or looped yarns, or such as have the curl or loop formed during the process of weaving, are often used in the figuring with good results. In such cases, the most suitable designs

FIG. 110.

are those of an irregular character—for instance, Fig. 102 in last chapter is somewhat in the style of thing which may be employed. The general run of patterns, either floral or ornamental, hitherto given in these chapters, are much too regular in formation to be of service for the particular type of mantle fabric under consideration. Fig. 109 illustrates the method of drafting that may be employed in this instance. The cloth would have a navy blue satin face weft, with the warp figuring in blue and red, black being the curl or loop yarn. The warping would be of these three colours alternately, as shown upon the draft in black, in lines and in crosses. The odd picks shown in black dots on the draft represent a ground weft, and the white or even picks show the satin face weft.

AN EXAMPLE IN WOOLLEN.

A very good class of reversible fabric for mantlings may

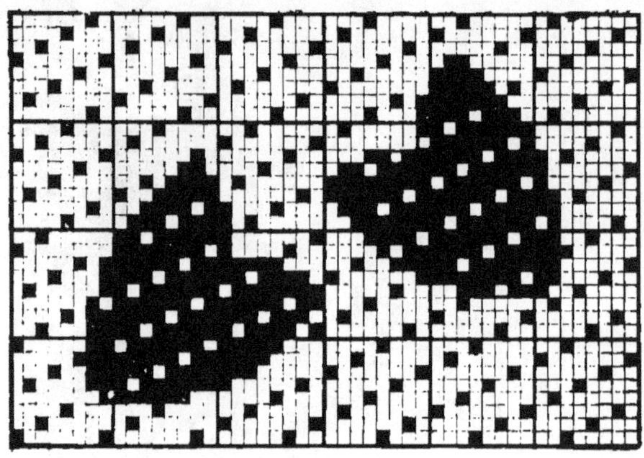

Fig. 111.

be manufactured from woollen yarns, either in a plain or figured cloth. For the latter the design, Fig. 110, will be found suitable. The method of drafting is shown in Fig. 111, which is simply a weft satin figure on a warp satin ground. A warp of 12 skeins brown woollen and a weft of 9 skeins pale blue woollen would be a good combination of colour—of course, giving a blue figure on one side and a brown one on the other. For a 56 inch finished cloth 2240 ends would be required in the warp, 34 ends per inch, woven 35 picks per inch. Lift all black.

A WOOLLEN SHAWL.

The pattern, Fig. 110, is exactly the style of design employed in the manufacture of woollen shawls so much in use amongst a certain section of the population. These tissues are produced with the body of the shawl ornamented and the border plain, or *vice versâ*. In the latter case stripes in various colours are introduced, as well as the ornamental figuring. Such cloths are reversible and may be manufactured by the aid of the following figure and ground weave, Fig. 112, which has been extensively employed for this purpose. The draft is for weft figure, and requires two

Fig. 112.

shuttles in weaving. By turning the draft on end it can be used for warp figure with one shuttle, but end and end warping would be required. The double satin weave given in a previous chapter could also be used for a warp figure for this class of cloth, if warped end and end, or by making the bottom of the draft the side and using two shuttles, a weft figure would result.

PATENT RAISING MACHINE.

Fabrics such as the woollen mantle cloth and the woollen shawl require to have a special velvety finish imparted to them, such as that afforded by teaseling, or by passing through the patent raising machine invented by E. Moser and manufactured by James Tomlinson. This raising machine performs its work in such an admirable manner and has gained such a wide popularity that a description of it here will be found advantageous.

For the information of those readers who may not be familiar with the mechanical construction and principle of this machine it will be well to explain that it consists of a

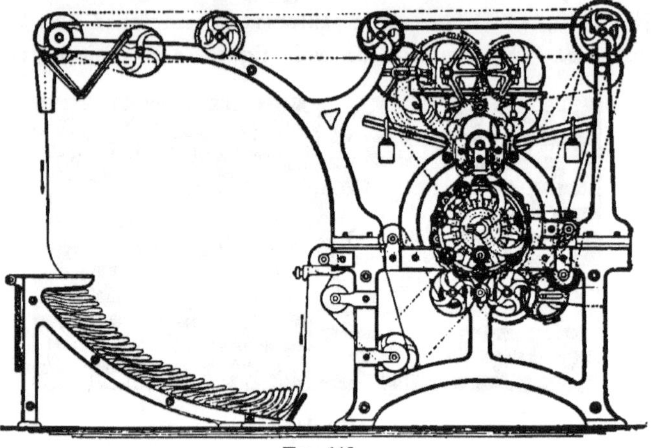

FIG. 113.

cylinder or drum, upon which is mounted a series of rollers, each covered with suitable raising cards made of steel or brass, as may be most suitable for the fabric to be raised. The machine illustrated in Fig. 113 has fourteen of these card-covered rollers; seven of these have their card points inclined in a forward direction, while the remaining seven have their points inclined in a backward direction. The cylinder is made to revolve in a forward direction and at a speed of about 800 feet per minute, carrying of course the fourteen card rollers with it. The cloth to be raised travels through the machine in the same direction, but at a speed of about 1-20th of that of the cylinder. Upon the cylinder being set in motion, as will be easily understood, the rollers receive a rotating movement in a direction opposite to that of the cylinder itself, and, as this movement is of the character of a rolling action, no raising or napping of the fabric could be effected until the speed of the planetary rollers is increased over and above that which they receive from the cylinder itself. To do this and to accomplish the raising or napping of a variety of goods, such as are found in textile factories, the speed of each card roller is accelerated or retarded, thus the raising energy of the card rollers is more or less severe according to the nature of the fabric and to the amount of nap it is desirous to obtain. The raising rollers being furnished, as mentioned above, with card points working in opposite directions to each other, the nap obtained is very short and full, and any tendency there may be in the operation of raising to drive the weft or otherwise weaken the fabric is practically overcome.

CHAPTER XVI.

FIGURED PLUSH.

In dealing with this subject some reference will, no doubt, be expected in relation to figured plushes, those beautiful fabrics which are of such infinite value for the decoration of the home. What can be more effective or in better taste than a suite of furniture upholstered in a neatly designed plush fabric? The manufacture of plush has made great strides towards perfection, owing, in no small degree, to the skill, high inventive faculties and perseverance of Lord Masham, who, as is well known, has built up a gigantic manufacturing concern at Manningham, Bradford, and who has never wearied in bringing his machinery to the highest possible state of efficiency, as is evidenced by the great number of patented inventions in which he is interested. It is scarcely necessary to say anything further by way of introduction.

A PLUSH DESIGN.

The illustration given in Fig. 114 represents a design for plush, and is shown mainly with a view to demonstrate to what degree ornament for this class of fabric may be worked up. From this it will be noticed that too much detail is objectionable, and should therefore be avoided. A fairly balanced quantity of figure and ground, with the former carefully surrounded by the latter, may be considered as an essential feature in designs of this class. The ornament should not be too fine in drawing. In weaving this pattern, the white, of course, represents the plush, the ground being in satin or in some similar weave, and it will easily be noticed that the marking of the centres of the flowers, the veins of the leaves, etc., are so bold that when woven they will show clearly between the pile of the plush. This is likewise the case in the lines which divide one portion of ornament from another. By following this course, an

FIG. 114.

effective pattern results, when otherwise there would be a heavy mass of indistinct and objectionable figuring, with no artistic or ornamental formation about it. Therefore, let the ornament be clear and bold, and thus it will be found possible to work it out properly upon the ruled paper, which would not be the case if too much detail were attempted upon a sketch.

PLUSH WOVEN SINGLE.

Patterns of this character may be woven in a loom either single (*i.e.*, one piece at a time) or double (*i.e.*, two pieces woven face to face), the latter being by far the more favoured method. It is, of course, understood that, in weaving plushes singly, wires are used upon which the pile is formed, much as in the case of Brussels and tapestry

FIG. 115.

carpets. The withdrawal of each wire severs the pile, each of the former being supplied with a knife-like termination which accomplishes this. The diagram, Fig. 115, gives a cross section of plush, the heavy black dots, A,

FIG. 116.

representing the wires, the line, B, the pile warp, and the dots, C, the weft. The draft given in Fig. 116 further explains the construction of the cloth. The black is the satin ground, the round dots represent the plush warp, which rises for the wire to pass under it wherever it is desired to make plush, but where it is desired to make satin, the plush warp lies down for the wire to pass over it. The

× on the second pick of the black is employed to bind the plush warp at the back of the cloth, and thus prevent floating.

PLUSH WOVEN DOUBLE.

In the weaving of two pieces of plush face to face, it is scarcely necessary to remark that no wires are requisite, the pile being formed in the loom by the plush warp passing from the upper to the lower piece of fabric, and *vice versâ*. The two pieces are, of course, severed by a cutter, as mentioned later. The diagram given in Fig. 117 shows the working of the plush warp, and also the satin ground, the black lines representing the former, and the fine lines the latter. The small dots represent the weft. Fig. 118 is a draft which will further explain matters. The black is the

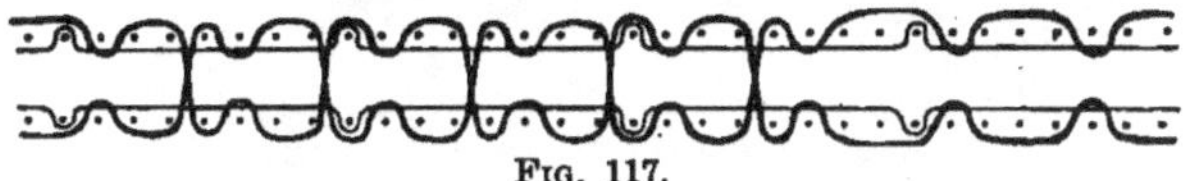

FIG. 117.

satin ground, and the dots and crosses show the plush warp. In these figures satin grounds only have been mentioned, but others are employed, such, for instance, as twills and some of the fancy effects common to the silk and ribbon trades, amongst those being the one known as the Barathea, shown in Fig. 119, which is in formation similar to a hopsack. Here again the black is the ground and the dots and crosses the plush warp. It is necessary that some particulars should be given of the looms employed in the plush industry, and, therefore, the following short description of one for the weaving of two pieces of plush face to face will be both interesting and instructive.

A FIGURED PLUSH LOOM.

In Fig. 120 an illustration is given representing a side elevation of a loom for the weaving of two pieces of plush face to face, at one operation. A Jacquard machine is employed for producing the figures by means of the pile warp, each thread of which is fixed in a creel, placed behind the loom. The Jacquard is in the usual position, and has, therefore, been omitted from the illustration. Whilst the figure is produced by the Jacquard acting upon each thread of the pile warp, the ground is made by a set of tappets, which also regulate the

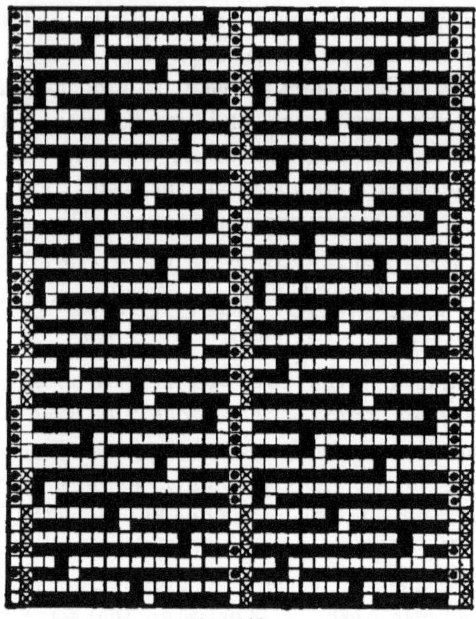

Fig. 118.

length of the pile. The ground may, of course, be in a satin, a twill, or otherwise, as above described. The tappets are so arranged that, whilst weaving the top piece, the healds belonging to the lower are kept at rest at the bottom, and, when weaving the bottom piece, the healds which control the top piece remain at rest likewise, thus causing the two pieces to separate, and by so doing taking up the length of pile given.

There are two rollers at the back of the loom, one for each ground warp, to open the said warps to a certain angle in combination with the healds. The healds belonging to the top piece are kept at a higher level than those which belong to the bottom piece. These two levels, and the angles given by the above-named rollers, keep the pile tight between the two pieces. A movable rail or shelf is attached in front of

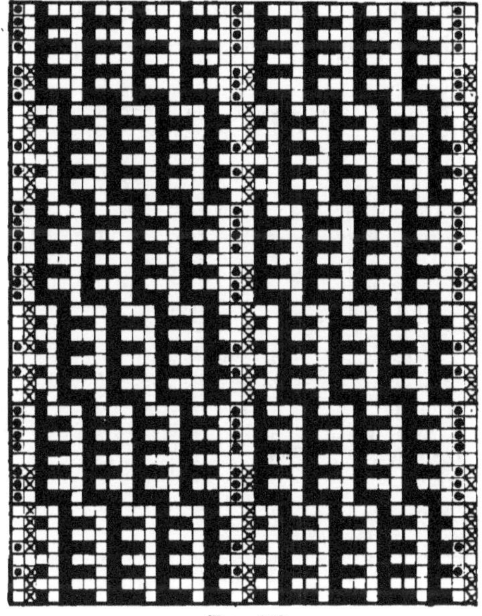

FIG. 119.

the reed in the shuttle race of the going part for the shuttle to traverse over it. The object of this is to permit the rail or shelf to descend as soon as it comes near the pile gauge, which is placed close to the fell or edge of the cloth, and to raise it again to its proper level, as the going part recedes after beating up, thereby keeping clear of the pile gauge each time the going part beats up. This rail or shelf is carried by two pivots close up to the reed, and its front part only may be raised or lowered, or the whole rail may be raised or lowered, by means of a positive parallel motion.

Utrecht velvets may be woven, two pieces face to face, by using three combinations of tappets. Each combination makes the weft to form the loop for the temples, and also fastens all the selvages of the two pieces.

By reference to the illustration, it will be seen that A is the side of the loom which carries the crank shaft, B; the swords, C, of the going part, E, are connected with the crank

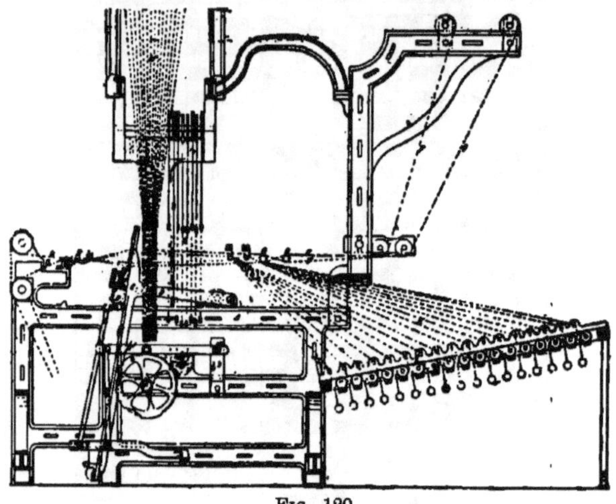

FIG. 120.

shaft, B, by the crank arm, D, which gives motion to the going part, E. The ground warps to form the back of the pile fabric are marked F, F. These warps are acted upon by the healds, G, the said healds being worked by tappets. The creel, I, is required to carry the bobbins, J, upon which the threads of the pile, K, are wound. The weights, L, are to give tension to the pile threads, K, worked by the harness, N, which is, of course, operated by the Jacquard. It has been already stated that the tappets which work the healds, G, are so constructed that, whilst weaving the top piece, the healds belonging to the bottom piece are kept at rest at the bottom, thus causing an opening between the two pieces which take up the length of pile. Two rollers, Q Q, are placed between the warps, F, to keep them open to such an angle as to take up the length of the pile in combination with the tappets, such length of pile being given by the bobbins, J, and regulated by a swing pile gauge, R. The swing rail or shelf, S, in front of the reed in the shuttle race of the going part, E, is connected by rods, T, to levers, U, mounted on the shaft, V, which is carried across the going part, E. Upon the same shaft is mounted another lever, W, connected by the rod, X, to the lever, Y, which lever works on its fulcrum, Y^1. This is fixed to the loom side, A. The lever, Y, is also connected by the rod, b, to the lever, b^1. The lever, b^1, works on the stud, b^2, carried by the stand, b^3, fixed to the loom side, A. The lever, b^1, receives its motion from the tappet, Z. This tappet is keyed on a toothed wheel, both of which revolve upon the stud, d, fixed on the loom side, A. The tappet, Z, and wheel receive their motion from the pinion, d^1, keyed on picking shaft, d^2, which is driven from the crank shaft in the ordinary manner. The tappet, Z, is divided into six parts, each part giving the required movement to meet the swing gauge, R, and the shuttle at its proper time as follows: Whilst weaving the top piece, the swing rail or shelf, S, in the going part, E, is kept down by the tappet, Z, in order to clear the swing pile gauge when beating up, there being sufficient warp down to carry the shuttle. Whilst weaving the bottom piece, the shelf, S, is caused to rise and depress at each pick—it rises to carry the shuttle across, there not being sufficient warp down to carry it, and it depresses to clear the swing pile gauge, R, at the time of beating up.

It is most important in a figured pile fabric woven face to face to obtain a smooth back and an equal length of pile.

The swing pile gauge, in combination with the swing or movable rail or shelf, accomplishes this.

In the endeavour to give a description of a loom for the weaving of two pieces of plush face to face, it has been advisable to refer to an invention emanating from a firm well known throughout the whole textile world.

In the above description there is no mention made of the manner in which the two pieces of plush are severed, but the same firm has a method which may be briefly alluded to. A cutter is mounted upon a rail and drawn backwards and forwards by cords attached to drums, which are rotated by means of racks and pinions driven by a double cam. When the knife comes to a rest at one side of the loom, it enters between two sharpening rollers, one of which is brought into contact with the knife as it slowly passes over it, and, as the knife returns, the other roller is brought into action. The rollers consist of metal spindles, upon which are firm concave barrels, covered with india-rubber, which is again covered with leather, or a similar substance, and over this the grinding material is spread.

CHAPTER XVII.

BED QUILTS.

THE manufacture of bed quilts or counterpanes is one of the most important of the Lancashire cotton industries, there being some thousands of looms running upon this type of ornamental fabric in Bolton and the district. In Scotland there is also a considerable trade done in counterpanes. They are made in many varieties, from the very finest to the lowest quality of fabric, and are known by various names, such as the toilet, the honey-comb, the Marseilles, the Grecian, the satin, the Alhambra, and the tapestry, in the designing of which there is much scope for the production of good ornamental effects; it is, therefore, requisite, in treating upon ornamental textile fabrics, to give special attention to this subject.

THE QUILT LOOM.

It is not necessary to make many preliminary remarks with reference to the loom, as the mechanism employed will be understood by a perusal of the information given in treating upon the various makes of quilts. The warp threads are controlled by the Jacquard, in combination with healds. The former is of various capacities, ranging from 400 to 1200 needles for ordinary makes of goods. In some cases the harness is tied up for ordinary repeating patterns, whilst in others it is arranged so as to control one half the width of the cloth woven, the pattern being drawn to turn over from the centre. In the course of this chapter both these types of designs are given.

SATIN QUILTS.

Fig. 121 illustrates the class specially suitable for a satin quilt, and is an example of a pattern that turns over from the centre, both in the width and the length; in other words,

Fig. 121.

there is just one quarter of the pattern shown. In the manufacture of satin quilts, two yarn beams are employed and two shuttles, one of the latter using fine and the other coarse weft, and two picks of each are made at one time. The best satins are woven with two ends of Jacquard to one of healds. Both grey warp and weft are employed, the quilts being bleached after weaving. In preparing a ruled-paper design for a satin quilt, it is necessary to draft the ornamentation only, as the ground and binders are made by the healds, but in order that the whole system may be properly understood, a small draft is given in Fig. 122. In this the black squares represent the figure weft and the black dots indicate the ground weft, whilst the crosses show a binder warp for the figure weft. This gives a detailed draft for a small spot, but,

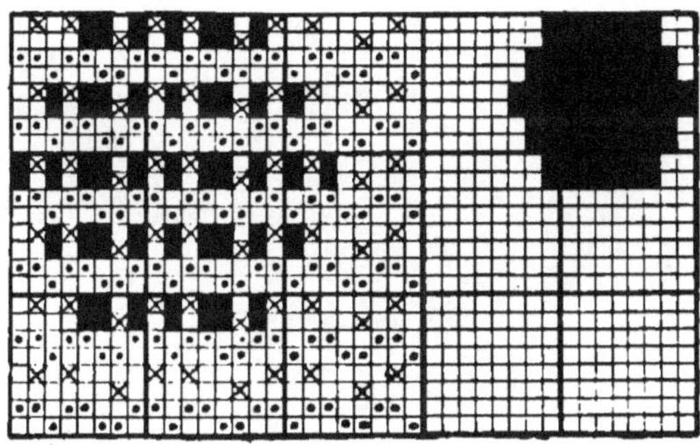

Fig. 122.

in actual practice, only the spot itself would be drafted, as shown to the right of Fig. 122. A very pretty effect may be gained by employing a coloured ground, a good way to do this being to use a striped warp. Thus the first, third, fifth, twelfth, thirteenth and fifteenth ends may be in red or pink, and the sixth, eighth, tenth, seventeenth, nineteenth, and twentieth ends in white. The draft, Fig. 123, is for the same class of cloth, but in this case the binder warp threads are more regular. The black is the figure weft, the dots are the ground weft, and the crosses are the binder warp ends for the figure weft. Here, again, it is scarcely necessary to remark that only the actual figure requires drafting, as shown by the spot to the right of the draft.

TOILET QUILTS.

The design shown in Fig. 124 represents a toilet quilt, in preparing drafts for which there is again no necessity to show the binders. Thus the drafting becomes a very simple matter of good freehand drawing. Toilet quilts are usually made with a 1200 Jacquard machine and two shafts of healds, so that plain cloth can we woven with fine weft upon the face side of the cloth. Two yarn beams are employed,

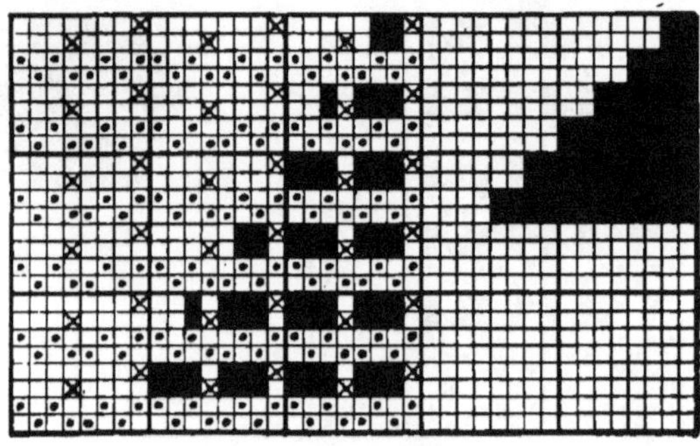

FIG. 123.

one for the Jacquard and one for the healds. There are two heald or face ends for one Jacquard end. The Jacquard ends are drawn in two comber boards one after the other, but there are always two heald ends between each Jacquard end. The comber boards work when the fifth and tenth picks are going in, in order to bind the Jacquard yarn at the back of the cloth, that is, under the figure which is made on the face side. Two shuttles also are employed, one weaving fine weft, which gives the quilt a good appearance, and the other coarse weft, which forces the pattern up, and at the same time gives weight to the fabric.

There are generally five picks to each Jacquard card, as follows :—

First pick : Jacquard up, fine weft, first heald up.

Second pick : Jacquard up, fine weft, second heald up.

Fig. 124.

Third pick : Jacquard up, coarse weft, both healds up.

Fourth pick : Jacquard up, coarse weft, both healds up. This latter is a repeat of the third pick, as it returns in the same shed.

Fifth pick: Jacquard down, fine weft, both healds up, and one of the pressure, lifting half the figure warp. This makes plain cloth at the back where the figure is.

Sixth pick: Jacquard up, fine weft, first heald up.

Seventh pick: Jacquard up, fine weft, second heald up.

Eighth pick: Jacquard up, coarse weft, both healds up.

Ninth pick: Jacquard up, coarse weft, both healds up. Repeat of eighth pick.

Tenth pick: Jacquard down, fine weft, both healds up, and one of the pressure up, lifting one half the Jacquard yarn which was not lifted by the fifth pick.

Numbers five and ten are termed pressure picks. They are both fine picks, and make plain cloth at the back of the quilt, where the Jacquard yarn has not been raised. Were it not for these, the Jacquard yarn would be loose at the back of the cloth, behind the figure. Grey yarn for warp and weft is employed, and the quilts are bleached after being woven.

HONEYCOMB QUILTS.

Honeycomb quilts, so called from the cellular appearance of the fabric, rank amongst the most effective of the many varieties of quilts manufactured. Good bold patterns are the best for this class of cloth, in order that the honeycomb may be used to the greatest advantage. Various fancy weaves are likewise employed, and when they are combined with the honeycomb, a handsome reversible fabric results. This style of quilt is made with the Jacquard alone, only one yarn beam and one shuttle being needed. The Jacquard rises and falls at every pick. The warp is always a two or threefold yarn, and in the better qualities of cloths, the weft is the same as the warp, but, in the lower qualities, poor single yarns are used. Both warp and weft are bleached before weaving.

A draft for making the honeycomb effect is given in Fig.

125. In this, the black represents the warp and the white the weft. The dots show the longest floats of each, and it is these that produce the cellular appearance, as those portions which are more tightly bound naturally fall in. Good geometrical patterns, repeating in the ordinary manner, with bold outlines and clear spaces at intervals, for the introduction of the honeycomb, and with lesser spaces filled in with other fancy weaves, form good designs for this variety of quilt. Borders of a similar character to the body pattern may be employed, and where the ground of such is made in

FIG. 125.

the cellular effect, a very handsome fabric results, which is much enhanced by allowing a few inches of plain honeycomb around the border as a termination to the quilt.

GRECIAN QUILTS.

In the manufacture of Grecian quilts, no healds are required, and only one yarn beam and one shuttle are used, the Jacquard rising and falling at every pick, as in the case of honeycombs. Of course, the appearance of the cloth is not the same. In Fig. 126, a design suitable for a Grecian quilt is shown, in which the body of the pattern centres or turns over at each side, and a border may be so constructed that each side of it may be the same, although the centre

Fig. 126.

portion may not turn over. By this method, a freer and easier effect is given to the border than would be the case if it turned over from the centre. But in Fig. 126, an ordinary flowing border is shown. As a termination to the quilt, the bars may be repeated for a few inches. In preparing a ruled paper for a Grecian quilt, the ground should be in, say, a five shaft satin, but the figure may be more loosely bound, say, in a ten shaft satin. The bars may be suitably bound with a twill. A Grecian makes a very good reversible quilt.

FIG. 127.

ALHAMBRA QUILTS.

Alhambras are amongst the cheapest varieties of quilts manufactured; they are also the most popular, if the number made and sold is any criterion. There are more Alhambras sold than of all other kinds combined. The value of full-sized quilts, measuring about 108 × 84 inches, ranges from 2s. 9d. to 6s. 6d. There are two yarn beams employed in the weaving—one for the Jacquard, in which there is a coloured warp, making the pattern or figure, and the other containing a white warp, worked by two healds, which makes the plain cloth. In the lower qualities of cloth, a grey warp is used in place of the white. The Jacquard rises and falls at every pick, and one heald also changes at every pick. There are as many white ends in the warp as there are mails for the Jacquard, but there are two, three or four ends in each mail, according to the quality of the quilt—four ends are more expensive, but look much better than two. The weft is a very common bleached yarn, generally of from 80 to 100 yards to the ounce. One shuttle only is required, and, as a rule, a 600 Jacquard machine is employed, or a 400 is used, providing the harness is tied up specially for small repeats. There are usually twenty white ends to twenty mail ends per inch. In Fig. 127, a design is given showing an ordinary repeating pattern suitable for an Alhambra quilt. In preparing the ruled paper, draft the figure for the body pattern in red. This may be tied, to prevent an unnecessary length of float, in a suitable manner. Veins of leaves may be continued to their edges in single lines, a satin here and there where required, and in such-like manner the binding may be accomplished. The ground may be in half-and-half effect, that is equal portions of warp and weft up and down. The border should then be drafted in white, the ground being red, tied with a satin, say, of eight shafts. The border figure may be bound in a similar manner to that adopted for the body.

The small diaper pattern shown around the border must be repeated several times, in order to form a good termination to the quilt. This introduction of small diaper patterns is a common practice in the manufacture of any class of quilt, but, as one example is sufficient, the diaper has not been shown in the other figures illustrating this chapter.

Of course, in drafting, only one repeat of the diaper is necessary around the border.

With these few particulars and figures illustrating the satin, the toilet, the honeycomb, the Grecian and the Alhambra, this chapter on the subject of quilts may be concluded.

In Figs. 121 and 124, one quarter only of the design is given, but, in order that the reader may better judge of the effect, the whole of each pattern is given on our separate plates.

CHAPTER XVIII.

CALICO PRINTING.

THE subject of colour printing as applied to textile fabrics is one that would fill a large volume if dealt with adequately. It is necessary in treating upon ornamental textile fabrics to say something upon this highly interesting process, but it is obvious that, within the scope of a single chapter, it will not be possible to do more than treat upon those points which are of the most use to the student and designer. The printing of textile fabrics is a very ancient art, having been practised in olden times by the Egyptians and Chinese. We also find that the printing of calico was carried on in India at an early date. "Prints" were so much worn in this country that the Government prohibited their use. Such obstacles were, however, afterwards removed, so that in the year 1765 calico printing had been established as a regular branch of Lancashire industry. Of course, it is scarcely necessary to state that many other fabrics besides cotton are printed—that silk, linen, woollen, etc., are extensive branches of the art, but the processes in each case are mainly the same as that in use for calico printing.

BLOCK PRINTING.

Probably there are many who suppose that, in consequence of the inventive genius of the present age, machine printing has entirely superseded the older and more primitive method of block printing, but this is by no means the case. The latter process is extensively practised to this day, and there are those who consider themselves competent judges who will assert that the result produced by block printing is greatly superior to that gained by the more modern and speedier method of machine printing. However, there is no necessity to inquire into the relative merits of these assertions and methods, still there is no doubt that

FIG. 128.

some very beautiful fabrics are printed by the primitive system. In this process as many wooden blocks are employed as there are colours in a design—that is to say, each colour is separately engraved upon a block of fir, pear tree, sycamore, or boxwood. Impressions of these blocks are often cast in type metal, and thus made use of. Each portion of the pattern stands out in relief, and where fine effects, such as lines, etc., are employed, copper wire is used. The blocks are supplied with pins at the corner, in order that each one may successively fit exactly upon the space occupied by the previous one, and thus produce a perfect pattern. The cloth to be operated upon is stretched over a table, upon which a blanket is first laid, in order to ensure the necessary degree of softness in the foundation for printing. Each block is dipped into a colour and impressed upon the fabric. One class of block printing which may be mentioned is that commonly employed for table covers. The cloth in this case is usually of woollen, and by reason of its being easy distinguishable, and therefore forming a subject for examination by the designer or student, it is mentioned here. The fabric is usually of red or green, with a design impressed upon it in black, and to give gradation and softness of tone to the pattern, stippling is largely resorted to. In the printing of these goods the cloth is stretched over a table. A slab, upon which the colour is laid, is placed in a convenient position, and so that the block may be easily operated, a little mechanical contrivance of weighted cords is employed, by which the printer, with little manual exertion, raises the block from the cloth, swings it forward to the colour slab, and back again to the fabric. With this brief reference, the subject of block printing may be dismissed.

MACHINE PRINTING.

In times of keen competition it is apparent to all that, in order to cater for the million, block printing, however perfect it may be in its results, would be much too slow from a productive point of view. Thus, machine printing has become a very extensive industry, and the apparatus employed has attained to the very highest pitch of excellence. The illustration given in Fig. 128 represents an eight-colour duplex calico printing machine, made by Mr. Thomas Gadd. It has been specially constructed for the production of cloths up to sixty inches wide, having a pattern on both sides, and so perfect is it in its action that the colours accurately register or come exactly opposite each other on each side of the cloth. But not only is this machine adapted for producing an eight-colour reversible fabric, but it is likewise capable of printing sixteen colours on one side only. This appears a great number to print at one operation, but it is by no means unusual, as an examination of some cretonnes will easily demonstrate; indeed, the såme maker constructs machines to print as many as twenty colours. The illustration gives a perspective view of the eight-colour duplex machine, one end and side being clearly visible. Upon the latter portion of the view two drums will be noticeable, and at the end the rollers or cylinders corresponding with one of these drums are shown. At the opposite end of the machine are the rollers corresponding with the second drum. This mode of construction differs in one important point from that employed for a single-colour machine, as in the latter case there is but one drum, the rollers being arranged at each side of this instead of at one side of each drum, as in the duplex machine. A colour box with furnishing roller is fixed immediately under each roller, and steel blades called doctors are employed to remove the colour from the plain portions of the rollers. Blankets for printing upon are employed, as in the case of block printing. In this particular machine every possible improvement which can tend towards its more perfect operation has been made, but as it would be impossible to particularise these without a comparison with other machines, there is no necessity to speak of them here. Each roller employed is engraved around its circumference with the ornamentation represented by one colour of the design. In the case under notice there are eight differently engraved rollers, and these eight are duplicated, a complete set being required at each end of the machine. The fabric to be printed upon runs tightly around the drums, and as it runs it receives the impressions from the rollers. The printing of two sides at one operation is easily understood. Supposing the fabric comes up the side and over the top of one drum during its progress, it is receiving the imprint of the pattern on one side of the fabric. When the cloth passes down between the two drums, and, crossing over to the other one, passes under and up the side of this, it receives the imprint on the reverse side. Such is a simple and brief description of one of these interesting and valuable pieces of mechanism.

INTERMITTENT MACHINE.

But a more ingenious apparatus is the intermittent calico printing machine, employed in the production of fabrics where one continuous pattern is not requisite—for instance, in dado curtains, shawls and sarees. This latter, it may be mentioned, is the principal garment of a Hindoo woman, and is wrapped around the body, one portion being taken over the left shoulder, and the other hanging down in front. These sarees are of considerable length, and certain portions are of different ornamentation. Now it is obvious that to change from one pattern to another, whilst printing upon one and the same piece of fabric, some other arrangement must be employed than that usual in ordinary calico printing, and here comes in the intermittent system. In the machine constructed by Mr. Thomas Gadd, three rollers are required for each colour, one for the border, one for the crossbar, and one for the main portion of the pattern. By the adoption of ingenious mechanism, these rollers are caused to come into, or retire from, contact with the cloth, just whenever required, so that no two are in operation at one and the same time. As soon as the pattern engraved upon one roller has been impressed upon the fabric, the next roller is brought into contact with the cloth, and continues running and printing a new design, until it is succeeded by another roller. The crossbar patterns may be printed from rollers of 36, 45 or 54 inch circumference, and the border and body patterns from rollers of 18 inch circumference. After the crossbar design has been imparted to the cloth once, the roller is caused to retire, and in its place the

FIG. 129.

body or filling roller comes into operation and continues running until the necessary length has been acted upon. In other words, whilst the crossbar roller may revolve once only, the filling roller may make several revolutions before another change is required. With this machine, different combinations of rollers are possible—for instance, 18 inch border and body rollers can be used with crossbar rollers of any of the above-named dimensions, and various body or filling designs may be printed between one crossbar and another. Sarees are made of varying lengths, up to ten yards, but, by the addition of change wheels, a greater length can be printed.

CRETONNE DESIGNS.

The production of cretonne patterns calls for the utmost artistic skill and ability, and in this respect French designers take the palm. Many of the patterns which come from the studios of Paris are really nothing less than

FIG. 130.

works of art. In a previous chapter, it was stated that, for certain purposes, French patterns were not at all practical —too much being attempted, with the result that, when produced in the cloth, much of the beauty had vanished. But in the case of cretonnes, this is not so. When an artist has scarcely a limit placed upon the number of colours he can use, when he can employ 12, 16 or 20 colours, or even more than these, by what is known as super-position, it will be obvious that, with ability, such as French designers as a rule possess, the production of an artistic pattern for a cretonne becomes a much easier matter than where a design is controlled within the narrow limits of striped warps and changing shuttles. But granting to Frenchmen great skill in this direction, it is open to doubt whether English designers receive sufficient encouragement from the general run of cretonne printers. Representatives of the best English

FIG. 191.

houses make periodical visits to Paris, where they spend some time in the studios purchasing designs, and, possibly, in other ways having a happy time. The English designer calls upon these firms and is lucky if he does business. There is little doubt that, with due encouragement, much of the French trade might pass into the hands of English artists at no distant period. The trade in cretonne designs is quite worthy of the attention of home artists, the main consideration being the price paid, which is good. It has been stated over and over again that the charge for one of these patterns runs to a sovereign for each colour used, and, as calico printing machines are made to print up to twenty colours, the charges are easily estimated. In designing for calico prints, it is scarcely necessary to state that the pattern is in all respects an exact facsimile of the finished fabric. For every colour in the design, an engraved roller or cylinder is re-

Fig. 132.

quired, and, whilst in block printing the engravings are raised, those used in machine printing are sunk. It would be impossible to give a good example of a cretonne pattern, as these are usually too extensive in repeat and contain too many colours to be reproduced in an engraving. Fig. 129 is a simple pattern in imitation of a woven design, and although this is by no means offered as a fair example, for the reason above stated, it will, nevertheless, serve the purpose of illustrating these remarks. The figure represents the finished cretonne. Fig. 130 shows the light grey portion of the pattern, which would be engraved on a roller by itself. Fig. 131 is the dark grey roller, and Fig. 132 represents the black roller. Thus there is a three-colour pattern on a white ground, as seen in Fig. 129. But if such a pattern were actually to be employed, it would be usually printed upon a coloured ground—pale blue, pink, primrose, or some such shade. In order to do this, the ground colour would be "padded," that is to say, it would be printed on a machine with one roller, and the pattern would be printed upon this in suitable colours. In some cases, designers of cretonnes exercise a method whereby more colours are obtained in a design than there are rollers in the machine upon which it is to be printed. This is known as super-position and is easily understood. Suppose in a certain pattern there are five colours—black, red, blue, yellow and orange. This could be printed in a four-colour machine by engraving that portion required in orange both on the yellow and the red rollers, so that, in the actual printing, the red would fall upon the yellow and thus produce orange. But this method requires the exercise of a great amount of experience before it can be successfully employed to any extent, and it is therefore better left alone by the student, or he might end in the production of patterns which would be worthless, from a practical point of view. In designing for cretonnes, nature is more closely followed, both in form and colour, than in any other branch. It is therefore essential that the designer should have a good knowledge of plant form, with undoubted ability in the use of his pencil and brush.

Catalogue
OF
Special Technical Books
FOR
MANUFACTURERS, TECHNICAL STUDENTS AND WORKERS, SCHOOLS, COLLEGES, ETC.
BY EXPERT WRITERS

INDEX TO SUBJECTS.

	PAGE
Agricultural Chemistry	10
Air, Industrial Use of	12
Alum and its Sulphates	9
Ammonia	9
Aniline Colours	3
Animal Fats	6
Anti-corrosive Paints	4
Architecture, Terms in	29
Architectural Pottery	15
Artificial Perfumes	7
Balsams	10
Bibliography	32
Bleaching	23
Bone Products	8
Bookbinding	31
Brick-making	14, 15
Burnishing Brass	27
Carpet Yarn Printing	21
Casein	4
Celluloid	31
Ceramic Books	14, 15, 16
Charcoal	9
Chemical Essays	9
Chemistry of Pottery	16
Chemistry of Dye-stuffs	23
Clay Analysis	16
Coal-dust Firing	26
Colour Matching	22
Colliery Recovery Work	25
Colour-mixing for Dyers	22
Colour Theory	22
Combing Machines	24
Compounding Oils	6
Condensing Apparatus	26
Cosmetics	8
Cotton Dyeing	23
Cotton Spinning	24
Damask Weaving	20
Dampness in Buildings	29
Decorators' Books	28
Decorative Textiles	20
Dental Metallurgy	25
Dictionary of Paint Materials	2
Drying Oils	5
Drying with Air	12
Dyeing Marble	30
Dyeing Woollen Fabrics	23
Dyers' Materials	22
Dye-stuffs	23
Electric Wiring	27
Electricity in Collieries	25
Enamelling Metal	18
Enamels	18
Engraving	31

	PAGE
Essential Oils	7
Extracts, Wood	29
Evaporating Apparatus	26
External Plumbing	27
Fats	5, 6
Faults in Woollen Goods	21
Flax Spinning	24
Fruit Preserving	30
Gas Firing	26
Glass-making Recipes	16
Glass Painting	17
Glue Making and Testing	8
Greases	5
Hat Manufacturing	20
Hemp Spinning	24
History of Staffs Potteries	16
Hops	28
Hot-water Supply	28
How to make a Woollen Mill Pay	21
India-rubber	13
Industrial Alcohol	10
Inks	3, 11
Iron-corrosion	4
Iron, Science of	26
Japanning	28
Jute Spinning	24
Lace-Making	20
Lacquering	27
Lake Pigments	2
Lead and its Compounds	11
Leather Industry	13
Leather-working Materials	14
Lithography	31
Lubricants	5, 6
Manures	8, 10
Meat Preserving	30
Mineral Pigments	3
Mineral Waxes	6
Mine Ventilation	25
Mine Haulage	25
Mining, Electricity	25
Needlework	20
Oil and Colour Recipes	3
Oil Boiling	5
Oil Merchants' Manual	6
Oils	5
Ozone, Industrial Use of	12
Paint Manufacture	2
Paint Materials	3
Paint-material Testing	4
Paint Mixing	28
Paper-Mill Chemistry	17
Paper-pulp Dyeing	17

	PAGE
Petroleum	6
Pigments, Chemistry of	2
Plumbers' Work	27
Porcelain Painting	17
Pottery Clays	16
Pottery Decorating	15
Pottery Manufacture	14
Power-loom Weaving	19
Preserved Foods	30
Printers' Ready Reckoner	31
Printing Inks	3
Recipes for Oilmen, etc.	3
Resins	10
Risks of Occupations	12
Riveting China, etc.	16
Sanitary Plumbing	27
Scheele's Essays	9
Sealing Waxes	11
Silk Dyeing	22
Silk Throwing	18
Smoke Prevention	26
Soaps	7
Spinning	21
Staining Marble, and Bone	30
Steam Drying	12
Sugar Refining	32
Steel Hardening	26
Sweetmeats	30
Tanning Extracts	29
Technical Schools, Handbook to the	32
Terra-cotta	15
Testing Paint Materials	4
Testing Yarns	20
Textile Fabrics	20
Textile Materials	19, 20
Timber	29
Varnishes	5
Vegetable Fats	7
Vegetable Preserving	30
Waste Utilisation	11
Water, Industrial Use	12
Waterproofing Fabrics	21
Waxes	6
Weaving Calculations	21
White Lead and Zinc	4
Wood Distillation	29
Wood Waste Utilisation	29
Wood Dyeing	30
Wool Dyeing	22, 23
Writing Inks	11
X-Ray Work	13
Yarn Testing	20
Zinc White Paints	4

PUBLISHED BY

SCOTT, GREENWOOD & SON,

8 BROADWAY, LUDGATE HILL,
LONDON, E.C.

Telephone, Bank 5403. Telegraphic Address, "Printeries, London".

Paints, Colours and Printing Inks.

THE CHEMISTRY OF PIGMENTS. By ERNEST J. PARRY, B.Sc. (Lond.), F.I.C., F.C.S., and J. H. COSTE, F.I.C., F.C.S. Demy 8vo. Five Illustrations. 285 pp. Price 10s. 6d. net. (Post free, 10s. 10d. home; 11s. 3d. abroad.)

Contents.

Introductory. Light—White Light—The Spectrum—The Invisible Spectrum—Normal Spectrum—Simple Nature of Pure Spectral Colour—The Recomposition of White Light—Primary and Complementary Colours—Coloured Bodies—Absorption Spectra—**The Application of Pigments.** Uses of Pigments: Artistic, Decorative, Protective—Methods of Application of Pigments: Pastels and Crayons, Water Colour, Tempera Painting, Fresco, Encaustic Painting, Oil-colour Painting, Keramic Art, Enamel, Stained and Painted Glass, Mosaic—**Inorganic Pigments.** White Lead—Zinc White—Enamel White—Whitening—Red Lead—Litharge—Vermilion—Royal Scarlet—The Chromium Greens—Chromates of Lead, Zinc, Silver and Mercury—Brunswick Green—The Ochres—Indian Red—Venetian Red—Siennas and Umbers—Light Red—Cappagh Brown—Red Oxides—Mars Colours—Terre Verte—Prussian Brown—Cobalt Colours—Cœruleum—Smalt—Copper Pigments—Malachite—Bremen Green—Scheele's Green—Emerald Green—Verdigris—Brunswick Green—Non-arsenical Greens—Copper Blues—Ultramarine—Carbon Pigments—Ivory Black—Lamp Black—Bistre—Naples Yellow—Arsenic Sulphides: Orpiment, Realgar—Cadmium Yellow—Vandyck Brown—**Organic Pigments.** Prussian Blue—Natural Lakes—Cochineal—Carmine—Crimson—Lac Dye—Scarlet—Madder—Alizarin—Campeachy—Quercitron—Rhamnus—Brazil Wood—Alkanet—Santal Wood—Archil—Coal-tar Lakes—Red Lakes—Alizarin Compounds—Orange and Yellow Lakes—Green and Blue Lakes—Indigo—Dragon's Blood—Gamboge—Sepia—Indian Yellow, Puree—Bitumen, Asphaltum, Mummy—**Index.**

THE MANUFACTURE OF PAINT. A Practical Handbook for Paint Manufacturers, Merchants and Painters. By J. CRUICKSHANK SMITH, B.Sc. Demy 8vo. 200 pp. Sixty Illustrations and One Large Diagram. Price 7s. 6d. net. (Post free, 7s. 10d. home; 8s. abroad.)

Contents.

Preparation of Raw Material—Storing of Raw Material—Testing and Valuation of Raw Material—Paint Plant and Machinery—The Grinding of White Lead—Grinding of White Zinc—Grinding of other White Pigments—Grinding of Oxide Paints—Grinding of Staining Colours—Grinding of Black Paints—Grinding of Chemical Colours—Yellows—Grinding of Chemical Colours—Blues—Grinding Greens—Grinding Reds—Grinding Lakes—Grinding Colours in Water—Grinding Colours in Turpentine—The Uses of Paint—Testing and Matching Paints—Economic Considerations—Index.

DICTIONARY OF CHEMICALS AND RAW PRODUCTS USED IN THE MANUFACTURE OF PAINTS, COLOURS, VARNISHES AND ALLIED PREPARATIONS. By GEORGE H. HURST, F.C.S. Demy 8vo. 380 pp. Price 7s. 6d. net. (Post free, 8s. home; 8s. 6d. abroad.)

THE MANUFACTURE OF LAKE PIGMENTS FROM ARTIFICIAL COLOURS. By FRANCIS H. JENNISON, F.I.C., F.C.S. **Sixteen Coloured Plates, showing Specimens of Eighty-nine Colours, specially prepared from the Recipes given in the Book.** 136 pp. Demy 8vo. Price 7s. 6d. net. (Post free, 7s. 10d. home; 8s. abroad.)

Contents.

The Groups of the Artificial Colouring Matters—The Nature and Manipulation of Artificial Colours—Lake-forming Bodies for Acid Colours—Lake-forming Bodies' Basic Colours—Lake Bases—The Principles of Lake Formation—Red Lakes—Orange, Yellow, Green, Blue, Violet and Black Lakes—The Production of Insoluble Azo Colours in tne Form of Pigments—The General Properties of Lakes Produced from Artificial Colours—Washing, Filtering and Finishing—Matching and Testing Lake Pigments—Index.

PAINTS, COLOURS, ETC.—*continued.*

THE MANUFACTURE OF MINERAL AND LAKE PIGMENTS. Containing Directions for the Manufacture of all Artificial, Artists and Painters' Colours, Enamel, Soot and Metallic Pigments. A Text-book for Manufacturers, Merchants, Artists and Painters. By Dr. JOSEF BERSCH. Translated by A. C. WRIGHT, M.A. (Oxon.), B.Sc. (Lond.). Forty-three Illustrations. 476 pp., demy 8vo. Price 12s. 6d. net. (Post free, 13s. home; 13s. 6d. abroad.)

Contents.

Introduction—Physico-chemical Behaviour of Pigments—Raw Materials Employed in the Manufacture of Pigments—Assistant Materials—Metallic Compounds—The Manufacture of Mineral Pigments—The Manufacture of White Lead—Enamel White—Washing Apparatus—Zinc White—Yellow Mineral Pigments—Chrome Yellow—Lead Oxide Pigments—Other Yellow Pigments—Mosaic Gold—Red Mineral Pigments—The Manufacture of Vermilion—Antimony Vermilion—Ferric Oxide Pigments—Other Red Mineral Pigments—Purple of Cassius—Blue Mineral Pigments—Ultramarine—Manufacture of Ultramarine—Blue Copper Pigments—Blue Cobalt Pigments—Smalts—Green Mineral Pigments—Emerald Green—Verdigris—Chromium Oxide—Other Green Chromium Pigments—Green Cobalt Pigments—Green Manganese Pigments—Compounded Green Pigments—Violet Mineral Pigments—Brown Mineral Pigments—Brown Decomposition Products—Black Pigments—Manufacture of Soot Pigments—Manufacture of Lamp Black—The Manufacture of Soot Black without Chambers—Indian Ink—Enamel Colours—Metallic Pigments—Bronze Pigments—Vegetable Bronze Pigments.

PIGMENTS OF ORGANIC ORIGIN—Lakes—Yellow Lakes—Red Lakes—Manufacture of Carmine—The Colouring Matter of Lac—Safflower or Carthamine Red—Madder and its Colouring Matters—Madder Lakes—Manjit (Indian Madder)—Lichen Colouring Matters—Red Wood Lakes—The Colouring Matters of Sandal Wood and Other Dye Woods—Blue Lakes—Indigo Carmine—The Colouring Matter of Log Wood—Green Lakes—Brown Organic Pigments—Sap Colours—Water Colours—Crayons—Confectionery Colours—The Preparation of Pigments for Painting—The Examination of Pigments—Examination of Lakes—The Testing of Dye-Woods—The Design of a Colour Works—Commercial Names of Pigments—Appendix: Conversion of Metric to English Weights and Measures—Centigrade and Fahrenheit Thermometer Scales—Index.

RECIPES FOR THE COLOUR, PAINT, VARNISH, OIL, SOAP AND DRYSALTERY TRADES. Compiled by AN ANALYTICAL CHEMIST. 350 pp. Demy 8vo. Price 7s. 6d. net. (Post free, 8s. home; 8s. 3d. abroad.)

Contents.

Pigments or Colours for Paints, Lithographic and Letterpress Printing Inks, etc.—Mixed Paints and Preparations for Paint-making, Painting, Lime-washing, Paperhanging, etc.—Varnishes for Coach-builders, Cabinetmakers, Wood-workers, Metal-workers, Photographers, etc.—Soaps for Toilet, Cleansing, Polishing, etc.—Perfumes—Lubricating Greases, Oils, etc.—Cements, Pastes, Glues and Other Adhesive Preparations—Writing, Marking, Endorsing and Other Inks—Sealing-wax and Office Requisites—Preparations for the Laundry, Kitchen, Stable and General Household Uses—Disinfectant Preparations—Miscellaneous Preparations—Index.

OIL COLOURS AND PRINTERS' INKS. By LOUIS EDGAR ANDÉS. Translated from the German. 215 pp. Crown 8vo. 56 Illustrations. Price 5s. net. (Post free, 5s. 4d. home; 5s. 6d. abroad.)

Contents.

Linseed Oil—Poppy Oil—Mechanical Purification of Linseed Oil—Chemical Purification of Linseed Oil—Bleaching Linseed Oil—Oxidizing Agents for Boiling Linseed Oil—Theory of Oil Boiling—Manufacture of Boiled Oil—Adulterations of Boiled Oil—Chinese Drying Oil and Other Specialities—Pigments for House and Artistic Painting and Inks—Pigment for Printers' Black Inks—Substitutes for Lampblack—Machinery for Colour Grinding and Rubbing—Machines for mixing Pigments with the Vehicle—Paint Mills—Manufacture of House Oil Paints—Ship Paints—Luminous Paint—Artists Colours—Printers' Inks:—VEHICLES—Printers' Inks:—PIGMENTS and MANUFACTURE—Index.

(*See also Writing Inks, p.* 11.)

THREE HUNDRED SHADES AND HOW TO MIX THEM. For Architects, Decorators and Painters.

(*See page* 28.)

PAINTS, COLOURS, ETC.—*continued.*

CASEIN. By ROBERT SCHERER. Translated from the German by CHAS. SALTER. Demy 8vo. Illustrated. 160 pp. Price 7s. 6d. net. (Post free, 7s. 10d. home; 8s. abroad.)

Contents.

Casein: Its Origin, Preparation and Properties. Various Methods of Preparing Casein. Composition and Properties of Casein. Casein Paints.—"Marble-Lime" Colour for Outside Work—Casein Enamel Paint—Casein Façade Paint—Cold-Water Paint in Powder Form—Kistory's Recipe for Casein Paint and Varnish—Pure Casein Paints for Walls, etc.—Casein Paints for Woodwork and Iron—Casein-Silicate Paints—Milk Paints—Casein-Silicate Paint Recipes—Trojel's Boiled Oil Substitute—Calsomine Wash—Quick-Drying Casein Paint—Boiled Oil Substitute—Ring's Cold-Water Paint—Formolactin—Waterproof Paint for Playing Cards—Casein Colour Lake—Casein-Cement Paint. **The Technics of Casein Painting. Casein Adhesives and Putties.**—Casein Glue in Plates or Flakes—Jeromin's Casein Adhesive—Hall's Casein Glue—Waterproof Glue—Liquid Casein Glue—Casein and Borax Glue—Solid Casein Adhesive—Casein Solution—Glue Powder—Casein Putties—Washable Cement for Deal Boards—Wenk's Casein Cement—Casein and Lime Cement—"Pitch Barm"—Casein Stopping—Casein Cement for Stone. **The Preparation of Plastic Masses from Casein.**—Imitation Ivory—Anti-Radiation and Anti-Corrosive Composition—Dickmann's Covering for Floors and Walls—Imitation Linoleum—Imitation Leather—Imitation Bone—Plastic Mass of Keratin and Casein—Insulating Mass—Plastic Casein Masses—Horny Casein Mass—Plastic Mass from Celluloid—Casein Cellulose Composition—Fireproof Cellulose Substitute—Nitrocellulose and Casein Composition—Franquet's Celluloid Substitute—Galalith. **Uses of Casein in the Textile Industry, for Finishing Colour Printing, etc.**—Caseogum—"Glutin"—Casein Dressing for Linen and Cotton Fabrics—Printing Colour with Metallic Lustre—Process for Softening, Sizing and Loading—Fixing Casein and Other Albuminoids on the Fibre—Fixing Insoluble Colouring Matters—Waterproofing and Softening Dressing—Casein for Mercerising Crêpe—Fixing Zinc White on Cotton with Formaldehyde—Casein-Magnesia—Casein Medium for Calico Printing—Loading Silk. **Casein Foodstuffs.**—Casein Food—Synthetic Milk—Milk Food—Emulsifiable Casein—Casein Phosphate for Baking—Making Bread, Low in Carbohydrates, from Flour and Curd—Preparing Soluble Casein Compounds with Citrates—Casein Food. **Sundry Applications of Casein.**

SIMPLE METHODS FOR TESTING PAINTERS' MATERIALS. By A. C. WRIGHT, M.A. (Oxon.), B.Sc. (Lond.). Crown 8vo. 160 pp. Price 5s. net. (Post free, 5s. 3d. home; 5s. 6d. abroad.)

IRON-CORROSION, ANTI-FOULING AND ANTI-CORROSIVE PAINTS. Translated from the German of LOUIS EDGAR ANDÉS. Sixty-two Illustrations. 275 pp. Demy 8vo. Price 10s. 6d. net. (Post free, 10s. 10d. home; 11s. 3d. abroad.)

Contents.

Iron-rust and its Formation—Protection from Rusting by Paint—Grounding the Iron with Linseed Oil, etc.—Testing Paints—Use of Tar for Painting on Iron—Anti-corrosive Paints—Linseed Varnish—Chinese Wood Oil—Lead Pigments—Iron Pigments—Artificial Iron Oxides—Carbon—Preparation of Anti-corrosive Paints—Results of Examination of Several Anti-corrosive Paints—Paints for Ship's Bottoms—Anti-fouling Compositions—Various Anti-corrosive and Ship's Paints—Official Standard Specifications for Ironwork Paints—Index.

THE TESTING AND VALUATION OF RAW MATERIALS USED IN PAINT AND COLOUR MANUFACTURE. By M. W. JONES, F.C.S. A Book for the Laboratories of Colour Works. 88 pp. Crown 8vo. Price 5s. net. (Post free, 5s. 3d. home and abroad.)

THE MANUFACTURE AND COMPARATIVE MERITS OF WHITE LEAD AND ZINC WHITE PAINTS. By G. PETIT, Civil Engineer, etc. Translated from the French. Crown 8vo. 100 pp. Price 4s. net. (Post free, 4s. 3d. home; 4s. 4d. abroad.)

Contents.

Chapters I., The Fundamental Principles of Painting in Oil. II., The Different Varieties of White Leads—The Dutch Process—Grinding White Lead in Oil. III., Other Processes of Manufacturing White Lead. IV., White Lead Substitutes—Sophistication of White Lead—Analysis of White Lead. V., White Lead Paints—Their Merits and Defects. VI., Toxicology of White Lead—Hygienic Measures in its Manufacture and Use. VII., Zinc White—Its Preparation. IX., Zinc White Paint and Zinc White Coatings—Their Merits and Defects.

STUDENTS' HANDBOOK OF PAINTS, COLOURS, OILS AND VARNISHES. By JOHN FURNELL. Crown 8vo. 12 Illustrations. 96 pp. Price 2s. 6d. net. (Post free, 2s. 9d. home and abroad.)

Varnishes and Drying Oils.

OIL CRUSHING, REFINING AND BOILING, THE MANUFACTURE OF LINOLEUM, PRINTING AND LITHOGRAPHIC INKS, AND INDIA-RUBBER SUBSTITUTES. By JOHN GEDDES McINTOSH. Being Volume I. of the Second, greatly enlarged, English Edition, in three Volumes, of "The Manufacture of Varnishes and Kindred Industries," based on and including the work of Ach. Livache. Demy 8vo. 150 pp. 29 Illustrations. Price 7s. 6d. net. (Post free, 7s. 10d. home; 8s. abroad.)

VARNISH MATERIALS AND OIL-VARNISH MAKING. By J. G. McINTOSH. Being Vol. II. of "The Manufacture of Varnishes and Kindred Industries". Demy 8vo. 70 Illustrations. 220 pp. Price 10s. 6d. net. (Post free, 10s. 10d. home; 11s. 3d. abroad.)

Contents.

Chapter I., Introduction. II., Amber and Amber Oil Varnishes. III., Copal, etc. IV., Resins—Assorting, Cleaning and Fusing. V., Asphaltum, Coal-Tar, Pitch, Rubber, etc. VI., Oil-Varnish Making—General Instructions. VII., Copal Oil Varnish. VIII., Rosin Oil Varnish—Brunswick Black—Super Black Japan. IX., Testing Varnish—Utilisation of Residues.

DRYING OILS, BOILED OIL AND SOLID AND LIQUID DRIERS. By L. E. ANDÉS. Expressly Written for this Series of Special Technical Books, and the Publishers hold the Copyright for English and Foreign Editions. Forty-two Illustrations. 342 pp. Demy 8vo. Price 12s. 6d. net. (Post free, 13s. home; 13s. 3d. abroad.)

Contents.

Properties of the Drying Oils; Cause of the Drying Property; Absorption of Oxygen; Behaviour towards Metallic Oxides, etc.—The Properties of and Methods for obtaining the Drying Oils—Production of the Drying Oils by Expression and Extraction; Refining and Bleaching; Oil Cakes and Meal; The Refining and Bleaching of the Drying Oils; The Bleaching of Linseed Oil—The Manufacture of Boiled Oil; The Preparation of Drying Oils for Use in the Grinding of Paints and Artists' Colours and in the Manufacture of Varnishes by Heating over a Fire or by Steam, by the Cold Process, by the Action of Air, and by Means of the Electric Current; The Driers used in Boiling Linseed Oil; The Manufacture of Boiled Oil and the Apparatus therefor; Livache's Process for Preparing a Good Drying Oil and its Practical Application—The Preparation of Varnishes for Letterpress, Lithographic and Copper-plate Printing, for Oilcloth and Waterproof Fabrics; The Manufacture of Thickened Linseed Oil, Burnt Oil, Stand Oil by Fire Heat, Superheated Steam, and by a Current of Air—Behaviour of the Drying Oils and Boiled Oils towards Atmospheric Influences, Water, Acids and Alkalies—Boiled Oil Substitutes—The Manufacture of Solid and Liquid Driers from Linseed Oil and Rosin; Linolic Acid Compounds of the Driers—The Adulteration and Examination of the Drying Oils and Boiled Oil.

Oils, Fats, Waxes, Greases, Petroleum.

LUBRICATING OILS, FATS AND GREASES: Their Origin, Preparation, Properties, Uses and Analyses. A Handbook for Oil Manufacturers, Refiners and Merchants, and the Oil and Fat Industry in General. By GEORGE H. HURST, F.C.S. Second Revised and Enlarged Edition. Sixty-five Illustrations. 317 pp. Demy 8vo. Price 10s. 6d. net. (Post free, 11s. home; 11s. 3d. abroad.)

Contents.

Introductory—Hydrocarbon Oils—Scotch Shale Oils—Petroleum—Vegetable and Animal Oils—Testing and Adulteration of Oils—Lubricating Greases—Lubrication—Appendices—Index.

TECHNOLOGY OF PETROLEUM: Oil Fields of the World—Their History, Geography and Geology—Annual Production and Development—Oil-well Drilling—Transport. By HENRY NEUBERGER and HENRY NOALHAT. Translated from the French by J. G. McINTOSH. 550 pp. 153 Illustrations. 26 Plates. Super Royal 8vo. Price 21s. net. (Post free, 21s. 9d. home; 23s. 6d. abroad.)

Contents.

Study of the Petroliferous Strata.
Excavations—Hand Excavation or Hand Digging of Oil Wells.
Methods of Boring.
Accidents—Boring Accidents—Methods of preventing them—Methods of remedying them—Explosives and the use of the "Torpedo" Levigation—Storing and Transport of Petroleum—General Advice—Prospecting, Management and carrying on of Petroleum Boring Operations.
General Data—Customary Formulæ—Memento. Practical Part. General Data bearing on Petroleum—Glossary of Technical Terms used in the Petroleum Industry—Copious Index.

MINERAL WAXES: Their Preparation and Uses. By RUDOLF GREGORIUS. Translated from the German. Crown 8vo. 250 pp. 32 Illustrations. Price 6s. net. (Post free, 6s. 4d. home; 6s. 6d. abroad.)

Contents.

Ozokerite—Ceresine—Paraffin—Refining Paraffin—Mineral Wax—Appliances for Extracting, Distilling and Refining Ozokerite—Uses of Ceresine, Paraffin and Mineral Waxes—Paint and Varnish Removers—Leather and Piston-Rod Greases—Recipes for Silk, Cotton and Linen Dressings—Candles.

THE PRACTICAL COMPOUNDING OF OILS, TALLOW AND GREASE FOR LUBRICATION, ETC. By AN EXPERT OIL REFINER. Second Edition. 100 pp. Demy 8vo. Price 7s. 6d. net. (Post free, 7s. 10d. home; 8s. abroad.)

Contents.

Introductory Remarks on the General Nomenclature of Oils, Tallow and Greases suitable for Lubrication—**Hydrocarbon Oils—Animal and Fish Oils—Compound Oils—Vegetable Oils—Lamp Oils—Engine Tallow, Solidified Oils and Petroleum Jelly—Machinery Greases**: **Loco and Anti-friction—Clarifying and Utilisation of Waste Fats, Oils, Tank Bottoms, Drainings of Barrels and Drums, Pickings Up, Dregs, etc.—The Fixing and Cleaning of Oil Tanks, etc.—Appendix and General Information.**

ANIMAL FATS AND OILS: Their Practical Production, Purification and Uses for a great Variety of Purposes. Their Properties, Falsification and Examination. Translated from the German of LOUIS EDGAR ANDÉS. Sixty-two Illustrations. 240 pp. Second Edition, Revised and Enlarged. Demy 8vo. Price 10s. 6d. net. (Post free, 10s. 10d. home; 11s. 3d. abroad.)

THE MANUFACTURE OF LUBRICANTS, SHOE POLISHES AND LEATHER DRESSINGS. By RICHARD BRUNNER. Translated from the Sixth German Edition by CHAS. SALTER. 10 Illustrations. Crown 8vo. 170 pp. Price 7s. 6d. net. (Post free, 7s. 10d. home; 8s. abroad.)

THE OIL MERCHANTS' MANUAL AND OIL TRADE READY RECKONER. Compiled by FRANK F. SHERRIFF. Second Edition Revised and Enlarged. Demy 8vo. 214 pp. 1904. With Two Sheets of Tables. Price 7s. 6d. net. (Post free, 7s. 10d. home; 8s. 3d. abroad.)

Contents.

Trade Terms and Customs—Tables to Ascertain Value of Oil sold per cwt. or ton—Specific Gravity Tables—Percentage Tare Tables—Petroleum Tables—Paraffine and Benzoline Calculations—Customary Drafts—Tables for Calculating Allowance for Dirt, Water, etc.—Capacity of Circular Tanks, Tables, etc., etc.

VEGETABLE FATS AND OILS: Their Practical Preparation, Purification and Employment for Various Purposes, their Properties, Adulteration and Examination. Translated from the German of LOUIS EDGAR ANDÉS. Ninety-four Illustrations. 340 pp. Second Edition. Demy 8vo. Price 10s. 6d. net. (Post free, 11s. home; 11s. 6d. abroad.)

Essential Oils and Perfumes.

THE CHEMISTRY OF ESSENTIAL OILS AND ARTIFICIAL PERFUMES. By ERNEST J. PARRY, B.Sc. (Lond.), F.I.C., F.C.S. Second Edition, Revised and Enlarged. 552 pp. 20 Illustrations. Demy 8vo. Price 12s. 6d. net. (Post free, 13s. home; 13s. 6d. abroad.)

Contents.

Chapter I. **The General Properties of Essential Oils.** II. **Compounds occurring in Essential Oils**; (I.) The Terpenes—Sesquiterpenes—Olefinic Terpenes and Sesquiterpenes—Pinene—(II.) The Camphor Series—(III.) The Geraniol and Citronellol Group—The Geraniol and Citronellol Series—(IV.) Benzene Compounds: Cymene—Phenols and their Derivatives—Phenols with Nine Carbon Atoms—Phenols with Ten Carbon Atoms—Alcohols—Aldehydes—Ketones—Acids—(V.) Aliphatic Compounds: Alcohols—Acids—Aldehydes—Sulphur Compounds—Other Bodies. III. **The Preparation of Essential Oils**: Expression—Distillation—Extraction. IV. **The Analysis of Essential Oils**: Specific Gravity—Optical Methods: (1) Refraction (2) Polarimetry, Melting and Solidifying Points—Boiling Point and Distillation—Quantitative Estimations of Constituents—Aldehydes, Ketones and Oils on which a Direct Determination can be made. V. **Systematic Study of the Essential Oils**: Oils of the Gymnosperms—(I.) Wood Oils—(II.) Fruit Oils—(III.) Leaf Oils—Oils of the Angiosperms: (I.) Monocotyledons: N. O. Gramineæ, Geraniol, N. O. Ariodeæ, N. O. Liliaceæ, N. O. Irideæ, N. O. Zingiberaceæ—(II.) Dicotyledons: (A) *Monochlamydeæ*, N. O. Piperaceæ, N. O. Cannabinaceæ, N. O. Myricaceæ, N. O. Salicineæ, N. O. Chenopodiaceæ, N. O. Laurineæ, N. O. Myristiceæ, N. O. Euphorbiaceæ, N. O. Cupuliferæ, N. O. Santalaceæ, N. O. Aristolochieæ—(B) *Gamopetalæ*, N. O. Labiatæ, N. O. Verbenaceæ, N. O. Convolvulaceæ, N. O. Jasmineæ, N. O. Ericaceæ, N. O. Valerianeæ, N. O. Compositæ, N. O. Caprifoliaceæ, Polypetalæ, N. O. Umbelliferæ, N. O. Myrtaceæ, N. O. Rosaceæ, N. O. Rutaceæ, N. O. Zygophylleæ, N. O. Anacardiaceæ, N. O. Leguminosæ, N. O. Burseraceæ, N. O. Geraniaceæ, N. O. Tropæoleæ, N. O. Meliaceæ, N. O. Cruciferæ, N. O. Cistineæ, N. O. Magnoliaceæ, N. O. Resedaceæ, N. O. Turneraceæ, N. O. Clusiaceæ, N. O. Dipterocarpeæ, N. O. Ternstrœmiaceæ, N. O. Malvaceæ, N. O. Ranunculaceæ, N. O. Anonaceæ. VI. **Chemistry of Artificial Perfumes.** Appendix I. Table on Constants of the more important Essential Oils. Appendix II. Table of Pharmacopœial Standards. Index.

Soaps.

SOAPS. A Practical Manual of the Manufacture of Domestic, Toilet and other Soaps. By GEORGE H. HURST, F.C.S. 2nd edition. 390 pp. 66 Illustrations. Price 12s. 6d. net. (Post free, 13s. home; 13s. 6d. abroad.)

Contents.

Introductory—Soap-maker's Alkalies—Soap Fats and Oils—Perfumes—Water as a Soap Material—Soap Machinery—Technology of Soap-making—Glycerine in Soap Lyes—Laying out a Soap Factory—Soap Analysis—Appendices.

TEXTILE SOAPS AND OILS. Handbook on the Preparation, Properties and Analysis of the Soaps and Oils used in Textile Manufacturing, Dyeing and Printing. By GEORGE H. HURST, F.C.S. Crown 8vo. 195 pp. 1904. Price 5s. net. (Post free, 5s. 4d. home; 5s. 6d. abroad.)

THE HANDBOOK OF SOAP MANUFACTURE. By WM. H. SIMMONS, B.Sc. (Lond.), F.C.S. and H. A. APPLETON. Demy 8vo. 160 pp. 27 Illustrations. Price 8s. 6d. net. (Post free, 8s. 10d. home; 9s. abroad.)

Contents.

Definition of Soap.—Properties—Hydrolysis—Detergent Action. **Constitution of Oils and Fats, and their Saponification.**—Researches of Chevreul and Berthelot—Mixed Glycerides—Modern Theories of Saponification—Hydrolysis accelerated by (1) **Heat or Electricity,** (2) **Ferments,** Castor-seed Ferment, Steapsin, Emulsin, and (3) **Chemical**

Reagents, Sulphuric Acid, Twitchell's Reagent, Hydrochloric Acid, Lime, Magnesia, Zinc Oxide, Soda and Potash. **Raw Materials used in Soap-making.**—Fats and Oils—Waste Fats—Fatty Acids—Less-known Oils and Fats of Limited Use—Various New Fats and Oils Suggested for Soap-making—Rosin—Alkali (Caustic and Carbonated)—Water— alt—Soap-stock. **Bleaching and Treatment of Raw Materials Intended for Soap-making.**—Palm Oil—Cottonseed Oil—Cottonseed "Foots"—Vegetable Oils—Animal Fats—Bone Fat—Rosin. **Soap-making.**—Classification of Soaps—Direct combination of Fatty Acids with Alkali—Cold Process Soaps—Saponification under Increased or Diminished Pressure—Soft Soap—Marine Soap—Hydrated Soaps, Smooth and Marbled—Pasting or Saponification—Graining Out—Boiling on Strength—Fitting—Curd Soaps—Curd Mottled—Blue and Grey Mottled Soaps—Milling Base—Yellow Household Soaps—Resting of Pans and Settling of Soap—Utilisation of Nigres—Transparent Soaps—Saponifying Mineral Oil—Electrical Production of Soap. **Treatment of Settled Soap.**—Cleansing—Crutching—Liquoring of Soaps—Filling—Neutralising, Colouring and Perfuming—Disinfectant Soaps—Framing—Slabbing—Barring—Open and Close Piling—Drying—Stamping—Cooling. **Toilet, Textile and Miscellaneous Soaps.**—Toilet Soaps—Cold Process Soaps—Settled Boiled Soap—Remelted Soaps—Milled Soaps—Drying, Milling and Incorporating Colour, Perfumes, or Medicaments—Perfumes—Colouring Matter—Neutralising and Super-fatting Material—Compressing—Cutting—Stamping—Medicated Soaps—Ether Soap—Floating Soaps—Shaving Soaps—Textile Soaps—Soaps for Woollen, Cotton and Silk Industries—Patent Textile Soaps—Miscellaneous Soaps. **Soap Perfumes.**—Essential Oils—Source and Preparation—Properties—Artificial and Synthetic Perfumes. **Glycerine Manufacture and Purification.**—Treatment of Lyes—Evaporation—Crude Glycerine—Distillation—Distilled and Dynamite Glycerine—Chemically Pure Glycerine—Animal Charcoal for Decolorisation—Glycerine resultant from other methods of Saponification—Yield of Glycerine from Fats and Oils. **Analysis of Raw Materials, Soap and Glycerine.**—Fats and Oils—Alkalies and Alkali Salts—Essential Oils—Soap—Lyes—Crude Glycerine. **Statistics of the Soap Industry.** Appendix A.—**Comparison of Degrees Twaddell, Beaume and Actual Densities.** Appendix B.—**Comparison of Different Thermometric Scales.** Appendix C.—**Table of the Specific Gravities of Solutions of Caustic Soda.** Appendix D.—**Table of Strength of Caustic Potash Solutions at 60° F. Index.**

Cosmetical Preparations.

COSMETICS: MANUFACTURE, EMPLOYMENT AND TESTING OF ALL COSMETIC MATERIALS AND COSMETIC SPECIALITIES. Translated from the German of Dr. THEODOR KOLLER. Crown 8vo. 262 pp. Price 5s. net. (Post free, 5s. 4d. home; 5s. 6d. abroad.)

Contents.

Purposes and Uses of, and Ingredients used in the Preparation of Cosmetics—Preparation of Perfumes by Pressure, Distillation, Maceration, Absorption or Enfleurage, and Extraction Methods—Chemical and Animal Products used in the Preparation of Cosmetics—Oils and Fats used in the Preparation of Cosmetics—General Cosmetic Preparations—Mouth Washes and Tooth Pastes—Hair Dyes, Hair Restorers and Depilatories—Cosmetic Adjuncts and Specialities—Colouring Cosmetic Preparations—Antiseptic Washes and Soaps—Toilet and Hygienic Soaps—Secret Preparations for Skin, Complexion, Teeth, Mouth, etc.—Testing and Examining the Materials Employed in the Manufacture of Cosmetics—Index.

Glue, Bone Products and Manures.

GLUE AND GLUE TESTING. By SAMUEL RIDEAL, D.Sc. (Lond.), F.I.C. Fourteen Engravings. 144 pp. Demy 8vo. Price 10s. 6d. net. (Post free, 10s. 10d. home; 11s. abroad.)

Contents.

Constitution and Properties: Definitions and Sources, Gelatine, Chondrin and Allied Bodies, Physical and Chemical Properties, Classification, Grades and Commercial Varieties—**Raw Materials and Manufacture:** Glue Stock, Lining, Extraction, Washing and Clarifying, Filter Presses, Water Supply, Use of Alkalies, Action of Bacteria and of Antiseptics Various Processes, Cleansing, Forming, Drying, Crushing, etc., Secondary Products—**Uses of Glue:** Selection and Preparation for Use, Carpentry, Veneering, Paper-Making, Book-binding, Printing Rollers, Hectographs, Match Manufacture, Sandpaper, etc., Substitutes for other Materials, Artificial Leather and Caoutchouc—**Gelatine:** General Characters, Liquid Gelatine, Photographic Uses, Size, Tanno-, Chrome and Formo-Gelatine, Artificial Silk, Cements, Pneumatic Tyres, Culinary, Meat Extracts, Isinglass, Medicinal and other Uses, Bacteriology—**Glue Testing:** Review of Processes, Chemical Examination, Adulteration, Physical Tests, Valuation of Raw Materials—**Commercial Aspects.**

BONE PRODUCTS AND MANURES: An Account of the most recent Improvements in the Manufacture of Fat, Glue, Animal Charcoal, Size, Gelatine and Manures. By THOMAS LAMBERT, Technical and Consulting Chemist. Illustrated by Twenty-one Plans and Diagrams. 162 pp. Demy 8vo. Price 7s. 6d. net. (Post free, 7s. 10d. home; 8s. abroad.)

Contents.

Chemical Composition of Bones—Arrangement of Factory—Properties of Glue—Glutin and Chondrin—Skin Glue—Liming of Skins—Washing—Boiling of Skins—Clarification of Glue Liquors—Glue-Boiling and Clarifying-House—Specification of a Glue—Size—Uses and Preparation and Composition of Size—Concentrated Size—Properties of Gelatine—Preparation of Skin Gelatine—Drying—Bone Gelatine—Selecting Bones—Crushing—Dissolving—Bleaching—Boiling—Properties of Glutin and Chondrin—Testing of Glues and Gelatines—The Uses of Glue, Gelatine and Size in Various Trades—Soluble and Liquid Glues—Steam and Waterproof Glues—**Manures**—Importation of Food Stuffs—Soils—Germination—Plant Life—**Natural Manures**—Water and Nitrogen in Farmyard Manure—Full Analysis of Farmyard Manure—Action on Crops—Water-Closet System—Sewage Manure—Green Manures—**Artificial Manures**—**Mineral Manures**—Nitrogenous Matters—Shoddy—Hoofs and Horns—Leather Waste—Dried Meat—Dried Blood—Superphosphates—Composition—Manufacture—Common Raw Bones—Degreased Bones—Crude Fat—Refined Fat—Degelatinised Bones—Animal Charcoal—Bone Superphosphates—Guanos—Dried Animal Products—Potash Compounds—Sulphate of Ammonia—Extraction in Zacuo—French and British Gelatines compared—Index.

Chemicals, Waste Products and Agricultural Chemistry.

REISSUE OF **CHEMICAL ESSAYS OF C. W. SCHEELE**. First Published in English in 1786. Translated from the Academy of Sciences at Stockholm, with Additions. 300 pp. Demy 8vo. Price 5s. net. (Post free, 5s. 6d. home; 5s. 9d. abroad.)

Contents.

Memoir: C. W. Scheele and his work (written for this edition by J. G. McIntosh)—On Fluor Mineral and its Acid—On Fluor Mineral—Chemical Investigation of Fluor Acid, with a View to the Earth which it Yields, by Mr. Wiegler—Additional Information Concerning Fluor Minerals—On Manganese, Magnesium, or Magnesia Vitrariorum—On Arsenic and its Acid—Remarks upon Salts of Benzoin—On Silex, Clay and Alum—Analysis of the Calculus Vesical—Method of Preparing Mercurius Dulcis Via Humida—Cheaper and more Convenient Method of Preparing Pulvis Algarothi—Experiments upon Molybdæna—Experiments on Plumbago—Method of Preparing a New Green Colour—Of the Decomposition of Neutral Salts by Unslaked Lime and Iron—On the Quantity of Pure Air which is Daily Present in our Atmosphere—On Milk and its Acid—On the Acid of Saccharum Lactis—On the Constituent Parts of Lapis Ponderosus or Tungsten—Experiments and Observations on Ether—Index.

THE MANUFACTURE OF ALUM AND THE SULPHATES AND OTHER SALTS OF ALUMINA AND IRON. Their Uses and Applications as Mordants in Dyeing and Calico Printing, and their other Applications in the Arts, Manufactures, Sanitary Engineering, Agriculture and Horticulture. Translated from the French of LUCIEN GESCHWIND. 195 Illustrations. 400 pp. Royal 8vo. Price 12s. 6d. net. (Post free, 13s. home; 13s. 6d abroad.)

AMMONIA AND ITS COMPOUNDS: Their Manufacture and Uses. By CAMILLE VINCENT, Professor at the Central School of Arts and Manufactures, Paris. Translated from the French by M. J. SALTER. Royal 8vo. 114 pp. Thirty-two Illustrations. Price 5s. net. (Post free, 5s. 4d. home; 5s. 6d. abroad.)

Contents.

General Considerations: Various Sources of Ammoniacal Products; Human Urine as a Source of Ammonia—**Extraction of Ammoniacal Products from Sewage—Extraction of Ammonia from Gas Liquor—Manufacture of Ammoniacal Compounds from Bones, Nitrogenous Waste, Beetroot Wash and Peat—Manufacture of Caustic Ammonia, and Ammonium Chloride, Phosphate and Carbonate—Recovery of Ammonia from the Ammonia-Soda Mother Liquors—Index.**

INDUSTRIAL ALCOHOL. A Practical Manual on the Production and Use of Alcohol for Industrial Purposes and for Use as a Heating Agent, as an Illuminant and as a Source of Motive Power. By J. G. M'INTOSH, Lecturer on Manufacture and Applications of Industrial Alcohol at The Polytechnic, Regent Street, London. Demy 8vo. 1907. 250 pp. With 75 Illustrations and 25 Tables. Price 7s. 6d. net. (Post free, 7s. 9d. home; 8s. abroad.)

Contents.

Alcohol and its Properties.—Ethylic Alcohol—Absolute Alcohol—Adulterations—Properties of Alcohol—Fractional Distillation—Destructive Distillation—Products of Combustion—Alcoholometry—Proof Spirit—Analysis of Alcohol—Table showing Correspondence between the Specific Gravity and Per Cents. of Alcohol over and under Proof—Other Alcohol Tables. **Continuous Aseptic and Antiseptic Fermentation and Sterilisation in Industrial Alcohol Manufacture. The Manufacture of Industrial Alcohol from Beets.**—Beet Slicing Machines—Extraction of Beet Juice by Maceration, by Diffusion—Fermentation in Beet Distilleries—Plans of Modern Beet Distillery. **The Manufacture of Industrial Alcohol from Grain.**—Plan of Modern Grain Distillery. **The Manufacture of Industrial Alcohol from Potatoes. The Manufacture of Industrial Alcohol from Surplus Stocks of Wine,** Spoilt Wine, Wine Marcs, and from Fruit in General. The Manufacture of Alcohol from the Sugar Cane and Sugar Cane Molasses—Plans. **Plant, etc., for the Distillation and Rectification of Industrial Alcohol.**—The Caffey and other "Patent" Stills—Intermittent versus Continuous Rectification—Continuous Distillation—Rectification of Spent Wash. **The Manufacture and Uses of Various Alcohol Derivatives,** Ether, Haloid Ethers, Compound Ethers, Chloroform—Methyl and Amyl Alcohols and their Ethereal Salts, Acetone—Barbet's Ether, Methyl Alcohol and Acetone Rectifying Stills. **The Uses of Alcohol in Manufactures, etc.**—List of Industries in which Alcohol is used, with Key to Function of Alcohol in each Industry. **The Uses of Alcohol for Lighting, Heating, and Motive Power.**

ANALYSIS OF RESINS AND BALSAMS. Translated from the German of Dr. KARL DIETERICH. Demy 8vo. 340 pp. Price 7s. 6d. net. (Post free, 7s. 10d. home; 8s. 3d. abroad.)

MANUAL OF AGRICULTURAL CHEMISTRY. By HERBERT INGLE, F.I.C., Late Lecturer on Agricultural Chemistry, the Leeds University; Lecturer in the Victoria University. Second Edition, with additional matter relating to Tropical Agriculture, etc. 438 pp. 11 Illustrations. Demy 8vo. Price 7s. 6d. net. (Post free, 8s. home; 8s. 6d. abroad.)

Contents.

Properties and Characteristics of the Elements.—Hydrogen—Oxygen—Heat of Combustion—Nitrogen—Carbon—Sulphur—Phosphorous—Potassium—Sodium—Fluorine—Magnesium—Iron—Chlorine—Aluminium—Silicon—Borax. **The Atmosphere.**—Nitrogen—Oxygen—Argon—Carbon Dioxide—Ammonia—Nitric Acid—Ozone—Solid Matter. **The Soil.**—Classification of Rocks—Quartz—Felspar—Mica—Clay—Sandstones—Shales—Limestones—Calcareous Rocks—Transported Soils. **Formation of Soils.**—By Water, Air, Earth Worms, Vegetation and Bacteria—Sand—Clay—Limestone—Humus—Classification of Soils. **Reactions in Soils.**—Diffusion—Gravitation—Nitrification—Soil Gases—Water of the Soil—Biology of the Soil—Electrolytic Dissociation Theory—Mass Action. **Analysis of Soils.**—Sampling—Mechanical and Chemical Analyses—Determination of Silica, Alumina, Ferric Oxide, Total Potash and Phosphoric Acid, Lime, Magnesia, Calcium Carbonate, Sulphuric Acid, Nitrates and Nitrites. **Natural Manures.**—Improvement of Soils—Farmyard Manure—Composition of Animal Excreta—Use of Litter, Straw, Peat, Bracken, Leaves, Sawdust, Tanners' Refuse—Fermentation and Preservation of Farmyard Manure. **Other Organic Manures.**—Guano—Poultry and Fish Manures—Seaweed—Dried Blood—Bones—Meat Guano—Hair—Soot—Oil-cakes. **Nitrogenous Manures.**—Sodium Nitrate—Ammonium Sulphate—**Phosphatic Manures**—Tricalcum Phosphate—Coprolites—Phosphorites—Mineral Superphosphates—Basic Slag—**Potash Manures**—Composition of Principal Potash Salts—**Various Manures**—Common Salt—Gypsum—Limestone—Ferrous Sulphate—Gas Lime—Copper Sulphate. **Analysis of Manures.**—Constituents—Determination of Nitrogen—Phosphoric Acid—Potassium—Valuation of Manures from Analysis. **Constituents of Plants.**—Carbohydrates—Sugars—Starch—Dextrin—Glycogen—Inulin—Gums—Cellulose—Glucose—Fructose—Cane Sugar—Meletrose—Arabinose—Xylose—Lignose—Pectose—Glycerol—Waxes—Organic Acids and their Salts. **Essential Oils and Resins.**—Terpenes—Oxygenated Essential Oils—Essential Oils containing Sulphur—Resins. **Nitrogenous Substances.**—Albuminoids—Amides—Alkaloids—Chlorophyll. **The Plant.**—Germination—Roots—Osmotic Pressure—Leaves—Assimilation—Flowers. **Crops.**—Cereals—Root Crops—Fodder Crops—Hay—Ventilating Stacks—Silage—Composition of Crops. **The Animal.**—Blood—Bones—Fatty Tissue—Muscle—Digestion—Bile—Urine. **Foods and Feeding.**—Composition of Oil-cake—Bye-Products as Foods—Digestibility of Foods—Calorific Value of Foods—Feeding Standards—Manurial Value of Foods. **Milk and Milk Products.**—Fat—Albuminoids—Milk Sugar—Chemical Composition of Cow's Milk—Influence of Food, Season and Milking Time—Milk Products—Cream—Skimmed Milk—Butter—Butter-milk—Cheese—Condensed Milk—Koumiss—Milk Preservation. **Analysis of Milk and Milk Products.**—

Milk—Amount of Fat—Determination of Total Solids, Specific Gravity, Proteids, Milk Sugar —Adulteration of Milk—Detection of Preservatives—Butter—Butter Colouring—Cheese—Milk Standards. **Various Products used in Agriculture.**—Arsenious Oxide—Bleaching Powder—Copper Salts—Disinfectants—Fungicides—Iron Sulphate—Mercuric Chloride—Plant Poisons. **Appendix.**—Atomic Weights—Hydrometer Scales—Metric System—Solubilities. **Tropical Agriculture, etc.**—Composition of Rain Water—Irrigation Water—Earth Worms—Motion of Water in Soil—Analysis of Soils—Green Manuring—Kraal Manure—Bats' Guano—Artificial Manures—The Plant—Rice—Maize—Millet—Cotton—Flax—Castor Seeds—Sunflower—Composition of Various South African Grown Crops—Ash Constituents of Foods—Variations in the Composition of Milk—Butter—Fat—Bordeaux Mixture—Insecticides.

THE UTILISATION OF WASTE PRODUCTS. A Treatise on the Rational Utilisation, Recovery and Treatment of Waste Products of all kinds. By Dr. THEODOR KOLLER. Translated from the Second Revised German Edition. Twenty-two Illustrations. Demy 8vo. 280 pp. Price 7s. 6d. net. (Post free, 7s. 10d. home; 8s. 3d. abroad.)

Writing Inks and Sealing Waxes.

INK MANUFACTURE: Including Writing, Copying, Lithographic, Marking, Stamping, and Laundry Inks. By SIGMUND LEHNER. Three Illustrations. Crown 8vo. 162 pp. Translated from the German of the Fifth Edition. Price 5s. net. (Post free, 5s. 3d. home; 5s. 6d. abroad.)

Contents.

Varieties of Ink—Writing Inks—Raw Materials of Tannin Inks—The Chemical Constitution of the Tannin Inks—Recipes for Tannin Inks—Logwood Tannin Inks—Ferric Inks—Alizarine Inks—Extract Inks—Logwood Inks—Copying Inks—Hektographs—Hektograph Inks—Safety Inks—Ink Extracts and Powders—Preserving Inks—Changes in Ink and the Restoration of Faded Writing—Coloured Inks—Red Inks—Blue Inks—Violet Inks—Yellow Inks—Green Inks—Metallic Inks—Indian Ink—Lithographic Inks and Pencils—Ink Pencils—Marking Inks—Ink Specialities—Sympathetic Inks—Stamping Inks—Laundry or Washing Blue—Index.

SEALING-WAXES, WAFERS AND OTHER ADHESIVES FOR THE HOUSEHOLD, OFFICE, WORKSHOP AND FACTORY. By H. C. STANDAGE. Crown 8vo. 96 pp. Price 5s. net. (Post free, 5s. 3d. home; 5s. 4d. abroad.)

Contents.

Materials Used for Making Sealing-Waxes—The Manufacture of Sealing-Waxes—Wafers—Notes on the Nature of the Materials Used in Making Adhesive Compounds—Cements for Use in the Household—Office Gums, Pastes and Mucilages—Adhesive Compounds for Factory and Workshop Use.

Lead Ores and Compounds.

LEAD AND ITS COMPOUNDS. By THOS. LAMBERT, Technical and Consulting Chemist. Demy 8vo. 226 pp. Forty Illustrations. Price 7s. 6d. net. (Post free, 7s. 10d. home; 8s. 3d. abroad.)

Contents.

History—Ores of Lead—Geographical Distribution of the Lead Industry—Chemical and Physical Properties of Lead—Alloys of Lead—Compounds of Lead—Dressing of Lead Ores—Smelting of Lead Ores—Smelting in the Scotch or American Ore-hearth—Smelting in the Shaft or Blast Furnace—Condensation of Lead Fume—Desilverisation, or the Separation of Silver from Argentiferous Lead—Cupellation—The Manufacture of Lead Pipes and Sheets—Protoxide of Lead—Litharge and Massicot—Red Lead or Minium—Lead Poisoning—Lead Substitutes—Zinc and its Compounds—Pumice Stone—Drying Oils and Siccatives—Oil of Turpentine Resin—Classification of Mineral Pigments—Analysis of Raw and Finished Products—Tables—Index.

NOTES ON LEAD ORES: Their Distribution and Properties. By JAS. FAIRIE, F.G.S. Crown 8vo. 64 pages. Price 1s. net. (Post free, 1s. 3d. home; 1s. 4d. abroad.)

(*White Lead and Zinc White Paints, see p. 4.*)

Industrial Hygiene.

THE RISKS AND DANGERS TO HEALTH OF VARIOUS OCCUPATIONS AND THEIR PREVENTION. By LEONARD A. PARRY, M.D., B.Sc. (Lond.). 196 pp. Demy 8vo. Price 7s. 6d. net. (Post free, 7s. 10d. home; 8s. abroad.)

Contents.

Occupations which are Accompanied by the Generation and Scattering of Abnormal Quantities of Dust—Trades in which there is Danger of Metallic Poisoning—Certain Chemical Trades—Some Miscellaneous Occupations—Trades in which Various Poisonous Vapours are Inhaled—General Hygienic Considerations—Index.

Industrial Uses of Air, Steam and Water.

DRYING BY MEANS OF AIR AND STEAM. Explanations, Formulæ, and Tables for Use in Practice. Translated from the German of E. HAUSBRAND. Two folding Diagrams and Thirteen Tables. Crown 8vo. 72 pp. Price 5s. net. (Post free, 5s. 3d. home; 5s. 6d. abroad.)

Contents.

British and Metric Systems Compared—Centigrade and Fahr. Thermometers—Estimation of the Maximum Weight of Saturated Aqueous Vapour which can be contained in 1 kilo. of Air at Different Pressure and Temperatures—Calculation of the Necessary Weight and Volume of Air, and of the Least Expenditure of Heat, per Drying Apparatus with Heated Air, at the Atmospheric Pressure: *A*, With the Assumption that the Air is *Completely Saturated* with Vapour both before Entry and after Exit from the Apparatus—*B*, When the Atmospheric Air is Completely Saturated *before entry*, but at its *exit* is *only* ¾, ½ or ¼ Saturated—*C*, When the Atmospheric Air is *not* Saturated with Moisture before Entering the Drying Apparatus—Drying Apparatus, in which, in the Drying Chamber, a Pressure is Artificially Created, Higher or Lower than that of the Atmosphere—Drying by Means of Superheated Steam, without Air—Heating Surface, Velocity of the Air Current, Dimensions of the Drying Room, Surface of the Drying Material, Losses of Heat—Index.

(*See also "Evaporating, Condensing and Cooling Apparatus," p. 26.*)

PURE AIR, OZONE AND WATER. A Practical Treatise of their Utilisation and Value in Oil, Grease, Soap, Paint, Glue and other Industries. By W. B. COWELL. Twelve Illustrations. Crown 8vo. 85 pp. Price 5s. net. (Post free, 5s. 3d. home; 5s. 6d. abroad.)

Contents.

Atmospheric Air; Lifting of Liquids; Suction Process; Preparing Blown Oils; Preparing Siccative Drying Oils—Compressed Air; Whitewash—Liquid Air; Retrocession—Purification of Water; Water Hardness—Fleshings and Bones—Ozonised Air in the Bleaching and Deodorising of Fats, Glues, etc.; Bleaching Textile Fibres—Appendix: Air and Gases; Pressure of Air at Various Temperatures; Fuel; Table of Combustibles; Saving of Fuel by Heating Feed Water; Table of Solubilities of Scale Making Minerals; British Thermal Units Tables; Volume of the Flow of Steam into the Atmosphere; Temperature of Steam—Index.

THE INDUSTRIAL USES OF WATER. COMPOSITION—EFFECTS—TROUBLES—REMEDIES—RESIDUARY WATERS—PURIFICATION—ANALYSIS. By H. DE LA COUX. Royal 8vo. Translated from the French and Revised by ARTHUR MORRIS. 364 pp. 135 Illustrations. Price 10s. 6d. net. (Post free, 11s. home; 11s. 6d. abroad.)

Contents.

Chemical Action of Water in Nature and in Industrial Use—Composition of Waters—Solubility of Certain Salts in Water Considered from the Industrial Point of View—Effects on the Boiling of Water—Effects of Water in the Industries—Difficulties with Water—Feed Water for Boilers—Water in Dyeworks, Print Works, and Bleach Works—Water in the Textile Industries and in Conditioning—Water in Soap Works—Water in Laundries and Washhouses—Water in Tanning—Water in Preparing Tannin and Dyewood Extracts—Water in Papermaking—Water in Photography—Water in Sugar Refining—Water in Making Ices and Beverages—Water in Cider Making—Water in Brewing—Water in Distilling—Preliminary Treatment and Apparatus—Substances Used for Preliminary Chemical Purification—Commercial Specialities and their Employment—Precipitation of Matters in Suspension in Water—Apparatus for the Preliminary Chemical Purification of Water—Industrial Filters—Industrial Sterilisation of Water—Residuary Waters and their Purification—Soil Filtration—Purification by Chemical Processes—Analyses—Index.

(*See Books on Smoke Prevention, Engineering and Metallurgy, p. 26, etc.*)

X Rays.

PRACTICAL X RAY WORK. By FRANK T. ADDYMAN, B.Sc. (Lond.), F.I.C., Member of the Roentgen Society of London; Radiographer to St. George's Hospital; Demonstrator of Physics and Chemistry, and Teacher of Radiography in St. George's Hospital Medical School. Demy 8vo. Twelve Plates from Photographs of X Ray Work. Fifty-two Illustrations. 200 pp. Price 10s. 6d. net. (Post free, 10s. 10d. home; 11s. 3d. abroad.)

Contents.

Historical—Work leading up to the Discovery of the X Rays—The Discovery—**Apparatus and its Management**—Electrical Terms—Sources of Electricity—Induction Coils—Electrostatic Machines—Tubes—Air Pumps—Tube Holders and Stereoscopic Apparatus—Fluorescent Screens—**Practical X Ray Work**—Installations—Radioscopy—Radiography—X Rays in Dentistry—X Rays in Chemistry—X Rays in War—Index.

List of Plates.

Frontispiece—Congenital Dislocation of Hip-Joint.—I., Needle in Finger.—II., Needle in Foot.—III., Revolver Bullet in Calf and Leg.—IV., A Method of Localisation.—V, Stellate Fracture of Patella showing shadow of "Strapping".—VI., Sarcoma.—VII., Six-weeks-old Injury to Elbow showing new Growth of Bone.—VIII., Old Fracture of Tibia and Fibula badly set.—IX., Heart Shadow.—X., Fractured Femur showing Grain of Splint.—XI., Barrell's Method of Localisation.

India-Rubber and Gutta Percha.

INDIA-RUBBER AND GUTTA PERCHA. Second Edition, Revised and Enlarged. Based on the French work of T. SEELIGMANN, G. LAMY TORVILHON and H. FALCONNET by JOHN GEDDES MCINTOSH. Royal 8vo. [*In the press.*

Contents.

India-Rubber—Botanical Origin—Climatology—Soil—Rational Culture and Acclimation of the Different Species of India-Rubber Plants—Methods of Obtaining the Latex—Methods of Preparing Raw or Crude India-Rubber—Classification of the Commercial Species of Raw Rubber—Physical and Chemical Properties of the Latex and of India-Rubber—Mechanical Transformation of Natural Caoutchouc into Washed or Normal Caoutchouc (Purification) and Normal Rubber into Masticated Rubber—Softening, Cutting, Washing, Drying—Preliminary Observations—Vulcanisation of Normal Rubber—Chemical and Physical Properties of Vulcanised Rubber—General Considerations—Hardened Rubber or Ebonite—Considerations on Mineralisation and other Mixtures—Coloration and Dyeing—Analysis of Natural or Normal Rubber and Vulcanised Rubber—Rubber Substitutes—Imitation Rubber.

Gutta Percha—Botanical Origin—Climatology—Soil—Rational Culture—Methods of Collection—Classification of the Different Species of Commercial Gutta Percha—Physical and Chemical Properties—Mechanical Transformation—Methods of Analysing—Gutta Percha Substitutes—Index.

Leather Trades.

PRACTICAL TREATISE ON THE LEATHER INDUSTRY. By A. M. VILLON. Translated by FRANK T. ADDYMAN, B.Sc. (Lond.), F.I.C., F.C.S.; and Corrected by an Eminent Member of the Trade. 500 pp., royal 8vo. 123 Illustrations. Price 21s. net. (Post free, 21s. 6d. home; 22s. 6d. abroad.)

Contents.

Preface—Translator's Preface—List of Illustrations.

Part I., **Materials used in Tanning**—Skins: Skin and its Structure; Skins used in Tanning; Various Skins and their Uses—Tannin and Tanning Substances: Tannin; Barks (Oak); Barks other than Oak; Tanning Woods; Tannin-bearing Leaves; Excrescences; Tan-bearing Fruits; Tan-bearing Roots and Bulbs; Tanning Juices; Tanning Substances used in Various Countries; Tannin Extracts; Estimation of Tannin and Tannin Principles.

Part II., **Tanning**—The Installation of a Tannery: Tan Furnaces; Chimneys, Boilers, etc.; Steam Engines—Grinding and Trituration of Tanning Substances: Cutting up Bark; Grinding Bark; The Grinding of Tan Woods; Powdering Fruit, Galls and Grains; Notes on the Grinding of Bark—Manufacture of Sole Leather: Soaking; Sweating and Unhairing; Plumping and Colouring; Handling; Tanning; Tanning Elephants' Hides; Drying; Striking or Pinning—Manufacture of Dressing Leather: Soaking; Depilation; New Processes for the Depilation of Skins; Tanning; Cow Hides; Horse Hides; Goat Skins; Manufacture of Split Hides—On Various Methods of Tanning: Mechanical Methods; Physical Methods; Chemical Methods; Tanning with Extracts—Quantity and Quality; Quantity; Net Cost; Quality of Leather—Various Manipulations of Tanned Leather: Second Tanning; Grease Stains; Bleaching Leather; Waterproofing Leather; Weighting Tanned Leather; Preservation of Leather—Tanning Various Skins.

Part III., **Currying** — Waxed Calf: Preparation; Shaving; Stretching or Slicking; Oiling the Grain; Oiling the Flesh Side; Whitening and Graining; Waxing; Finishing; Dry Finishing; Finishing in Colour; Cost — White Calf: Finishing in White—Cow Hide for Upper Leathers: Black Cow Hide; White Cow Hide; Coloured Cow Hide—Smooth Cow Hide—Black Leather—Miscellaneous Hides: Horse; Goat; Waxed Goat Skin; Matt Goat Skin—Russia Leather: Russia Leather; Artificial Russia Leather.

Part IV., **Enamelled, Hungary and Chamoy Leather, Morocco, Parchment, Furs and Artificial Leather**—Enamelled Leather: Varnish Manufacture; Application of the Enamel; Enamelling in Colour—Hungary Leather: Preliminary; Wet Work or Preparation; Aluming; Dressing or Loft Work; Tallowing; Hungary Leather from Various Hides—Tawing: Preparatory Operations; Dressing; Dyeing Tawed Skins; Rugs—Chamoy Leather—Morocco: Preliminary Operations, Morocco Tanning; Mordants used in Morocco Manufacture; Natural Colours used in Morocco Dyeing; Artificial Colours; Different Methods of Dyeing; Dyeing with Natural Colours; Dyeing with Aniline Colours; Dyeing with Metallic Salts; Leather Printing; Finishing Morocco; Shagreen; Bronzed Leather—Gilding and Silvering: Gilding; Silvering; Nickel and Cobalt—Parchment—Furs and Furriery: Preliminary Remarks; Indigenous Furs; Foreign Furs from Hot Countries; Foreign Furs from Cold Countries; Furs from Birds' Skins; Preparation of Furs; Dressing; Colouring; Preparation of Birds' Skins; Preservation of Furs—Artificial Leather: Leather made from Scraps; Compressed Leather; American Cloth; Pâpier Mâché; Linoleum; Artificial Leather.

Part V., **Leather Testing and the Theory of Tanning**—Testing and Analysis of Leather; Physical Testing of Tanned Leather; Chemical Analysis—The Theory of Tanning and the other Operations of the Leather and Skin Industry: Theory of Soaking; Theory of Unhairing; Theory of Swelling; Theory of Handling; Theory of Tanning; Theory of the Action of Tannin on the Skin; Theory of Hungary Leather Making; Theory of Tawing Theory of Chamoy Leather Making; Theory of Mineral Tanning.

Part VI., **Uses of Leather**—Machine Belts: Manufacture of Belting; Leather Chain Belts; Various Belts; Use of Belts—Boot and Shoe-making: Boots and Shoes; Laces—Saddlery: Composition of a Saddle; Construction of a Saddle—Harness: The Pack Saddle Harness—Military Equipment—Glove Making—Carriage Building—Mechanical Uses.

Appendix, **The World's Commerce in Leather**—Europe; America; Asia; Africa; Australasia—Index.

THE LEATHER WORKER'S MANUAL. Being a Compendium of Practical Recipes and Working Formulæ for Curriers, Bootmakers, Leather Dressers, Blacking Manufacturers, Saddlers, Fancy Leather Workers. By H. C. STANDAGE. Demy 8vo. 165 pp. Price 7s. 6d. net. (Post free, 7s. 10d. home; 8s. abroad.)

Contents.

Blackings, Polishes, Glosses, Dressings, Renovators, etc., for Boot and Shoe Leather—Harness Blackings, Dressings, Greases, Compositions, Soaps, and Boot-top Powders and Liquids, etc., etc.—Leather Grinders' Sundries—Currier's Seasonings, Blacking Compounds, Dressings, Finishes, Glosses, etc.—Dyes and Stains for Leather—Miscellaneous Information—Chrome Tannage—Index.

(*See " Wood Products, Distillates and Extracts," p.* 29).

Books on Pottery, Bricks, Tiles, Glass, etc.

THE MANUAL OF PRACTICAL POTTING. Compiled by Experts, and Edited by CHAS. F. BINNS. Third Edition, Revised and Enlarged. 200 pp. Demy 8vo. Price 17s. 6d. net. (Post free, 17s. 10d. home; 18s. 3d. abroad.)

Contents.

Introduction. The Rise and Progress of the Potter's Art—**Bodies.** China and Porcelain Bodies, Parian Bodies, Semi-porcelain and Vitreous Bodies, Mortar Bodies, Earthenwares Granite and C.C. Bodies, Miscellaneous Bodies, Sagger and Crucible Clays, Coloured Bodies, Jasper Bodies, Coloured Bodies for Mosaic Painting, Encaustic Tile Bodies, Body Stains, Coloured Dips—**Glazes.** China Glazes, Ironstone Glazes, Earthenware Glazes, Glazes without Lead, Miscellaneous Glazes, Coloured Glazes, Majolica Colours—**Gold and Gold Colours.** Gold, Purple of Cassius, Marone and Ruby, Enamel Coloured Bases, Enamel Colour Fluxes, Enamel Colours, Mixed Enamel Colours, Antique and Vellum Enamel Colours, Underglaze Colours, Underglaze Colour Fluxes, Mixed Underglaze Colours, Flow Powders, Oils and Varnishes—**Means and Methods.** Reclamation of Waste Gold, The Use of Cobalt, Notes on Enamel Colours, Liquid or Bright Gold—**Classification and Analysis.** Classification of Clay Ware, Lord Playfair's Analysis of Clays, The Markets of the World, Time and Scale of Firing, Weights of Potter's Material, Decorated Goods Count—Comparative Loss of Weight of Clays—Ground Felspar Calculations—The Conversion of Slop Body Recipes into Dry Weight—The Cost of Prepared Earthenware Clay—**Forms and Tables.** Articles of Apprenticeship, Manufacturer's Guide to Stocktaking, Table of Relative Values of Potter's Materials, Hourly Wages Table, Workman's Settling Table, Comparative Guide for Earthenware and China Manufacturers in the use of Slop Flint and Slop Stone, Foreign Terms applied to Earthenware and China Goods, Table for the Conversion of Metrical Weights and Measures on the Continent and South America—**Index.**

CERAMIC TECHNOLOGY: Being some Aspects of Technical Science as Applied to Pottery Manufacture. Edited by CHARLES F. BINNS. 100 pp. Demy 8vo. Price 12s. 6d. net. (Post free, 12s. 10d. home; 13s. abroad.)

Contents.

Preface—The Chemistry of Pottery—Analysis and Synthesis—Clays and their Components—The Biscuit Oven—Pyrometry—Glazes and their Composition—Colours and Colour-making—Index.

POTTERY DECORATING. A Description of all the Processes for Decorating Pottery and Porcelain. By R. HAINBACH. Translated from the German. Crown 8vo. 250 pp. Twenty-two Illustrations. Price 7s. 6d. net. (Post free, 7s. 10d. home; 8s. abroad.)

Contents.

Glazes and Engobes.—Glazes and Their Composition—Glaze Materials—The Preparation of Glazes—Coloured Glazes—Engobes and Glazes for same—Porcelain Glazes. **Ceramic Colours.**—Preparation of Pure Colours—Underglaze Colours—Applying the Colours on Earthenware—Glost Fire Colours—Muffle Colours—Decorating Porcelain with Metals—Decorating Porcelain by Electroplating—Lustre Decorating on Porcelain—Firing Muffle Colours—Imitation of Paintings on Porcelain—Index.

ARCHITECTURAL POTTERY. Bricks, Tiles, Pipes, Enamelled Terra-cottas, Ordinary and Incrusted Quarries, Stoneware Mosaics, Faïences and Architectural Stoneware. By LEON LEFÊVRE. Translated from the French by K. H. BIRD, M.A., and W. MOORE BINNS. With Five Plates. 950 Illustrations in the Text, and numerous estimates. 500 pp., royal 8vo. Price 15s. net. (Post free, 15s. 6d. home; 16s. 6d. abroad.)

Contents.

Part I., **Plain Undecorated Pottery.**—Chapter I., Clays: Sec. 1, Classification, General Geological Remarks—Classification, origin, locality; Sec. 2, General Properties and Composition: physical properties, contraction, analysis, influence of various substances on the properties of clays; Sec. 3, Working of Clay Pits—I. Open pits—II. Underground pits—Mining Laws. Chapter II., Preparation of the Clay: Crushing cylinders and mills, pounding machines—Damping: damping machines—Soaking, Shortening, Pugging: horse and steam pug-mills, rolling cylinders—Particulars of the above machines. Chapter III., Bricks: Sec. 1, Manufacture—(1) Hand and machine moulding.—I. Machines working by compression: on soft clay, on semi-firm clay, on firm clay, on dry clay.—II. Expression machines—Dies—Cutting-tables—Particulars of the above machines—Types of installations—Estimates—Planishing, hand and steam presses, particulars—(2) Drying—Drying-rooms in tiers, closed drying-rooms, in tunnels, in galleries—Detailed estimates of the various drying-rooms, comparison of prices—Transport from the machines to the drying-rooms—(3) Firing—I. In clamps—II. In intermittent kilns. *A*. Open: *a*. using wood; *b*. coal; *b'*. in clamps; *b''*. flame—*B*. Closed: *c*. direct flame; *c'*. rectangular; *c''*. round; *d*. reverberatory—III. Continuous kilns. *C*. With solid fuel: round kiln, rectangular kiln, chimneys (plans and estimates)—*D*. With gas fuel, Fillard kiln (plans and estimates), Schneider kiln (plans and estimates), water-gas kiln—Heat production of the kilns; Sec. 2, Dimensions, Shapes, Colours, Decoration and Quality of Bricks—Hollow bricks—Dimensions and prices of bricks, various shapes, qualities—Various hollow bricks, dimensions, resistance qualities; Sec. 3, Applications—History—Asia, Africa, America, Europe: Greek, Roman, Byzantine, Turkish, Romanesque, Gothic, Renaissance. Chapter IV., Tiles: Sec. 1, History; Sec. 2, Manufacture—(1) Moulding: preparation of the clay, soft paste, firm paste, hard paste—Preparation of the slabs—Screw, cam and revolver presses—Particulars of tile-presses—(2) Drying—(3) Firing—Divided kilns—Installation of mechanical tileworks—Estimates; Sec. 3, Shapes, Dimensions and Uses of the Principal Types of Tile—Ancient tiles—Modern tiles—Foreign tiles—Special tiles—Roofing accessories—Qualities of tiles—Black tiles—Stoneware tiles—Particulars of tiles. Chapter V., Pipes: I. Conduit Pipes—Manufacture—Moulding: horizontal machines, vertical machines—Particulars of these machines—Drying—Firing—II. Chimney Flues—Ventiducts and "boisseaux," "waggons"—Particulars of these products. Chapter VI., Quarries: 1, Plain quarries of ordinary clay; 2, of cleaned clay—Machines, cutting, mixing, polishing—Drying and Firing—Applications—Particulars of Quarries. Chapter VII., Terra-cottas: History—Manufacture—Application—Appendix: Official methods of testing terra-cottas.

Part II., **Made-up or Decorated Pottery.**—Chapter I., General Remarks on the Decoration of Pottery: Dips—Glazes: composition, colouring, preparation, harmony with pastes—Special processes of decoration—Enamels, opaque, transparent, colours, under-glaze, over-glaze—Other processes. Chapter II., Glazed and Enamelled Bricks—History: Glazing—Enamelling—Applications—Enamelled tiles. Chapter III., Decorated Quarries: I. Paving Quarries—1. Decorated with dips—2. Stoneware: *A*. Fired to stoneware; *a*. of slag base—Applications; *b*. of melting clay—Applications—*B*. Plain or incrusted stoneware; *a*. of special clay (Stoke-on-Trent)—Manufacture—Application—*b*. Of felspar base—Colouring, manufacture, moulding, drying, firing—Applications. II. Facing Quarries—1. In faïence—*A*. Of limestone paste—*B*. Of silicious paste—*C*. Of felspar paste—Manufacture, firing—2. Of glazed stoneware—3. Of porcelain—Applications of facing quarries. III. Stove Quarries—Preparation of the pastes, moulding, firing, enamelling, decoration—Applications. Chapter IV., Architectural Decorated Pottery: Sec. 1, Faïences; Sec. 2, Stoneware; Sec. 3, Porcelain. Chapter V., Sanitary Pottery: Stoneware Pipes—Manufacture, firing—Applications—Sinks—Applications—Urinals, seats and pans—Applications—Drinking fountains, wash-stands. Index.

THE ART OF RIVETING GLASS, CHINA AND EARTHENWARE. By J. HOWARTH. Second Edition. Paper Cover. Price 1s. net. (By post, home or abroad, 1s. 1d.)

NOTES ON POTTERY CLAYS. The Distribution, Properties, Uses and Analyses of Ball Clays, China Clays and China Stone. By JAS. FAIRIE, F.G.S. 132 pp. Crown 8vo. Price 3s. 6d. net. (Post free, 3s. 9d. home; 3s. 10d. abroad.)

A Reissue of

THE HISTORY OF THE STAFFORDSHIRE POTTERIES; AND THE RISE AND PROGRESS OF THE MANUFACTURE OF POTTERY AND PORCELAIN. With References to Genuine Specimens, and Notices of Eminent Potters. By SIMEON SHAW. (Originally Published in 1829.) 265 pp. Demy 8vo. Price 5s. net. (Post free, 5s. 4d. home; 5s. 9d. abroad.)

Contents.

Introductory Chapter showing the position of the Pottery Trade at the present time (1899)—**Preliminary Remarks**—**The Potteries**, comprising Tunstall, Brownhills, Greenfield and New Field, Golden Hill, Latebrook, Green Lane, Burslem, Longport and Dale Hall, Hot Lane and Cobridge, Hanley and Shelton, Etruria, Stoke, Penkhull, Fenton, Lane Delph, Foley, Lane End—**On the Origin of the Art**, and its Practice among the early Nations—**Manufacture of Pottery**, prior to 1700—**The Introduction of Red Porcelain** by Messrs. Elers, of Bradwell, 1690—**Progress of the Manufacture** from 1700 to Mr. Wedgwood's commencement in 1760—**Introduction of Fluid Glaze**—Extension of the Manufacture of Cream Colour—Mr. Wedgwood's Queen's Ware—Jasper, and Appointment of Potter to Her Majesty—Black Printing—**Introduction of Porcelain.** Mr. W. Littler's Porcelain—Mr. Cookworthy's Discovery of Kaolin and Petuntse, and Patent—Sold to Mr. Champion—resold to the New Hall Com.—Extension of Term—**Blue Printed Pottery.** Mr. Turner, Mr. Spode (1), Mr. Baddeley, Mr. Spode (2), Messrs. Turner, Mr. Wood, Mr. Wilson, Mr. Minton—Great Change in Patterns of Blue Printed—**Introduction of Lustre Pottery.** Improvements in Pottery and Porcelain subsequent to 1800.

A Reissue of

THE CHEMISTRY OF THE SEVERAL NATURAL AND ARTIFICIAL HETEROGENEOUS COMPOUNDS USED IN MANUFACTURING PORCELAIN, GLASS AND POTTERY. By SIMEON SHAW. (Originally published in 1837.) 750 pp. Royal 8vo. Price 10s. net. (Post free, 10s. 6d. home; 12s. abroad.)

Glassware, Glass Staining and Painting.

RECIPES FOR FLINT GLASS MAKING. By a British Glass Master and Mixer. Sixty Recipes. Being Leaves from the Mixing Book of several experts in the Flint Glass Trade, containing up-to-date recipes and valuable information as to Crystal, Demi-crystal and Coloured Glass in its many varieties. It contains the recipes for cheap metal suited to pressing, blowing, etc., as well as the most costly crystal and ruby. Second Edition. Crown 8vo. Price 10s. 6d. net. (Post free, 10s. 9d. home; 10s. 10d. abroad.)

Contents.

Ruby—Ruby from Copper—Flint for using with the Ruby for Coating—A German Metal—Cornelian, or Alabaster—Sapphire Blue—Crysophis—Opal—Turquoise Blue—Gold Colour—Dark Green—Green (common)—Green for Malachite—Blue for Malachite—Black for Melachite—Black—Common Canary Batch—Canary—White Opaque Glass—Sealing-wax Red—Flint—Flint Glass (Crystal and Demi)—Achromatic Glass—Paste Glass—White Enamel—Firestone—Dead White (for moons)—White Agate—Canary—Canary Enamel—Index.

A TREATISE ON THE ART OF GLASS PAINTING. Prefaced with a Review of Ancient Glass. By ERNEST R. SUFFLING. With One Coloured Plate and Thirty-seven Illustrations. Demy 8vo. 140 pp. Price 7s. 6d. net. (Post free, 7s. 10d. home; 8s. abroad.)

Contents.

A Short History of Stained Glass—Designing Scale Drawings—Cartoons and the Cut Line—Various Kinds of Glass Cutting for Windows—The Colours and Brushes used in Glass Painting—Painting on Glass, Dispersed Patterns—Diapered Patterns—Aciding—Firing—Fret Lead Glazing—Index.

PAINTING ON GLASS AND PORCELAIN AND ENAMEL PAINTING. A Complete Introduction to the Preparation of all the Colours and Fluxes used for Painting on Porcelain, Enamel, Faience and Stoneware, the Coloured Pastes and Coloured Glasses, together with a Minute Description of the Firing of Colours and Enamels. By FELIX HERMANN, Technical Chemist. With Eighteen Illustrations. 300 pp. Translated from the German second and enlarged Edition. Price 10s. 6d. net. (Post free, 10s. 10d. home; 11s. abroad.)

Paper Making, Paper Dyeing, and Testing.

THE DYEING OF PAPER PULP. A Practical Treatise for the use of Papermakers, Paperstainers, Students and others. By JULIUS ERFURT, Manager of a Paper Mill. Translated into English and Edited with Additions by JULIUS HÜBNER, F.C.S., Lecturer on Papermaking at the Manchester Municipal Technical School. With Illustrations and **157 patterns of paper dyed in the pulp.** Royal 8vo, 180 pp. Price 15s. net. (Post free, 15s. 6d. home; 16s. 6d abroad.)

Contents.

Behaviour of the Paper Fibres during the Process of Dyeing, Theory of the Mordant—Colour Fixing Mediums (Mordants)—Influence of the Quality of the Water Used—Inorganic Colours—Organic Colours—Practical Application of the Coal Tar Colours according to their Properties and their Behaviour towards the Different Paper Fibres—Dyed Patterns on Various Pulp Mixtures—Dyeing to Shade—Index.

THE PAPER MILL CHEMIST. By HENRY P. STEVENS, M.A., Ph.D., F.I.C. Royal 12mo. 60 Illustrations. 300 pp. Price 7s. 6d. net. (Post free, 7s. 9d. home; 7s. 10d. abroad.)

Contents.

Introduction.—Dealing with the Apparatus required in Chemical Work and General Chemical Manipulation, introducing the subject of Qualitative and Quantitative Analysis. **Fuels.**—Analysis of Coal, Coke and other Fuels—Sampling and Testing for Moisture, Ash, Calorific Value, etc.—Comparative Heating Value of different Fuels and Relative Efficiency. **Water.**—Analysis for Steam Raising and for Paper Making Purposes generally—Water Softening and Purification—A List of the more important Water Softening Plant, giving Power required, Weight, Space Occupied, Out-put and Approximate Cost. **Raw Materials and Detection of Adulterants.**—Analysis and Valuation of the more important Chemicals used in Paper Making, including Lime, Caustic Soda, Sodium Carbonate, Mineral Acids, Bleach Antichlor, Alum, Rosin and Rosin Size, Glue Gelatin and Casein, Starch, China Clay, Blanc Fixe, Satin White and other Loading Materials, Mineral Colours and Aniline Dyes. **Manufacturing Operations.**—Rags and the Chemical Control of Rag Boiling—Esparto Boiling—Wood Boiling—Testing Spent Liquors and Recovered Ash—Experimental Tests with Raw Fibrous Materials—Boiling in Autoclaves—Bleaching and making up Hand Sheets—Examination of Sulphite Liquors—Estimation of Moisture in Pulp and Half-stuff—Recommendations of the British Wood Pulp Association. **Finished Products.**—Paper Testing, including Physical, Chemical and Microscopical Tests, Area, Weight, Thickness, Apparent Specific Gravity, Bulk or Air Space. Determination of Machine Direction, Thickness, Strength, Stretch, Resistance to Crumpling and Friction, Transparency, Absorbency and other qualities of Blotting Papers—Determination of the Permeability of Filtering Papers—Detection and Estimation of Animal and Vegetable Size in Paper—Sizing Qualities of Paper—Fibrous Constituents—Microscopical Examination of Fibres—The Effect of Beating on Fibres—Staining Fibres—Mineral Matter—Ash—Qualitative and Quantitative Examination of Mineral Matter—Examination of Coated Papers and Colouring Matters in Paper.

CONTENTS OF "THE PAPER MILL CHEMIST"—*contd.*

Tables.—English and Metrical Weights and Measures with Equivalents—Conversion of Grams to Grains and *vice versâ*—Equivalent Costs per lb., cwt., and ton—Decimal Equivalents of lbs., qrs., and cwts.—Thermometric and Barometric Scales—Atomic Weights and Molecular Weights—Factors for Calculating the Percentage of Substance Sought from the Weight of Substance Found—Table of Solubilities of Substances Treated of in Paper Making—Specific Gravity Tables of such substances as are used in Paper Making, including Sulphuric Acid, Hydrochloric Acid, Bleach, Milk of Lime, Caustic Soda, Carbonate of Soda, etc., giving Percentage Strength with Specific Gravity and Degrees Tw.—Hardness Table for Soap Tests—Dew Point—Wet and Dry Bulb Tables—Properties of Saturated Steam, giving Temperature, Pressure and Volume—List of Different Machines used in the Paper Making Industry, giving Size, Weight, Space Occupied, Power to Drive, Out-put and Approximate Cost—Calculation of Moisture in Pulp—Rag-Boiling Tables, giving Percentages of Lime, Soda and Time required—Loss in Weight in Rags and other Raw Materials during Boiling and Bleaching—Conditions of Buying and Selling as laid down by the Paper Makers' Association—Table of Names and Sizes of Papers—Table for ascertaining the Weight per Ream from the Weight per Sheet—Calculations of Areas and Volumes—Logarithms—Blank pages for Notes.

THE TREATMENT OF PAPER FOR SPECIAL PURPOSES. By L. E. Andés. Translated from the German. Crown 8vo. 48 Illustrations. 250 pp. Price 6s. net. (Post free, 6s. 4d. home; 6s. 6d. abroad).

Contents.

I., **Parchment Paper, Vegetable Parchment.**—The Parchment Paper Machine—Opaque Supple Parchment Paper—Thick Parchment—Krugler's Parchment Paper and Parchment Slates—Double and Triple Osmotic Parchment—Utilising Waste Parchment Paper—Parchmented Linen and Cotton—Parchment Millboard—Imitation Horn and Ivory from Parchment Paper—Imitation Parchment Paper—Artificial Parchment—Testing the Sulphuric Acid. II., Papers for Transfer Pictures. III., **Papers for Preservative and Packing Purposes.**—Butter Paper—Wax Paper—Paraffin Paper—Wrapping Paper for Silverware—Waterproof Paper—Anticorrosive Paper. IV., Grained Transfer Papers. V., Fireproof and Antifalsification Papers. VI., **Paper Articles.**—Vulcanised Paper Maché—Paper Bottles—Plastic Articles of Paper—Waterproof Coverings for Walls and Ceilings—Paper Wheels, Roofing and Boats—Pa er Barrels—Paper Boxes—Paper Horseshoes. VII., Gummed Paper VIII., Hectograph Papers. IX., **Insecticide Papers.**—Fly Papers—Moth Papers. X., **Chalk and Leather Papers.**—Glacé Chalk Paper—Leather Paper—Imitation Leather. XI., Luminous Papers—Blue-Print Papers—Blotting Papers. XII., Metal Papers—Medicated Papers. XIII., Marbled Papers. XIV., Tracing and Copying Papers—Iridiscent or Mother of Pearl Papers. XV., Photographic Papers—Shellac Paper—Fumigating Papers—Test Papers. XVI., **Papers for Cleaning and Polishing Purposes**—Glass Paper—Pumic Paper—Emery Paper. XVII., Lithographic Transfer Papers. XIX., **Sundry Special Papers**—Satin Paper—Enamel Paper—Cork Paper—Split Paper—Electric Paper—Paper Matches—Magic Pictures—Laundry Blue Papers—Blue Paper for Bleachers. XX., Waterproof Papers—Washable Drawing Papers—Washable Card—Washable Coloured Paper—Waterproof Millboard—Sugar Paper. XXI., The Characteristics of Paper—Paper Testing.

Enamelling on Metal.

ENAMELS AND ENAMELLING. For Enamel Makers, Workers in Gold and Silver, and Manufacturers of Objects of Art. By Paul Randau. Translated from the German. With Sixteen Illustrations. Demy 8vo. 180 pp. Price 10s. 6d. net. (Post free, 10s. 10d. home; 11s. abroad.)

THE ART OF ENAMELLING ON METAL. By W. Norman Brown. Twenty-eight Illustrations. Crown 8vo. 60 pp. Price 2s. 6d. net. (Post free, 2s. 9d. home and abroad.)

Silk Manufacture.

SILK THROWING AND WASTE SILK SPINNING. By Hollins Rayner. Demy 8vo. 170 pp. 117 Illus. Price 5s. net. (Post free, 5s. 4d. home; 5s. 6d. abroad.)

Contents.

The Silkworm—Cocoon Reeling and Qualities of Silk—Silk Throwing—Silk Wastes—The Preparation of Silk Waste for Degumming—Silk Waste Degumming, Schapping and Discharging—The Opening and Dressing of Wastes—Silk Waste "Drawing" or "Preparing" Machinery—Long Spinning—Short Spinning—Spinning and Finishing Processes—Utilisation of Waste Products—Noil Spinning—Exhaust Noil Spinning.

Books on Textile and Dyeing Subjects.

THE CHEMICAL TECHNOLOGY OF TEXTILE FIBRES: Their Origin, Structure, Preparation, Washing, Bleaching, Dyeing, Printing and Dressing. By Dr. GEORG VON GEORGIEVICS. Translated from the German by CHARLES SALTER. 320 pp. Forty-seven Illustrations. Royal 8vo. Price 10s. 6d. net. (Post free, 11s. home; 11s. 3d. abroad.)

Contents.

The Textile Fibres—Washing, Bleaching, Carbonising—Mordants and Mordanting—Dyeing—Printing—Dressing and Finishing.

POWER-LOOM WEAVING AND YARN NUMBERING, According to Various Systems, with Conversion Tables. Translated from the German of ANTHON GRUNER. **With Twenty-six Diagrams in Colours.** 150 pp. Crown 8vo. Price 7s. 6d. net. (Post free, 7s. 9d. home; 8s. abroad.)

Contents.

Power-Loom Weaving in General. Various Systems of Looms—**Mounting and Starting the Power-Loom.** English Looms—Tappet or Treadle Looms—Dobbies—**General Remarks on the Numbering, Reeling and Packing of Yarn—Appendix—Useful Hints.** Calculating Warps—Weft Calculations—Calculations of Cost Price in Hanks.

TEXTILE RAW MATERIALS AND THEIR CONVERSION INTO YARNS. (The Study of the Raw Materials and the Technology of the Spinning Process.) By JULIUS ZIPSER. Translated from German by CHARLES SALTER. 302 Illustrations. 500 pp. Demy 8vo. Price 10s. 6d. net. (Post free, 11s home; 11s. 6d. abroad.)

Contents.

PART I.—The Raw Materials Used in the Textile Industry.

MINERAL RAW MATERIALS. VEGETABLE RAW MATERIALS. ANIMAL RAW MATERIALS.

PART II.—The Technology of Spinning or the Conversion of Textile Raw Materials into Yarn.

SPINNING VEGETABLE RAW MATERIALS. Cotton Spinning—Installation of a Cotton Mill—Spinning Waste Cotton and Waste Cotton Yarns—Flax Spinning—Fine Spinning—Tow Spinning—Hemp Spinning—Spinning Hemp Tow String—Jute Spinning—Spinning Jute Line Yarn—Utilising Jute Waste.

PART III.—Spinning Animal Raw Materials.

Spinning Carded Woollen Yarn—Finishing Yarn—Worsted Spinning—Finishing Worsted Yarn—Artificial Wool or Shoddy Spinning—Shoddy and Mungo Manufacture—Spinning Shoddy and other Wool Substitutes—Spinning Waste Silk—Chappe Silk—Fine Spinning—Index.

GRAMMAR OF TEXTILE DESIGN. By H. NISBET, Weaving and Designing Master, Bolton Municipal Technical School. Demy 8vo. 280 pp. 490 Illustrations and Diagrams. Price 6s. net. (Post free, 6s. 4d. home; 6s. 6d. abroad.)

Contents.

Chapter I., INTRODUCTION.—General Principle of Fabric Structure and the use of Design Paper.

Chapter II., THE PLAIN WEAVE AND ITS MODIFICATIONS.—**The Plain, Calico, or Tabby Weave.**—Firmness of Texture—Variety of Texture—Variety of Form: Ribbed Fabrics—Corded Fabrics—Matt Weaves.

Chapter III., TWILL AND KINDRED WEAVES.—Classification of Twill Weaves.—1. **Continuous Twills**—(a) *Warp-face Twills*—(b) *Weft-face Twills*—(c) *Warp and Weft-face Twills*—The Angle of Twill—Influences affecting the Prominence of Twills and Kindred Weaves (a) *Character of Weave*, (b) *Character of Yarn*, (c) *Number of Threads per Inch*, (d) *Direction of Twill in Relation to the Direction of Twist in Yarn*—2. **Zigzag or Wavy Twills**—3. **Rearranged Twills**: Satin Weaves—Table of Intervals of Selection for the Construction of Satin Weaves—Corkscrew Twills—Rearrangement of Twill Weaves on Satin and other Bases—4. **Combined Twills**—5. **Broken Twills**—6. **Figured or Ornamented Twills.**

Chapter IV., DIAMOND AND KINDRED WEAVES.—**Diamond Weaves.**—Honeycomb and Kindred Weaves—Brighton Weaves—Sponge Weaves—Huck-a-Back and Kindred Weaves—Grecian Weaves—Linear Zigzag Weaves.

Chapter V., BEDFORD CORDS.—Plain Calico-ribbed Bedford Cords—Plain Twill-ribbed Bedford Cords—Figured Bedford Cords—Tabulated Data of Particulars relating to the Manufacture of Seventeen Varieties of Bedford Cord Fabrics described in this Chapter.

[*Continued on next page.*

CONTENTS OF "GRAMMAR OF TEXTILE DESIGN"—*continued.*

Chapter VI., BACKED FABRICS.—Weft-backed Fabrics—Warp-backed Fabrics—Reversible or Double-faced Fabrics.

Chapter VII., FUSTIANS.—**Varieties of Fustians.**—Imperials or Swansdowns—Cantoons or Diagonals—Moleskins—Beaverteens—**Velveteens** and Velveteen Cutting—Ribbed or Corded Velveteen—Figured Velveteen—**Corduroy**—Figured Corduroy—Corduroy Cutting Machines.

Chapter VIII., TERRY PILE FABRICS.—Methods of producing Terry Pile on Textile Fabrics—Terry-forming Devices—Varieties of Terry Fabrics—Action of the Reed in Relation to Shedding—Figured Terry Weaving—Practical Details of Terry Weaving.

Chapter IX., GAUZE AND LENO FABRICS.—**Gauze, Net Leno, and Leno Brocade Varieties of Cross-Weaving.**—Plain Gauze, and a Heald Gauze or Leno Harness—Net Leno Fabrics—Gauze and Net Leno Figuring by means of several Back Standard Healds to each Doup Heald—**Leno Specialities produced by a System of Crossing Warp Ends in front of the Reed**—A Device for the Production of Special Leno Effects—Full Cross Leno Fabrics—Relative Merits of a Top and a Bottom Doup Harness—Relative Merits of Different Types of Dobbies for Gauze and Leno Fabrics—Shaking Devices for Leno Weaving—Practical Details of Leno Weaving—**Tempered Steel-wire Doup Harnesses for Cross-weaving**—Mock or Imitation Leno Fabrics.

Chapter X., TISSUE, LAPPET, AND SWIVEL FIGURING; ALSO ONDULÉ EFFECTS, AND LOOPED FABRICS.—**Tissue Figuring**—Madras Muslin Curtains—**Lappet Figuring**—Spot Lappet Figuring—**Swivel Figuring**—**Woven Ondulé Effects**—Loom for Weaving Ondulé Effects—Weft Ondulé Effects—**Looped Fabrics.**—INDEX.

ART NEEDLEWORK AND DESIGN. POINT LACE. A Manual of Applied Art for Secondary Schools and Continuation Classes. By M. E. WILKINSON. Oblong quarto. With 22 Plates. Bound in Art Linen. Price 3s. 6d. net. (Post free, 3s. 10d. home; 4s. abroad.)

Contents.

Sampler of Lace Stitches—Directions for working Point Lace, tracing Patterns, etc.—List of Materials and Implements required for working. Plates I., Simple Lines, Straight and Slanting, and Designs formed from them. II., Patterns formed from Lines in previous Lesson. III., Patterns formed from Lines in previous Lesson. IV., Simple Curves, and Designs formed from them. V., Simple Leaf form, and Designs formed from it. VI., Elementary Geometrical forms, with Definitions. VII., Exercises on previous Lessons. VIII., Filling of a Square, Oblong and Circle with Lace Stitches. IX., Design for Tie End, based on simple Leaf form. X., Lace Butterflies (Freehand). XI., Twenty simple Designs evolved from Honiton Braid Leaf. XII., Design for Lace Handkerchief, based on previous Lesson. XIII., Design for Tea-cosy. XIV., Freehand Lace Collar. XV., Freehand Lace Cuff (to match). XVI., Application of Spray from Lesson XI. XVII., Adaptation of Curves within a Square, for Lace Cushion Centre. XVIII., Conventional Spray for corner of Tea-cloth. XIX., Geometrical form for Rosebowl D'Oyley, to be originally filled in. XX., Geometrical form for Flower-vase D'Oyley, to be originally filled in. Each Lesson contains Instructions for Working, and application of new Stitches from Sampler.

HOME LACE-MAKING. A Handbook for Teachers and Pupils. By M. E. W. MILROY. Crown 8vo. 64 pp. With 3 Plates and 9 Diagrams. Price 1s. net. (Post free, 1s. 3d. home; 1s. 4d. abroad.)

THE CHEMISTRY OF HAT MANUFACTURING. Lectures delivered before the Hat Manufacturers' Association. By WATSON SMITH, F.C.S., F.I.C. Revised and Edited by ALBERT SHONK. Crown 8vo. 132 pp. 16 Illustrations. Price 7s. 6d. net. (Post free, 7s. 9d. home; 7s. 10d. abroad.)

THE TECHNICAL TESTING OF YARNS AND TEXTILE FABRICS. With Reference to Official Specifications. Translated from the German of Dr. J. HERZFELD. Second Edition. Sixty-nine Illustrations. 200 pp. Demy 8vo. Price 10s. 6d. net. (Post free, 10s. 10d. home; 11s. abroad.)

DECORATIVE AND FANCY TEXTILE FABRICS. By R. T. LORD. For Manufacturers and Designers of Carpets, Damask, Dress and all Textile Fabrics. 200 pp. Demy 8vo. 132 Designs and Illustrations. Price 7s. 6d. net. (Post free, 7s. 10d. home; 8s. abroad.)

THEORY AND PRACTICE OF DAMASK WEAVING. By H. KINZER and K. WALTER. Royal 8vo. Eighteen Folding Plates. Six Illustrations. Translated from the German. 110 pp. Price 8s. 6d. net. (Post free, 9s. home; 9s. 6d. abroad.)

TEXTILE BOOKS—*continued.*

Contents.

The Various Sorts of Damask Fabrics—Drill (Ticking, Handloom-made)—Whole Damask for Tablecloths—Damask with Ground- and Connecting-warp Threads—Furniture Damask—Lampas or Hangings—Church Damasks—**The Manufacture of Whole Damask**—Damask Arrangement with and without Cross-Shedding—The Altered Cone-arrangement—The Principle of the Corner Lifting Cord—The Roller Principle—The Combination of the Jacquard with the so-called Damask Machine—The Special Damask Machine—The Combination of Two Tyings.

FAULTS IN THE MANUFACTURE OF WOOLLEN GOODS AND THEIR PREVENTION. By NICOLAS REISER. Translated from the Second German Edition. Crown 8vo. Sixty-three Illustrations. 170 pp. Price 5s. net. (Post free, 5s. 4d. home; 5s. 6d. abroad.)

Contents.

Improperly Chosen Raw Material or Improper Mixtures—Wrong Treatment of the Material in Washing, Carbonisation, Drying, Dyeing and Spinning—Improper Spacing of the Goods in the Loom—Wrong Placing of Colours—Wrong Weight or Width of the Goods—Breaking of Warp and Weft Threads—Presence of Doubles, Singles, Thick, Loose, and too Hard Twisted Threads as well as Tangles, Thick Knots and the Like—Errors in Cross-weaving—Inequalities, *i.e.*, Bands and Stripes—Dirty Borders—Defective Selvedges—Holes and Buttons—Rubbed Places—Creases—Spots—Loose and Bad Colours—Badly Dyed Selvedges—Hard Goods—Brittle Goods—Uneven Goods—Removal of Bands, Stripes, Creases and Spots.

SPINNING AND WEAVING CALCULATIONS, especially relating to Woollens. From the German of N. REISER. Thirty-four Illustrations. Tables. 160 pp. Demy 8vo. 1904. Price 10s. 6d. net. (Post free, 10s. 10d. home; 11s. abroad.)

Contents.

Calculating the Raw Material—Proportion of Different Grades of Wool to Furnish a Mixture at a Given Price—Quantity to Produce a Given Length—Yarn Calculations—Yarn Number—Working Calculations—Calculating the Reed Count—Cost of Weaving, etc.

WATERPROOFING OF FABRICS. By Dr. S. MIERZINSKI. Crown 8vo. 104 pp. 29 Illus. Price 5s. net. (Post free, 5s. 3d. home; 5s. 4d. abroad.)

Contents.

Introduction—Preliminary Treatment of the Fabric—Waterproofing with Acetate of Alumina—Impregnation of the Fabric—Drying—Waterproofing with Paraffin—Waterproofing with Ammonium Cuprate—Waterproofing with Metallic Oxides—Coloured Waterproof Fabrics—Waterproofing with Gelatine, Tannin, Caseinate of Lime and other Bodies—Manufacture of Tarpaulin—British Waterproofing Patents—Index.

HOW TO MAKE A WOOLLEN MILL PAY. By JOHN MACKIE. Crown 8vo. 76 pp. Price 3s. 6d. net. (Post free, 3s. 9d. home; 3s. 10d. abroad.)

Contents.

Blends, Piles, or Mixtures of Clean Scoured Wools—Dyed Wool Book—The Order Book—Pattern Duplicate Books—Management and Oversight—Constant Inspection of Mill Departments—Importance of Delivering Goods to Time, Shade, Strength, etc.—Plums.

(For "Textile Soaps and Oils" see p. 7.)

Dyeing, Colour Printing, Matching and Dye-stuffs.

THE COLOUR PRINTING OF CARPET YARNS. Manual for Colour Chemists and Textile Printers. By DAVID PATERSON, F.C.S. Seventeen Illustrations. 136 pp. Demy 8vo. Price 7s. 6d. net. (Post free, 7s. 10d. home; 8s. abroad.)

Contents.

Structure and Constitution of Wool Fibre—Yarn Scouring—Scouring Materials—Water for Scouring—Bleaching Carpet Yarns—Colour Making for Yarn Printing—Colour Printing Pastes—Colour Recipes for Yarn Printing—Science of Colour Mixing—Matching of Colours—"Hank" Printing—Printing Tapestry Carpet Yarns—Yarn Printing—Steaming Printed Yarns—Washing of Steamed Yarns—Aniline Colours Suitable for Yarn Printing—Glossary of Dyes and Dye-wares used in Wood Yarn Printing—Appendix.

THE SCIENCE OF COLOUR MIXING. A Manual intended for the use of Dyers, Calico Printers and Colour Chemists. By DAVID PATERSON, F.C.S. Forty-one Illustrations, **Five Coloured Plates, and Four Plates showing Eleven Dyed Specimens of Fabrics.** 132 pp. Demy 8vo. Price 7s. 6d. net. (Post free, 7s. 10d. home; 8s. abroad.)

Contents.

Colour a Sensation; Colours of Illuminated Bodies; Colours of Opaque and Transparent Bodies; Surface Colour—Analysis of Light; Spectrum; Homogeneous Colours; Ready Method of Obtaining a Spectrum—Examination of Solar Spectrum; The Spectroscope and Its Construction; Colourists' Use of the Spectroscope—Colour by Absorption; Solutions and Dyed Fabrics; Dichroic Coloured Fabrics in Gaslight—Colour Primaries of the Scientist *versus* the Dyer and Artist; Colour Mixing by Rotation and Lye Dyeing; Hue, Purity, Brightness; Tints; Shades, Scales, Tones, Sad and Sombre Colours—Colour Mixing; Pure and Impure Greens, Orange and Violets; Large Variety of Shades from few Colours; Consideration of the Practical Primaries: Red, Yellow and Blue—Secondary Colours; Nomenclature of Violet and Purple Group; Tints and Shades of Violet; Changes in Artificial Light—Tertiary Shades; Broken Hues; Absorption Spectra of Tertiary Shades—Appendix: Four Plates with Dyed Specimens Illustrating Text—Index.

DYERS' MATERIALS: An Introduction to the Examination, Evaluation and Application of the most important Substances used in Dyeing, Printing, Bleaching and Finishing. By PAUL HEERMAN, Ph.D. Translated from the German by A. C. WRIGHT, M.A. (Oxon.), B.Sc. (Lond.). Twenty-four Illustrations. Crown 8vo. 150 pp. Price 5s. net. (Post free, 5s. 4d. home; 5s. 6d. abroad.)

COLOUR MATCHING ON TEXTILES. A Manual intended for the use of Students of Colour Chemistry, Dyeing and Textile Printing. By DAVID PATERSON, F.C.S. Coloured Frontispiece. Twenty-nine Illustrations and **Fourteen Specimens of Dyed Fabrics.** Demy 8vo. 132 pp. Price 7s. 6d. net. (Post free, 7s. 10d. home; 8s. abroad.)

Contents.

Colour Vision and Structure of the Eye—Perception of Colour—Primary and Complementary Colour Sensations—Daylight for Colour Matching—Selection of a Good Pure Light—Diffused Daylight, Direct Sunlight, Blue Skylight, Variability of Daylight, etc., etc.—Matching of Hues—Purity and Luminosity of Colours—Matching Bright Hues—Aid of Tinted Films—Matching Difficulties Arising from Contrast—Examination of Colours by Reflected and Transmitted Lights—Effect of Lustre and Transparency of Fibres in Colour Matching—Matching of Colours on Velvet Pile—Optical Properties of Dye-stuffs, Dichroism, Fluorescence—Use of Tinted Mediums—Orange Film—Defects of the Eye—Yellowing of the Lens—Colour Blindness, etc.—Matching of Dyed Silk Trimmings and Linings and Bindings—Its Difficulties—Behaviour of Shades in Artificial Light—Colour Matching of Old Fabrics, etc.—Examination of Dyed Colours under the Artificial Lights—Electric Arc, Magnesium and Dufton, Gardner Lights, Welsbach, Acetylene, etc.—Testing Qualities of an Illuminant—Influence of the Absorption Spectrum in Changes of Hue under the Artificial Lights—Study of the Causes of Abnormal Modifications of Hue, etc.

COLOUR: A HANDBOOK OF THE THEORY OF COLOUR. By GEORGE H. HURST, F.C.S. **With Ten Coloured Plates** and Seventy-two Illustrations. 160 pp. Demy 8vo. Price 7s. 6d. net. (Post free, 7s. 10d. home; 8s. abroad.)

Contents.

Colour and Its Production—Cause of Colour in Coloured Bodies—Colour Phenomena and Theories—The Physiology of Light—Contrast—Colour in Decoration and Design—Measurement of Colour.

Reissue of

THE ART OF DYEING WOOL, SILK AND COTTON. Translated from the French of M. HELLOT, M. MACQUER and M. LE PILEUR D'APLIGNY. First Published in English in 1789. Six Plates. Demy 8vo. 446 pp. Price 5s. net. (Post free, 5s. 6d. home; 6s. abroad.)

Contents.

Part I., The Art of Dyeing Wool and Woollen Cloth, Stuffs, Yarn, Worsted, etc. Part II., The Art of Dyeing Silk. Part III., The Art of Dyeing Cotton and Linen Thread, together with the Method of Stamping Silks, Cottons, etc.

THE CHEMISTRY OF DYE-STUFFS. By Dr. GEORG VON GEORGIEVICS. Translated from the Second German Edition. 412 pp. Demy 8vo. Price 10s. 6d. net. (Post free, 11s. home; 11s. 6d. abroad.)

Contents.

Introduction—Coal Tar—Intermediate Products in the Manufacture of Dye-stuffs—The Artificial Dye-stuffs (Coal-tar Dyes)—Nitroso Dye-stuffs—Nitro Dye-stuffs—Azo Dye-stuffs—Substantive Cotton Dye-stuffs—Azoxystilbene Dye-stuffs—Hydrazones—Ketoneimides—Triphenylmethane Dye-stuffs—Rosolic Acid Dye-stuffs—Xanthene Dye-stuffs—Xanthone Dye-stuffs—Flavones—Oxyketone Dye-stuffs—Quinoline and Acridine Dye-stuffs—Quinonimide or Diphenylamine Dye-stuffs—The Azine Group: Eurhodines, Safranines and Indulines—Eurhodines—Safranines—Quinoxalines—Indigo—Dye-stuffs of Unknown Constitution—Sulphur or Sulphine Dye-stuffs—Development of the Artificial Dye-stuff Industry—The Natural Dye-stuffs—Mineral Colours—Index.

THE DYEING OF COTTON FABRICS: A Practical Handbook for the Dyer and Student. By FRANKLIN BEECH, Practical Colourist and Chemist. 272 pp. Forty-four Illustrations of Bleaching and Dyeing Machinery. Demy 8vo. Price 7s. 6d. net. (Post free, 7s. 10d. home; 8s. abroad.)

Contents.

Structure and Chemistry of the Cotton Fibre—Scouring and Bleaching of Cotton—Dyeing Machinery and Dyeing Manipulations—Principles and Practice of Cotton Dyeing—Direct Dyeing; Direct Dyeing followed by Fixation with Metallic Salts; Direct Dyeing followed by Fixation with Developers; Direct Dyeing followed by Fixation with Couplers; Dyeing on Tannic Mordant; Dyeing on Metallic Mordant; Production of Colour Direct upon Cotton Fibres; Dyeing Cotton by Impregnation with Dye-stuff Solution—Dyeing Union (Mixed Cotton and Wool) Fabrics—Dyeing Half Silk (Cotton-Silk, Satin) Fabrics—Operations following Dyeing—Washing, Soaping, Drying—Testing of the Colour of Dyed Fabrics—Experimental Dyeing and Comparative Dye Testing—Index.

The book contains numerous recipes for the production on Cotton Fabrics of all kinds of a great range of colours.

THE DYEING OF WOOLLEN FABRICS. By FRANKLIN BEECH, Practical Colourist and Chemist. Thirty-three Illustrations. Demy 8vo. 228 pp. Price 7s. 6d. net. (Post free, 7s. 10d. home; 8s. abroad.)

Contents.

The Wool Fibre—Structure, Composition and Properties—Processes Preparatory to Dyeing—Scouring and Bleaching of Wool—Dyeing Machinery and Dyeing Manipulations—Loose Wool Dyeing, Yarn Dyeing and Piece Dyeing Machinery—The Principles and Practice of Wool Dyeing—Properties of Wool Dyeing—Methods of Wool Dyeing—Groups of Dyes—Dyeing with the Direct Dyes—Dyeing with Basic Dyes—Dyeing with Acid Dyes—Dyeing with Mordant Dyes—Level Dyeing—Blacks on Wool—Reds on Wool—Mordanting of Wool—Orange Shades on Wool—Yellow Shades on Wool—Green Shades on Wool—Blue Shades on Wool—Violet Shades on Wool—Brown Shades on Wool—Mode Colours on Wool—Dyeing Union (Mixed Cotton Wool) Fabrics—Dyeing of Gloria—Operations following Dyeing—Washing, Soaping, Drying—Experimental Dyeing and Comparative Dye Testing—Testing of the Colour of Dyed Fabrics—Index.

Bleaching and Washing.

A PRACTICAL TREATISE ON THE BLEACHING OF LINEN AND COTTON YARN AND FABRICS. By L. TAILFER, Chemical and Mechanical Engineer. Translated from the French by JOHN GEDDES MCINTOSH. Demy 8vo. 303 pp. Twenty Illus. Price 12s. 6d. net. (Post free, 13s. home; 13s. 6d. abroad.)

Cotton Spinning and Combing.

COTTON SPINNING (First Year). By THOMAS THORNLEY, Spinning Master, Bolton Technical School. 160 pp. Eighty-four Illustrations. Crown 8vo. Second Impression. Price 3s. net. (Post free, 3s. 4d. home; 3s. 6d. abroad.)

Contents.

Syllabus and Examination Papers of the City and Guilds of London Institute—Cultivation, Classification, Ginning, Baling and Mixing of the Raw Cotton—Bale-Breakers, Mixing Lattices and Hopper Feeders—Opening and Scutching—Carding—Indexes.

COTTON SPINNING (Intermediate, or Second Year). By THOMAS THORNLEY. Second Impression. 180 pp. Seventy Illustrations. Crown 8vo. Price 5s. net. (Post free, 5s. 4d. home; 5s. 6d. abroad.)

Contents.

Syllabuses and Examination Papers of the City and Guilds of London Institute—The Combing Process—The Drawing Frame—Bobbin and Fly Frames—Mule Spinning—Ring Spinning—General Indexes.

COTTON SPINNING (Honours, or Third Year). By THOMAS THORNLEY. 216 pp. Seventy-four Illustrations. Crown 8vo. Second Edition. Price 5s. net. (Post free, 5s. 4d. home; 5s. 6d. abroad.)

Contents.

Syllabuses and Examination Papers of the City and Guilds of London Institute—Cotton—The Practical Manipulation of Cotton Spinning Machinery—Doubling and Winding—Reeling—Warping—Production and Costs—Main Driving—Arrangement of Machinery and Mill Planning—Waste and Waste Spinning—Indexes.

COTTON COMBING MACHINES. By THOS. THORNLEY, Spinning Master, Technical School, Bolton. Demy 8vo. 117 Illustrations. 300 pp. Price 7s. 6d. net. (Post free, 8s. home; 8s. 6d. abroad.)

Contents.

The Sliver Lap Machine and the Ribbon Cap Machine—General Description of the Heilmann Comber—The Cam Shaft—On the Detaching and Attaching Mechanism of the Comber—Resetting of Combers—The Erection of a Heilmann Comber—Stop Motions: Various Calculations—Various Notes and Discussions—Cotton Combing Machines of Continental Make—Index.

Flax, Hemp and Jute Spinning.

MODERN FLAX, HEMP AND JUTE SPINNING AND TWISTING. A Practical Handbook for the use of Flax, Hemp and Jute Spinners, Thread, Twine and Rope Makers. By HERBERT R. CARTER, Mill Manager, Textile Expert and Engineer, Examiner in Flax Spinning to the City and Guilds of London Institute. Demy 8vo. 1907. With 92 Illustrations. 200 pp. Price 7s. 6d. net. (Post free, 7s. 9d. home; 8s. abroad.)

Contents.

Raw Fibre.—Origin of Flax—Hemp and Jute Fibre—Description of the Plants—Mode of Cultivation—Suitable Climate and Soil—Sowing—Harvesting—Rippling Flax and Hemp—Water Retting—Dew Retting—Extraction of the Fibre—Marketing the Fibre—Bracquing—Flax, Hemp and Jute Marks—Comparative Prices—Ports of Export—Trade Centres—Fibre Selling Conditions—Duty on Fibre—Fibre Exports. **Hackling.**—Sorting and Storing the Raw Fibre—Softening Hemp and Jute—Jute Batching—Cutting—Piecing Out—Roughing—Hackling by Hand and Machine—Tippling—Sorting—Ventilation of Hackling Rooms. **Sliver Formation.**—Spreading Line—Heavy Spreading System—Good's Combined Hackle and Spreader—Jute Breaking and Carding—Flax and Hemp Tow Carding—Bell Calculation—Clock System—Theory of Spreading. **Line and Tow Preparing.**—Drawing and Doubling—Draft Calculation—Set Calculation—Tow Combing—Compound Systems—Automatic Stop Motions and Independent Heads—Details of Preparing Machinery—Ventilation—Humidification. **Gill Spinning.**—Gill Spinning for Shoe Threads, Rope Yarns, Binder and Trawl Twines—The Automatic Gill Spinner—Rope and Reaper Yarn Numbering. **The Flax, Hemp and Jute Roving Frame.**—Bobbin Winding—Differential Motion—Twist Calculation—Practical Changing—Rove Stock. **Dry and Half-Dry Spinning.**—Flyer and Ring Frames—Draft and Twist Calculation—Bobbin Dragging—Reaches—Set of Breast Beam and Tin-rod. **Wet Spinning** of Flax, Hemp and Tow—Hot and Cold Water Spinning—Improvements in the Water Trough—Turn off and Speed of Spindles—Reaches—Belting—Band Tying—Tape Driving—Oiling—Black Threads—Cuts per Spindle—Ventilation of the Wet Spinning Room. **Yarn Department.**—Reeling—Cop Winding—Cheese and Spool Winding—Balling Shoe Thread, Reaper Yarn, etc.—Yarn Drying and Conditioning—Yarn Bundling—Yarn Baling—Weight of Yarn—Yarn Tables—Duty on Yarn Imports. **Manufacture of Threads, Twines and Cords.**—Hank Winding—Wet and Dry Twisting—Cabling—Fancy Yarns—Twine Laying—Sizing and Polishing Threads and Twines—Softening Threads—Skeining Threads—Balling Twines—Leeson's Universal Winder—Randing Twines—Spooling Sewing Threads—Comparative Prices of Flax and Hemp Cords, Lines and Threads. **Rope Making.**—Construction of Hawsers and Cables—Stranding—Laying and Closing—Compound Rope Machines—Rules for Rope Makers—Weight of Ropes—Balling and Coiling Ropes. **Mechanical Department.**—Boilers, Engines and Turbines—Power Transmission by Belts and Ropes—Electric Light and Power Transmission—Fans—Oils and Oiling—Repairs—Fluting. **Mill Construction.**—Flax, Hemp and Jute Spinning Mills and Ropeworks—Heating—Roofs—Chimneys, etc.

Collieries and Mines.

RECOVERY WORK AFTER PIT FIRES. By ROBERT LAMPRECHT, Mining Engineer and Manager. Translated from the German. Illustrated by Six large Plates, containing Seventy-six Illustrations. 175 pp., demy 8vo. Price 10s. 6d. net. (Post free, 10s. 10d. home; 11s. abroad.)

Contents.

Causes of Pit Fires—Preventive Regulations: (1) The Outbreak and Rapid Extension of a Shaft Fire can be most reliably prevented by Employing little or no Combustible Material in the Construction of the Shaft; (2) Precautions for Rapidly Localising an Outbreak of Fire in the Shaft; (3) Precautions to be Adopted in case those under 1 and 2 Fail or Prove Inefficient. Precautions against Spontaneous Ignition of Coal. Precautions for Preventing Explosions of Fire-damp and Coal Dust. Employment of Electricity in Mining, particularly in Fiery Pits. Experiments on the Ignition of Fire-damp Mixtures and Clouds of Coal Dust by Electricity—**Indications of an Existing or Incipient Fire—Appliances for Working in Irrespirable Gases:** Respiratory Apparatus; Apparatus with Air Supply Pipes; Reservoir Apparatus; Oxygen Apparatus—**Extinguishing Pit Fires:** (*a*) Chemical Means; (*b*) Extinction with Water. Dragging down the Burning Masses and Packing with Clay; (*c*) Insulating the Seat of the Fire by Dams. Dam Building. Analyses of Fire Gases. Isolating the Seat of a Fire with Dams: Working in Irrespirable Gases ("Gas-diving"): Air-Lock Work. Complete Isolation of the Pit. Flooding a Burning Section isolated by means of Dams. Wooden Dams: Masonry Dams. Examples of Cylindrical and Dome-shaped Dams. Dam Doors: Flooding the Whole Pit—**Rescue Stations:** (*a*) Stations above Ground; (*b*) Underground Rescue Stations—**Spontaneous Ignition of Coal in Bulk**—Index.

VENTILATION IN MINES. By ROBERT WABNER, Mining Engineer. Translated from the German. Royal 8vo. Thirty Plates and Twenty-two Illustrations. 240 pp. Price 10s. 6d. net. (Post free, 11s. home; 11s. 3d. abroad.)

HAULAGE AND WINDING APPLIANCES USED IN MINES. By CARL VOLK. Translated from the German. Royal 8vo. With Six Plates and 148 Illustrations. 150 pp. Price 8s. 6d. net. (Post free, 9s. home; 9s. 3d. abroad.)

Contents.

Haulage Appliances—Ropes—Haulage Tubs and Tracks—Cages and Winding Appliances—Winding Engines for Vertical Shafts—Winding without Ropes—Haulage in Levels and Inclines—The Working of Underground Engines—Machinery for Downhill Haulage.

THE ELECTRICAL EQUIPMENT OF COLLIERIES. By W. GALLOWAY DUNCAN, Electrical and Mechanical Engineer, Member of the Institution of Mining Engineers, Head of the Government School of Engineering, Dacca, India; and DAVID PENMAN, Certificated Colliery Manager, Lecturer in Mining to Fife County Committee. Demy 8vo. 310 pp. 155 Illustrations and Diagrams. Price 10s. 6d. net. (Post free, 11s. home; 11s. 3d. abroad.)

Contents.

General Principles, Magnetism, Units, Cells, etc.—Dynamos and Motors—Transmission and Distribution of Power—Prime Movers—Lighting by Electricity—Initial Outlay and Working Cost of Electrical Installations—Electricity Applied to Coal-cutting—Electric Haulage, Winding, and Locomotives—Electric Pumps and Pumping—Electric-power Drills and Underground Coal Conveyers—Typical Colliery Electrical Installations—Miscellaneous Applications of the Electric Current—Comparison of the Different Modes of Transmitting Power—Dangers Occurring from the Use of Electricity in Collieries—APPENDIX: Questions suitable for students preparing for colliery managers' examinations—INDEX.

Dental Metallurgy.

DENTAL METALLURGY: MANUAL FOR STUDENTS AND DENTISTS. By A. B. GRIFFITHS, Ph.D. Demy 8vo. Thirty-six Illustrations. 200 pp. Price 7s. 6d. net. (Post free, 7s. 10d. home; 8s. abroad.)

Contents.

Introduction—Physical Properties of the Metals—Action of Certain Agents on Metals—Alloys—Action of Oral Bacteria on Alloys—Theory and Varieties of Blowpipes—Fluxes—Furnaces and Appliances—Heat and Temperature—Gold—Mercury—Silver—Iron—Copper—Zinc—Magnesium—Cadmium—Tin—Lead—Aluminium—Antimony—Bismuth—Palladium—Platinum—Iridium—Nickel—Practical Work—Weights and Measures.

Engineering, Smoke Prevention and Metallurgy.

THE PREVENTION OF SMOKE. Combined with the Economical Combustion of Fuel. By W. C. POPPLEWELL, M.Sc., A.M.Inst., C.E., Consulting Engineer. Forty-six Illustrations. 190 pp. Demy 8vo. Price 7s. 6d. net. (Post free, 7s. 10d. home; 8s. 3d. abroad.)

Contents.

Fuel and Combustion— Hand Firing in Boiler Furnaces—Stoking by Mechanical Means—Powdered Fuel—Gaseous Fuel—Efficiency and Smoke Tests of Boilers—Some Standard Smoke Trials—The Legal Aspect of the Smoke Question—The Best Means to be adopted for the Prevention of Smoke—Index.

GAS AND COAL DUST FIRING. A Critical Review of the Various Appliances Patented in Germany for this purpose since 1885. By ALBERT PÜTSCH. 130 pp. Demy 8vo. Translated from the German. With 103 Illustrations. Price 5s. net. (Post free, 5s. 4d. home; 5s. 6d. abroad.)

Contents.

Generators—Generators Employing Steam—Stirring and Feed Regulating Appliances—Direct Generators—Burners—Regenerators and Recuperators—Glass Smelting Furnaces—Metallurgical Furnaces—Pottery Furnace—Coal Dust Firing—Index.

THE HARDENING AND TEMPERING OF STEEL IN THEORY AND PRACTICE. By FRIDOLIN REISER. Translated from the German of the Third Edition. Crown 8vo. 120 pp. Price 5s. net. (Post free, 5s. 3d. home; 5s. 4d. abroad.)

Contents.

Steel—Chemical and Physical Properties of Steel, and their Casual Connection—Classification of Steel according to Use—Testing the Quality of Steel — Steel-Hardening—Investigation of the Causes of Failure in Hardening—Regeneration of Steel Spoilt in the Furnace—Welding Steel—Index.

SIDEROLOGY: THE SCIENCE OF IRON (The Constitution of Iron Alloys and Slags). Translated from German of HANNS FREIHERR V. JÜPTNER. 350 pp. Demy 8vo. Eleven Plates and Ten Illustrations. Price 10s. 6d. net. (Post free, 11s. home; 11s. 6d. abroad.)

Contents.

The Theory of Solution.—Solutions—Molten Alloys—Varieties of Solutions—Osmotic Pressure—Relation between Osmotic Pressure and other Properties of Solutions—Osmotic Pressure and Molecular Weight of the Dissolved Substance—Solutions of Gases—Solid Solutions—Solubility—Diffusion—Electrical Conductivity—Constitution of Electrolytes and Metals—Thermal Expansion. **Micrography.**—Microstructure—The Micrographic Constituents of Iron—Relation between Micrographical Composition, Carbon-Content, and Thermal Treatment of Iron Alloys—The Microstructure of Slags. **Chemical Composition of the Alloys of Iron.**—Constituents of Iron Alloys—Carbon—Constituents of the Iron Alloys, Carbon—Opinions and Researches on Combined Carbon—Opinions and Researches on Combined Carbon—Applying the Curves of Solution deduced from the Curves of Recalescence to the Determination of the Chemical Composition of the Carbon present in Iron Alloys—The Constituents of Iron—Iron—The Constituents of Iron Alloys—Manganese—Remaining Constituents of Iron Alloys—A Silicon—Gases. **The Chemical Composition of Slag.**—Silicate Slags—Calculating the Composition of Silicate Slags—Phosphate Slags—Oxide Slags—Appendix—Index.

EVAPORATING, CONDENSING AND COOLING APPARATUS. Explanations, Formulæ and Tables for Use in Practice. By E. HAUSBRAND, Engineer. Translated by A. C. WRIGHT, M.A. (Oxon.), B.Sc. (Lond.). With Twenty-one Illustrations and Seventy-six Tables. 400 pp. Demy 8vo. Price 10s. 6d. net. (Post free, 11s. home; 11s. 6d. abroad.)

Contents.

*Re*Coefficient of Transmission of Heat, k/. and the Mean Temperature Difference, θ/m—Parallel and Opposite Currents—Apparatus for Heating with Direct Fire—The Injection of Saturated Steam—Superheated Steam—Evaporation by Means of Hot Liquids—The Transference of Heat in General, and Transference by means of Saturated Steam in Particular—The Transference of Heat from Saturated Steam in Pipes (Coils) and Double Bottoms—Evaporation in a Vacuum—The Multiple-effect Evaporator—Multiple-effect Evaporators

Contents of "Evaporating, Condensing and Cooling Apparatus".—*continued.*

from which Extra Steam is Taken—The Weight of Water which must be Evaporated from 100 Kilos. of Liquor in order its Original Percentage of Dry Materials from 1-25 per cent. up to 20-70 per cent.—The Relative Proportion of the Heating Surfaces in the Elements of the Multiple Evaporator and their Actual Dimensions—The Pressure Exerted by Currents of Steam and Gas upon Floating Drops of Water—The Motion of Floating Drops of Water upon which Press Currents of Steam—The Splashing of Evaporating Liquids—The Diameter of Pipes for Steam, Alcohol, Vapour and Air—The Diameter of Water Pipes—The Loss of Heat from Apparatus and Pipes to the Surrounding Air, and Means for Preventing the Loss—Condensers—Heating Liquids by Means of Steam—The Cooling of Liquids—The Volumes to be Exhausted from Condensers by the Air-pumps—A Few Remarks on Air-pumps and the Vacua they Produce—The Volumetric Efficiency of Air-pumps—The Volumes of Air which must be Exhausted from a Vessel in order to Reduce its Original Pressure to a Certain Lower Pressure—Index.

Sanitary Plumbing, Electric Wiring, Metal Work, etc.

EXTERNAL PLUMBING WORK. A Treatise on Lead Work for Roofs. By JOHN W. HART, R.P.C. 180 Illustrations. 272 pp. Demy 8vo. Second Edition Revised. Price 7s. 6d. net. (Post free, 7s. 10d. home; 8s. abroad.)

HINTS TO PLUMBERS ON JOINT WIPING, PIPE BENDING AND LEAD BURNING. Third Edition, Revised and Corrected. By JOHN W. HART, R.P.C. 184 Illustrations. 313 pp. Demy 8vo. Price 7s. 6d. net. (Post free, 8s. home; 8s. 6d. abroad.)

Contents.

Pipe Bending — Pipe Bending (continued) — Pipe Bending (continued) — Square Pipe Bendings—Half-circular Elbows—Curved Bends on Square Pipe—Bossed Bends—Curved Plinth Bends—Rain-water Shoes on Square Pipe—Curved and Angle Bends—Square Pipe Fixings—Joint-wiping—Substitutes for Wiped Joints—Preparing Wiped Joints—Joint Fixings—Plumbing Irons—Joint Fixings—Use of "Touch" in Soldering—Underhand Joints—Blown and Copper Bit Joints—Branch Joints—Branch Joints (continued)—Block Joints—Block Joints (continued)—Block Fixings—Astragal Joints—Pipe Fixings—Large Branch Joints—Large Underhand Joints—Solders—Autogenous Soldering or Lead Burning—Index.

SANITARY PLUMBING AND DRAINAGE. By JOHN W. HART. Demy 8vo. With 208 Illustrations. 250 pp. 1904. Price 7s. 6d. net. (Post free, 7s. 10d. home; 8s. abroad.)

ELECTRIC WIRING AND FITTING FOR PLUMBERS AND GASFITTERS. By SYDNEY F. WALKER, R.N., M.I.E.E., M.I.Min.E., A.M.Inst.C.E., etc., etc. Crown 8vo. 150 pp. With Illustrations and Tables. Price 5s. net. (Post free, 5s. 3d. home; 5s. 6d. abroad.)

Contents.

Chapter I., **Electrical Terms Used.**—Pressure and Current—The Volt—Ampère—Electrical Resistance—Earth—Continuous and Alternating Currents—The Electric Circuit—Leakage—Heating of Conductors—Size and Forms of Conductors—The Kilowatt—Loss of Pressure—Arrangement of Conductors—Looping In—The Three Wire System—Switches—Fuses—Circuit—Breakers. II., **The Insulation of Wires, Their Protection, Fixing, etc.** —Conductors Insulated with Paper and Similar Materials—Sparking between Conductors—Dialite Insulation—Flexible Cords—Concentric Conductors—Twin Conductors—Three-Core Cables—Fireproof Insulation for Conductors—Jointing—T Joints—Covering T Joints in Vulcanized Rubber Cables. III., **Fixing the Wiring and Cables.**—Laying Out the Route—The Protection of the Wires and Cables—Wood Casing—Metallic Conduits—Non-Metallic Conductors—Fixing the Conduits and Running Wires in Them—Drawing Wires into Tubes—To Avoid Shock. IV., **Lamps.**—The Incandescent Lamp—Lamp Holders—Lamp Fittings—The Nernst Lamp. V., **Switches, Fuses, Distribution Boards, etc.**—The Electricity Meter—Prepayment Meters.

THE PRINCIPLES AND PRACTICE OF DIPPING, BURNISHING, LACQUERING AND BRONZING BRASS WARE. By W. NORMAN BROWN. 35 pp. Crown 8vo. Price 2s. net. (Post free, 2s. 3d. home and abroad.)

THE PLUMBING, HEATING AND LIGHTING ANNUAL FOR 1910. *See page* 32.

A HANDBOOK ON JAPANNING AND ENAMELLING FOR CYCLES, BEDSTEADS, TINWARE, ETC. By William Norman Brown. 52 pp. and Illustrations. Crown 8vo. Price 2s. net. (Post free, 2s. 3d. home and abroad.)

THE PRINCIPLES OF HOT WATER SUPPLY. By John W. Hart, R.P.C. With 129 Illustrations. 177 pp., demy 8vo. Price 7s. 6d. net. (Post free, 7s. 10d. home; 8s. abroad.)

House Decorating and Painting.

THREE HUNDRED SHADES AND HOW TO MIX THEM. For Architects, Painters and Decorators. By A. Desaint, Artistic Interior Decorator of Paris. The book contains 100 folio Plates, measuring 12 in. by 7 in., each Plate containing specimens of three artistic shades. These shades are all numbered, and their composition and particulars for mixing are fully given at the beginning of the book. Each Plate is interleaved with grease-proof paper, and the volume is very artistically bound in art and linen with the Shield of the Painters' Guild impressed on the cover in gold and silver. Price 21s. net. (Post free, 21s. 6d. home; 22s. 6d. abroad.)

HOUSE DECORATING AND PAINTING. By W. Norman Brown. Eighty-eight Illustrations. 150 pp. Crown 8vo. Price 3s. 6d. net. (Post free, 3s. 9d. home and abroad.)

A HISTORY OF DECORATIVE ART. By W. Norman Brown. Thirty-nine Illustrations. 96 pp. Crown 8vo. Price 1s. net. (Post free, 1s. 3d. home and abroad.)

WORKSHOP WRINKLES for Decorators, Painters, Paperhangers and Others. By W. N. Brown. Crown 8vo. 128 pp. Second Edition. Price 2s. 6d. net. (Post free, 2s. 9d. home; 2s. 10d. abroad.)

Brewing and Botanical.

HOPS IN THEIR BOTANICAL, AGRICULTURAL AND TECHNICAL ASPECT, AND AS AN ARTICLE OF COMMERCE. By Emmanuel Gross, Professor at the Higher Agricultural College, Tetschen-Liebwerd. Translated from the German. Seventy-eight Illustrations. 340 pp. Demy 8vo. Price 10s. 6d. net. (Post free, 11s. home; 11s. 6d. abroad.)

Contents.

HISTORY OF THE HOP—THE HOP PLANT—Introductory—The Roots—The Stem—and Leaves—Inflorescence and Flower: Inflorescence and Flower of the Male Hop; Inflorescence and Flower of the Female Hop—The Fruit and its Glandular Structure: The Fruit and Seed—Propagation and Selection of the Hop—Varieties of the Hop: (*a*) Red Hops; (*b*) Green Hops; (*c*) Pale Green Hops—Classification according to the Period of Ripening: Early August Hops; Medium Early Hops; Late Hops—Injuries to Growth—Leaves Turning Yellow, Summer or Sunbrand, Cones Dropping Off, Honey Dew, Damage from Wind, Hail and Rain; Vegetable Enemies of the Hop: Animal Enemies of the Hop—Beneficial Insects on Hops—CULTIVATION—The Requirements of the Hop in Respect of Climate, Soil and Situation: Climate; Soil; Situation—Selection of Variety and Cuttings—Planting a Hop Garden: Drainage; Preparing the Ground: Marking-out for Planting; Planting; Cultivation and Cropping of the Hop Garden in the First Year—Work to be Performed Annually in the Hop Garden: Working the Ground; Cutting; The Non-cutting System; The Proper Performance of the Operation of Cutting: Method of Cutting: Close Cutting, Ordinary Cutting, The Long Cut, The Topping Cut; Proper Season for Cutting: Autumn Cutting, Spring Cutting; Manuring; Training the Hop Plant: Poled Gardens, Frame Training; Principal Types of Frames Pruning, Cropping, Topping, and Leaf Stripping the Hop Plant; Picking, Drying and Bagging—Principal and Subsidiary Utilisation of Hops and Hop Gardens—Life of a Hop Garden; Subsequent Cropping—Cost of Production, Yield and Selling Prices.

Preservation and Storage—Physical and Chemical Structure of the Hop Cone—Judging the Value of Hops.

Statistics of Production—The Hop Trade—Index.

Wood Products, Timber and Wood Waste.

WOOD PRODUCTS: DISTILLATES AND EXTRACTS. By P. DUMESNY, Chemical Engineer, Expert before the Lyons Commercial Tribunal, Member of the International Association of Leather Chemists; and J. NOYER. Translated from the French by DONALD GRANT. Royal 8vo. 320 pp. 103 Illustrations and Numerous Tables. Price 10s. 6d. net. (Post free, 11s. home; 11s. 6d. abroad.)

Contents.

Part I., **Wood Distillation—Principal Products from the Carbonisation of Wood—Acetates—Secondary Products of the Distillation of Wood—Acetone—Analysis of Raw Materials and Finished Products—Appendix**—The Destructive Distillation of Olive Oil Residuals. Part II., **Manufacture and Testing of Tan Wood Extracts and their Utilisation in Modern Tanneries—Plant and Equipment for Treating Chestnut Wood—Analysis of Tanning Substances**—The Official Method of the International Association of Leather Chemists, with Supplementary Notes.

TIMBER: A Comprehensive Study of Wood in all its Aspects (Commercial and Botanical), showing the Different Applications and Uses of Timber in Various Trades, etc. Translated from the French of PAUL CHARPENTIER. Royal 8vo. 437 pp. 178 Illustrations. Price 12s. 6d. net. (Post free, 13s. home; 14s. abroad.)

Contents.

Physical and Chemical Properties of Timber—Composition of the Vegetable Bodies—Chief Elements—M. Fremy's Researches—Elementary Organs of Plants and especially of Forests—Different Parts of Wood Anatomically and Chemically Considered—General Properties of Wood—**Description of the Different Kinds of Wood**—Principal Essences with Caducous Leaves—Coniferous Resinous Trees—**Division of the Useful Varieties of Timber in the Different Countries of the Globe**—European Timber—African Timber—Asiatic Timber—American Timber—Timber of Oceania—**Forests**—General Notes as to Forests; their Influence—Opinions as to Sylviculture—Improvement of Forests—Unwooding and Rewooding—Preservation of Forests—Exploitation of Forests—Damage caused to Forests—Different Alterations—**The Preservation of Timber**—Generalities—Causes and Progress of Deterioration—History of Different Proposed Processes—Dessication—Superficial Carbonisation of Timber—Processes by Immersion—Generalities as to Antiseptics Employed—Injection Processes in Closed Vessels—The Boucherie System, Based upon the Displacement of the Sap—Processes for Making Timber Uninflammable—**Applications of Timber**—Generalities—Working Timber—Paving—Timber for Mines—Railway Traverses—Accessory Products—Gums—Works of M. Fremy—Resins—Barks—Tan—Application of Cork—The Application of Wood to Art and Dyeing—Different Applications of Wood—Hard Wood—Distillation of Wood—Pyroligneous Acid—Oil of Wood—Distillation of Resins—Index.

THE UTILISATION OF WOOD WASTE. Translated from the German of ERNST HUBBARD. Crown 8vo. 192 pp. Fifty Illustrations. Price 5s. net. (Post free, 5s. 4d. home; 5s. 6d. abroad.)

Building and Architecture.

THE PREVENTION OF DAMPNESS IN BUILDINGS; with Remarks on the Causes, Nature and Effects of Saline, Efflorescences and Dry-rot, for Architects, Builders, Overseers, Plasterers, Painters and House Owners. By ADOLF WILHELM KEIM. Translated from the German of the second revised Edition by M. J. SALTER, F.I.C., F.C.S. Eight Coloured Plates and Thirteen Illustrations. Crown 8vo. 115 pp. Price 5s. net. (Post free, 5s. 3d. home; 5s. 4d. abroad.)

HANDBOOK OF TECHNICAL TERMS USED IN ARCHITECTURE AND BUILDING, AND THEIR ALLIED TRADES AND SUBJECTS. By AUGUSTINE C. PASSMORE. Demy 8vo. 380 pp. Price 7s. 6d. net. (Post free, 8s. home; 8s. 6d. abroad.)

The Preserving of Foods and Sweetmeats.

THE MANUFACTURE OF PRESERVED FOODS AND SWEETMEATS. By A. HAUSNER. With Twenty-eight Illustrations. Translated from the German of the third enlarged Edition. Crown 8vo. 225 pp. Price 7s. 6d. net. (Post free, 7s. 9d. home; 7s. 10d. abroad.)

Contents.

The Manufacture of Conserves—Introduction—The Causes of the Putrefaction of Food—The Chemical Composition of Foods—The Products of Decomposition—The Causes of Fermentation and Putrefaction—Preservative Bodies—The Various Methods of Preserving Food—The Preservation of Animal Food—Preserving Meat by Means of Ice—The Preservation of Meat by Charcoal—Preservation of Meat by Drying—The Preservation of Meat by the Exclusion of Air—The Appert Method—Preserving Flesh by Smoking—Quick Smoking—Preserving Meat with Salt—Quick Salting by Air Pressure—Quick Salting by Liquid Pressure—Gamgee's Method of Preserving Meat—The Preservation of Eggs—Preservation of White and Yolk of Egg—Milk Preservation—Condensed Milk—The Preservation of Fat—Manufacture of Soup Tablets—Meat Biscuits—Extract of Beef—The Preservation of Vegetable Foods in General—Compressing Vegetables—Preservation of Vegetables by Appert's Method—The Preservation of Fruit—Preservation of Fruit by Storage—The Preservation of Fruit by Drying—Drying Fruit by Artificial Heat—Roasting Fruit—The Preservation of Fruit with Sugar—Boiled Preserved Fruit—The Preservation of Fruit in Spirit, Acetic Acid or Glycerine—Preservation of Fruit without Boiling—Jam Manufacture—The Manufacture of Fruit Jellies—The Making of Gelatine Jellies—The Manufacture of "Sulzen"—The Preservation of Fermented Beverages—**The Manufacture of Candies**—Introduction—The Manufacture of Candied Fruit—The Manufacture of Boiled Sugar and Caramel—The Candying of Fruit—Caramelised Fruit—The Manufacture of Sugar Sticks, or Barley Sugar—Bonbon Making—Fruit Drops—The Manufacture of Dragées—The Machinery and Appliances used in Candy Manufacture—Dyeing Candies and Bonbons—Essential Oils used in Candy Making—Fruit Essences—The Manufacture of Filled Bonbons, Liqueur Bonbons and Stamped Lozenges—Recipes for Jams and Jellies—Recipes for Bonbon Making—Dragées—Appendix—Index.

RECIPES FOR THE PRESERVING OF FRUIT, VEGETABLES AND MEAT. By E. WAGNER. Translated from the German. Crown 8vo. 125 pp. With 14 Illustrations. Price 5s. net. (Post free, 5s. 3d. home; 5s. 4d. abroad.)

Contents.

Part I. Preserved Fruits.—Green Almonds—Gooseberries—Strawberries—Currants—Cherries—Black Nuts—White Nuts—Apricots—Greengages—Pears—Peaches—Plums—Figs—Melons—Apples—Chestnuts—Angelica—Pineapple. **Canned Fruit.**—Gooseberries—Cherries—Apricots—Plums—Rhubarb. **Glazed and Candied Fruits.**—Glazing Fruit—Candied Fruit—Blue Plums—Glazed Chestnuts—Glazed Pineapple Slices—Crystallised Strawberries. **Marmalades, Jams and Fruit Juices.**—Strawberry Marmalade—Cherry Marmalade—Jams—Fruit Jellies—Raspberry Juice—Cherry Juice—Lemon Syrup—Pineapple Juice. **Fruit Pulp for Ices. Citron Peel and Orange Peel. Part II. Preserved Vegetables.**—Asparagus—Peas—Beans—Carrots—Spinach—Artichokes—Tomatoes—Mixed Vegetables—Tinned Julienne—Celery—Mushrooms—Truffles—Pickled Gherkins—Gherkins in Mustard—Mixed Pickles. **Part III. Preserved Meats.**—Veal Cutlets—Fricondeau of Veal—Calves Head—Bouillon Meat—Ox Tongue—Beef à la Mode—Roast Hare—Roast Venison—Mutton and Cabbage—Savoury Paste—Beef Paste—Foie Gras Paste.

Dyeing Fancy Goods.

THE ART OF DYEING AND STAINING MARBLE, ARTIFICIAL STONE, BONE, HORN, IVORY AND WOOD, AND OF IMITATING ALL SORTS OF WOOD. A Practical Handbook for the Use of Joiners, Turners, Manufacturers of Fancy Goods, Stick and Umbrella Makers, Comb Makers, etc. Translated from the German of D. H. SOXHLET, Technical Chemist. Crown 8vo. 168 pp. Price 5s. net. (Post free 5s. 3d. home; 5s. 4d. abroad.)

Celluloid.

CELLULOID: Its Raw Material, Manufacture, Properties and Uses. A Handbook for Manufacturers of Celluloid and Celluloid Articles, and all Industries using Celluloid; also for Dentists and Teeth Specialists. By Dr. Fr. BÖCKMANN, Technical Chemist. Translated from the Third Revised German Edition. Crown 8vo. 120 pp. With 49 Illustrations. Price 5s. net. (Post free, 5s. 3d. home; 5s. 4d. abroad.)

Contents.

Chapters I., **Raw Materials for the Manufacture of Celluloid**: Cellulose and Pyroxylin—Gun-cotton—Properties of Gun-cotton—Special Gun-cottons for Celluloid Manufacture—Nitrating Centrifugalisers—Collodion Wool—Methods of Preparing Collodion Wool—Camphor—Japanese (Formosa) Camphor, Ordinary Camphor—Borneo Camphor (Borneol), Sumatra Camphor, Camphol, Baros Camphor)—Properties of Camphor—Artificial Camphor—Camphor Substitutes. II., **The Manufacture of Celluloid**: Manufacturing Camphor by the Aid of Heat and Pressure—Manufacture of Celluloid by Dissolving Gun-cotton in an Alcoholic Solution of Camphor—Preparing Celluloid by the Cold Process—Preparation with an Ethereal Solution of Camphor—Preparation with a Solution of Camphor and Wood Spirit. III., **The Employment of Pyroxylin for Artificial Silk**: Denitrating and Colouring Pyroxylin—Uninflammable Celluloid—Celluloid and Cork Composition—Incombustible Celluloid Substitute—Xylonite or Fibrolithoid. IV., **Properties of Celluloid**. V., **Testing Celluloid**. VI., **Application and Treatment of Celluloid**: Caoutchouc Industry—Making Celluloid Ornaments—Working by the Cold Process—Working by the Warm Process—Celluloid Combs—Celluloid as a Basis for Artificial Teeth—Stained Celluloid Sheets as a Substitute for Glass—Celluloid Printing Blocks and Stamps—Collapsible Seamless Vessels of Celluloid—Making Celluloid Balls—Celluloid Posters—Pressing Hollow Celluloid Articles—Casting Celluloid Articles—Method for Producing Designs on Plates or Sheets of Celluloid, Xylonite, etc.—Imitation Tortoiseshell—Metallic Incrustations—Imitation Florentine Mosaic—Celluloid Collars and Cuffs—Phonograph Cylinder Composition—Making Umbrella and Stick Handles of Celluloid—Celluloid Dolls—Celluloid for Ships' Bottoms—Celluloid Pens—Colouring Finished Celluloid Articles—Printing on Celluloid—Employment of Celluloid (and Pyroxylin) in Lacquer Varnishes—Index.

Lithography, Printing and Engraving.

PRACTICAL LITHOGRAPHY. By ALFRED SEYMOUR. Demy 8vo. With Frontispiece and 33 Illus. 120 pp. Price 5s. net. (Post free, 5s. 4d. home; 5s. 6d. abroad.)

Contents.

Stones—Transfer Inks—Transfer Papers—Transfer Printing—Litho Press—Press Work—Machine Printing—Colour Printing—Substitutes for Lithographic Stones—Tin Plate Printing and Decoration—Photo-Lithography.

PRINTERS' AND STATIONERS' READY RECKONER AND COMPENDIUM. Compiled by VICTOR GRAHAM. Crown 8vo. 112 pp. 1904. Price 3s. 6d. net. (Post free, 3s. 9d. home; 3s. 10d. abroad.)

Contents.

Price of Paper per Sheet, Quire, Ream and Lb.—Cost of 100 to 1000 Sheets at various Sizes and Prices per Ream—Cost of Cards—Quantity Table—Sizes and Weights of Paper, Cards, etc.—Notes on Account Books—Discount Tables—Sizes of spaces—Leads to a lb.—Dictionary—Measure for Bookwork—Correcting Proofs, etc.

ENGRAVING FOR ILLUSTRATION. HISTORICAL AND PRACTICAL NOTES. By J. KIRKBRIDE. 72 pp. Two Plates and 6 Illustrations. Crown 8vo. Price 2s. 6d. net. (Post free, 2s. 9d. home; 2s. 10d. abroad.)

Bookbinding.

PRACTICAL BOOKBINDING. By PAUL ADAM. Translated from the German. Crown 8vo. 180 pp. 127 Illustrations. Price 5s. net. (Post free, 5s. 4d. home; 5s. 6d. abroad.)

Sugar Refining.

THE TECHNOLOGY OF SUGAR: Practical Treatise on the Modern Methods of Manufacture of Sugar from the Sugar Cane and Sugar Beet. By JOHN GEDDES McINTOSH. Second Revised and Enlarged Edition. Demy 8vo. Fully Illustrated. 436 pp. Seventy-six Tables. 1906. Price 10s. 6d. net. (Post free, 11s. home; 11s. 6d. abroad.)

Contents.

Chemistry of Sucrose, Lactose, Maltose, Glucose, Invert Sugar, etc.—Purchase and Analysis of Beets—Treatment of Beets—Diffusion—Filtration—Concentration—Evaporation—**Sugar Cane**: Cultivation—Milling—Diffusion—Sugar Refining—Analysis of Raw Sugars—Chemistry of Molasses, etc.

(*See "Evaporating, Condensing, etc., Apparatus," p. 26.*)

Bibliography.

CLASSIFIED GUIDE TO TECHNICAL AND COMMERCIAL BOOKS. Compiled by EDGAR GREENWOOD. Demy 8vo. 224 pp. 1904. Being a Subject-list of the Principal British and American Books in print; giving Title, Author, Size, Date, Publisher and Price. Price 7s. 6d. net. (Post free, 7s. 10d. home; 8s. 3d. abroad.)

HANDBOOK TO THE TECHNICAL AND ART SCHOOLS AND COLLEGES OF THE UNITED KINGDOM. Containing particulars of nearly 1,000 Technical, Commercial and Art Schools throughout the United Kingdom, including Municipal Schools; Polytechnics; Schools of Art, Science and Technology; Colleges of Music and Elocution; Agricultural, Dairy Farming, Veterinary and Pharmacy Colleges; Domestic Economy, Cookery and Evening Classes; and Itinerant Technical Classes. With full particulars of the courses of instruction, names of principals, secretaries, etc. Demy 8vo. 150 pp. Price 3s. 6d. net. (Post free, 3s. 10d. home; 4s. abroad.)

THE PLUMBING, HEATING AND LIGHTING ANNUAL FOR 1910. The Trade Reference Book for Plumbers, Sanitary, Heating and Lighting Engineers, Builders' Merchants, Contractors and Architects. Quarto. Bound in cloth and gilt lettered. (Published in November, 1909.) Price 3s. net. (Post free, 3s. 4d. home; 3s. 8d. abroad.)

SCOTT, GREENWOOD & SON,

Technical Book and Trade Journal Publishers,

8 BROADWAY, LUDGATE HILL,

LONDON, E.C.

Telegraphic Address, "Printeries, London". Telephone, Bank 5403.

[*July*, 1909.

www.ingramcontent.com/pod-product-compliance
Lightning Source LLC
Chambersburg PA
CBHW030403270326
41926CB00009B/1241

* 9 7 8 3 7 4 1 1 2 5 3 1 7 *